Growing Up Muslim in Europe and the United States

G000097934

This volume brings together scholarship from two different, and until now, largely separate literatures – the study of the children of immigrants and the study of Muslim minority communities – in order to explore the changing nature of ethnic identity, religious practice, and citizenship in the contemporary Western world. With attention to the similarities and differences between the European and American experiences of growing up Muslim, the contributing authors ask what it means for young people to be both Muslim and American or European, how they reconcile these, at times, conflicting identities, how they reconcile the religious and gendered cultural norms of their immigrant families with the more liberal ideals of the Western societies that they live in, and how they deal with these issues through mobilization and political incorporation.

A transatlantic research effort that brings together work from the tradition in diaspora studies with research on the second generation, to examine social, cultural, and political dimensions of the second-generation Muslim experience in Europe and the United States, this book will appeal to scholars across the social sciences with interests in migration, diaspora, race and ethnicity, religion, and integration.

Mehdi Bozorgmehr is Professor of Sociology at the Graduate Center and City College, CUNY. He was the founding Co-Director of the Middle East and Middle Eastern American Center (MEMEAC) at the CUNY Graduate Center and is one of the pioneers of scholarly work on Middle Eastern Americans. He is the co-author of *Backlash 9/11: Middle Eastern and Muslim Americans Respond* and the co-editor of *Ethnic Los Angeles*, which won the best book award of the International Migration section of the American Sociological Association.

Philip Kasinitz is Presidential Professor of Sociology at the CUNY Graduate Center. He is the author of *Caribbean New York: Black Immigrants and the Politics of Race* and co-author of *Inheriting the City: The Children of Immigrants Come of Age*, which received the 2010 Distinguished Publication Award from the American Sociological Association. A former President of the Eastern Sociological Society, he is editor or co-editor of numerous collections, including *The Urban Ethnography Reader*, *Becoming New Yorkers: Ethnographies of the New Second Generation*, and *Global Cities, Local Streets*.

Studies in Migration and Diaspora

Series Editor Anne J. Kershen
Queen Mary University of London, UK

Studies in Migration and Diaspora is a series designed to showcase the interdisciplinary and multidisciplinary nature of research in this important field. Volumes in the series cover local, national and global issues and engage with both historical and contemporary events. The books will appeal to scholars, students and all those engaged in the study of migration and diaspora. Amongst the topics covered are minority ethnic relations, transnational movements and the cultural, social and political implications of moving from 'over there', to 'over here'.

International Marriages and Marital Citizenship
Southeast Asian Women on the Move
Edited by Asuncion Fresnoza-Flot and Gwénola Ricordeau

Belonging and Transnational Refugee Settlement
Unsettling the Everyday and the Extraordinary
Jay Marlowe

The Politics of Integration
Law, Race and Literature in Post-war Britain and France
Chloe A. Gill-Khan

Islamophobia and Everyday Multiculturalism in Australia
Randa Abdel-Fattah

Gender, Work and Migration
Agency in Gendered Labour Settings
Megha Amrith and Nina Sahraoui

Growing Up Muslim in Europe and the United States
Edited by Mehdi Bozorgmehr and Philip Kasinitz

Trajectories and Imaginaries in Migration
The Migrant Actor in Transnational Space
Edited by Felicitas Hillmann, Ton Van Naerssen and Ernst Spaan

For more information about this series, please visit: https://www.routledge.com/sociology/series/ASHSER1049

Growing Up Muslim in Europe and the United States

Edited by
Mehdi Bozorgmehr
and Philip Kasinitz

Routledge
Taylor & Francis Group

LONDON AND NEW YORK

First published 2018 by Routledge

2 Park Square, Milton Park, Abingdon, Oxfordshire OX14 4RN

52 Vanderbilt Avenue, New York, NY 10017

Routledge is an imprint of the Taylor & Francis Group, an informa business

First issued in paperback 2019

British Library Cataloguing-in-Publication Data
A catalogue record for this book is available from the British Library

Library of Congress Cataloging-in-Publication Data
Names: Bozorgmehr, Mehdi, editor. | Kasinitz, Philip, 1957– editor.
Title: Growing up Muslim in Europe and the United States / edited by Mehdi
    Bozorgmehr and Philip Kasinitz.
Description: First edition. | Abingdon, Oxon ; New York, NY : Routledge,
    2018. | Series: Studies in migration and diaspora | Includes bibliographical
    references and index.
Identifiers: LCCN 2018003147 | ISBN 9781138242166 (hbk) |
    ISBN 9781315279091 (ebk)
Subjects: LCSH: Muslims—Europe. | Muslims—United States. |
    Muslims—Cultural assimilation—Western countries.
Classification: LCC D1056.2.M87 G76 2018 | DDC 940.088/297—dc23
LC record available at https://lccn.loc.gov/2018003147

ISBN: 978-1-138-24216-6 (hbk)
ISBN: 978-0-367-89733-8 (pbk)

Typeset in Times New Roman
by Apex CoVantage, LLC

Contents

Illustrations

Tables

Figures

Acknowledgements

In a candid moment of commiseration, a colleague who has edited numerous books cautioned us that academics often underestimate how much work goes into them. We mention this remark not to get more credit than we deserve for putting this book together, but to point out the extent of debt one accrues in these time-consuming ventures. This book originated as an international conference held on two campuses of the City University of New York (i.e., City College and the Graduate Center) in April 2015. We are very grateful to Vincent Boudreau, at the time Dean of the Colin Powell School for Civic and Global Leadership, and to Dee Dee Mozeleski, its Chief of Staff, at the City College of New York for their enthusiastic support of the conference. We thank all conference participants for making it such a rich forum for exchange of ideas. Special thanks are due to our student assistants for their help with the logistics of the conference.

Further support for this project was generously provided by Donald Robotham, Director of the Advanced Research Collaborative (ARC) at the CUNY Graduate Center. Several of our European contributors have been affiliated with ARC as distinguished fellows, which made it feasible for us to collaborate with them. The Sociology Department at the CUNY Graduate Center provided additional support and a particularly conducive academic setting to work on this volume. In addition to a highly collegial environment, facilitated by Rati Kashyap, we benefitted from having great students to work with. In particular, doctoral sociology students Sarah Tosh, Christie Sillo and Eric Ketcham offered excellent research assistance. Two consecutive small grants from the Professional Staff Congress of the City University of New York (PSC-CUNY) enabled us to partially support our research assistants. Dirk Witteveen gave helpful feedback on the quantitative data analyses in the book. Outside of our academic setting, Terese Lyons provided indispensable help with editing the final manuscript.

Ultimately, we are indebted to our contributors for their wholehearted commitment to the project. Their willingness to respond to our nagging requests and make multiple revisions of chapters is deeply appreciated. Finally, we wish to thank Neil Jordan, Shannon Kneis, and Alice Salt of Routledge for their invaluable input at various stages of the production of this book.

Series editor's preface

The voyage from childhood to adulthood is a rite of passage that is rarely easy. Physically and emotionally it makes demands on each and every one of us, the challenges along the way creating the adults we become. As this timely volume highlights, young Muslims growing up in the United States and Europe in the early decades of the twenty-first century are now perceived by many Westerners as being enveloped within a miasma of terrorism. Second-generation followers of Islam are no longer considered simply as belonging to a separate religious group within the country of their birth. The Islamic religion has become fused with race, its followers considered a racial threat. Once comfortable within the country their parents migrated to, these young people have been 'othered' and often labelled 'the enemy'. The altered perception of Islam and Muslims has made the journey of their growing up far more testing. The young people have become victims of Islamophobia. Where once the second generation would not question their being American Muslim, Dutch Muslim or British Muslim, young Muslims in the West now have to dig deep within themselves in order to determine who they are and where they belong.

One factor which emerges from this book is that, in spite of the social and economic differences between Muslims in America and Europe, on both sides of the Atlantic the followers of Islam are being increasingly marginalised and alienated. The fusing of all Muslims into one hostile racial group ignores the diverse cultures, histories, languages, and colours which go to make up the *umma* – the global community of Islam bound by its *religious* ties. It is important to recognise that *umma* describes a bonding of religion, irrespective of race or culture, and is made up of many branches of Islam and many levels of religiosity.

A number of essays in this book identify a significant trend amongst the young second-generation Muslim communities, one which reflects a more intense level of religious purity and observance than that of their parents: this tendency is seemingly a reflex against the hostility that is emerging in some quarters of Western society. Male Muslim immigrant arrivals to London in the 1970s were far more concerned with earning a wage and making a home for their families than observing all the rites of their religion; commentators of those times recorded that the men drank, went with white women and did not always observe halal. It was as family reunification took place that the first-generation immigrants began to attend prayers on a more regular basis, if not every day. For some of the second generation this was not sufficient, and in the late 1990s and early 2000s, those not coming up to the level of religious attendance and behaviour expected were told threateningly by earnest young radicals 'you will regularly attend the mosque' – the threat implicit in the way it was articulated and the gestures accompanying the words![1]

This book's combination of comparative and specific chapters enables the reader to recognise the differences and similarities that are identifiable within the varied Muslim populations in the countries under the microscope. Several of the essays emphasise how in certain European countries concern over religious difference determines attitudes to Islam; others focus on the cultural divide. In Holland, for example, the concept of 'Dutchness' – which is underscored by that country's centuries-old sexual liberality – cannot accommodate devout Muslims, as Islam does not accept same sex relationships and other aspects of LGBT life. However, the cultural, as opposed to the religious, dimension of national identification has been undermined in America and other European countries. As the editors point out, recent terrorist attacks in Germany, Spain, France, Belgium, the United Kingdom and America, have resulted in a commonality of fear and the creation of a climate of Islamophobia. This has led to the marginalization of young, well-intentioned, unthreatening Muslims as well as to a disregard for the positive aspects of Muslim members of Western communities and their impressive contribution to the local and the national.

The simplicity and brevity of this book's title masks its high level of scholarship combined with a literary accessibility which makes it an outstanding collection of essays that go right to the heart of contemporary tensions and emotions. Significantly, the chapters are not committed to highlighting the impact of Islam on Western society, but rather they explore the way in which young Muslims have been disadvantaged and alienated by being associated with the horrendous crimes committed by those who hide under the carapace of Islam. This book is to be recommended for all those who wish truly to understand what it is like to 'Grow up Muslim' in twenty-first century Western society.

Anne J. Kershen
Queen Mary University of London
Winter 2017/18

Note

1 Information given to the series editor by a student in 2003.

Introduction

Second-generation Muslims in Europe and the United States

Mehdi Bozorgmehr and Philip Kasinitz

In December 2015, Donald Trump, already the leading contender in the Republican presidential primary elections, called for "a total and complete shutdown of Muslims entering the United States until our country's representatives can figure out what is going on."[1] The speech came soon after the mass shooting in San Bernardino, California, where 14 people were killed and another 22 seriously injured, at that time the deadliest terrorist incident in the U.S. since 9/11. The Federal Bureau of Investigation (FBI) called the shooting an act of "homegrown violent extremism," since it was perpetrated by a U.S.-born citizen of Pakistani descent and his wife, a lawful permanent resident of the United States.

In January 2017, barely a week into his presidency, President Trump acted on his anti-Muslim campaign promises and issued an Executive Order restricting immigration from seven predominantly Muslim countries (Iran, Iraq, Syria, Libya, Somalia, Sudan, and Yemen). This presidential initiative was met with widespread protest and was quickly blocked by the courts, forcing the administration to reissue a new and more streamlined travel ban. As of this writing, the ban has been revised several times and cases about its legality are still making their way through the judiciary. Yet whatever the outcome of these specific cases, for many Muslim Americans the ban signaled a new era in which their place in U.S. society was increasingly being questioned.

The U.S. is not alone in witnessing a rise in anti-immigrant and anti-Muslim sentiments and policies. Indeed, a perceptible surge in support for far-right anti-Muslim parties swept across Europe in 2017. While far-right candidates such as Marine Le Pen in France and Geert Wilders in the Netherlands did not fare as well as Trump in their own national elections, they nevertheless managed to bring far-right parties into the political mainstream to a degree not seen since World War II. Indeed, along with the UK Independence Party (UKIP), they succeeded in pushing more moderate candidates toward openly anti-immigrant and anti-Muslim positions (see Witteveen 2017 on the Netherlands).

While most of the existing literature has emphasized the differences in contexts between the U.S. and Western Europe (see Foner and Alba 2008), there are some indications that the contexts of reception for immigrants, and of integration for their descendants, are gradually and interdependently changing. On both sides of the Atlantic, longstanding attitudes about Islam and the status of

Muslim minorities have been shifting, and there now appears to be a degree of convergence between the United States and at least some European countries as they have become increasingly hostile to Muslim immigrants and their descendants. According to Marzouki (2017: 6), "Despite the well-known differences in political traditions, constitutional setups, and sociodemographic characteristics between Europe and the United States, the polemics and policies concerning Islam are increasingly interdependent." In the twenty-first century, she argues, there appears to be a standardization of anti-Muslim arguments, and "overlapping debates on Islam in the United States and Europe" engaged in by right-wing organizations. The danger of mosques as breeding grounds for terrorists, the threat of the alleged spread of Sharia Law, and the oppression of Muslim women, among similar themes, have become part and parcel of the discourse of right-wing organizations, which in turn have influenced the mainstream public debate about Islam and Muslims. Furthermore, counterarguments by Muslim groups and their allies are also becoming increasingly transnational, as ideas from one national setting are adopted by actors in other countries. In both cases, this convergence has been greatly accelerated by the Internet.

Recent acts of terrorism on European soil have undoubtedly stoked the flames of anti-Muslim sentiment across the continent. There were over a dozen terrorist attacks, including several major ones, in various European cities from 2015 to 2017. The so-called Islamic State of Iraq and Syria (ISIS) has claimed responsibility for most of these, often recruiting "operatives" through networks within Europe and training them on the battlegrounds of Iraq and Syria. The vicious cycle of lack of social mobility, sense of societal exclusion, and feelings of alienation among the most disadvantaged members of the second-generation Muslim Europeans has created a ready-made pool of potential recruits for extremist groups such as ISIS. Recruitment to violent extremism in the U.S. is more often through social media, and far fewer aspiring jihadists have travelled to the Middle East from the U.S. than from Europe.

In Europe, where Muslims typically make up a greater proportion of recent immigrants than in the U.S., much of the current debate concerns the social integration of Muslim immigrants and the second generation, whose values and norms are allegedly at odds with those of the modern and largely secular western societies around them. Conflicts have raged around a number of Muslim religious practices such as mosque construction, the Islamic call to prayer, public group prayer, ritual animal slaughter for halal meat, etc. The Islamic dress code is perhaps the most visibly controversial issue in Europe and has become a continuing source of cultural conflict. As of 2017, a number of European countries, including those covered in this book (i.e., France, Germany, the Netherlands, the United Kingdom, and Belgium) had at least proposed, and often passed, legislation at the national, regional, or municipal level to restrict wearing the *hijab* (headscarf), *niqab* (full-face veil), or *burqa* (an enveloping outer garment) in some or all public places (Banulesco-Bogdan and Benton 2017). Bans such as these are supported by the value placed on secularism in many Western European countries. Except perhaps in a handful of isolated cases, the issue of Islamic dress does not appear to be as contested in the United States. Furthermore, a long tradition of religious freedom in the U.S., as well as the principle of the separation of church and state central to the U.S. Constitution, makes it more difficult to legally regulate religious practices or to discriminate against people based on their religion. In that sense, the case of the so-called "Muslim Travel Ban," described above, serves as an example of both the presence of Islamophobia and the existence of legal safeguards against it in American society.

Islamophobia is best defined as "indiscriminate negative attitudes or emotions directed at Islam or Muslims" (Bleich 2011: 1585). Islamophobia in the U.S. is a pervasive and multifaceted phenomenon that spans American culture, politics, and policy (Love 2017). Bail (2015) argues and empirically demonstrates that, in the wake of 9/11, a coalition of anti-Muslim think tanks, religious groups, and social-movement organizations have dominated media discourse about Muslims and mobilized American public opinion against Islam. Sharia Law has become a "cause-célèbre" for these proliferating anti-Muslim organizations whose rhetoric depicts it as a looming threat to American society and culture. Between 2010 and 2012, legislators introduced anti-Sharia bills in two-thirds of the U.S. states. Moreover, there was an escalation over time of hostility directed against mosques (violent attacks on mosques and controversies revolving around their construction) across the United States (Bail 2015). According to a recent study, estimates of hate crimes against Muslim Americans reached their highest level (260) in 2015 since the record number (481) documented in 2001. While this surge in hate crimes is partly attributed to a series of terrorist attacks in the U.S. and Europe in that year, it is also due to the influence of anti-Muslim rhetoric central to the U.S. presidential campaign already under way at the time (Levin and Grisham 2016).

What does all of this mean for Muslims who were born or raised in the U.S. and Europe? Fearful right-wing rants notwithstanding, most Western nations are nowhere near having a Muslim majority population. However, for the first time, many of these countries are home to large, growing, and permanent Muslim minorities. Societies on both sides of the Atlantic face the challenges of accommodating and integrating sizable Muslim communities. At the same time, second-generation Muslims growing up in these societies are negotiating what it means to be both Muslim and American or Muslim and European in a politically charged climate of anti-Muslim sentiment espoused by nationalist politicians and right-wing parties.

Comparing the American and European experiences with these issues reveals many striking similarities and differences. While most of the literature thus far has stressed the differences (see Foner and Alba in this volume), more and more similarities and areas of convergence are attracting attention. A Policy Brief issued by the Migration Policy Institute, the foremost immigration think tank in the U.S., argues that cultural fears of Islam dominate in Western Europe, whereas in the U.S., Islam is often associated with security fears (Papademetriou et al. 2016; see also Foner and Simon 2015). Although the authors concede that these stark differences may have become blurred in light of recent terrorist attacks in Europe and the U.S., they contend that there are key distinctions between the two continents. We argue that these contextual distinctions are increasingly eroding with the remarkable rise of terrorism and the spread of Islamophobia.

In both settings, a disproportionate number of terrorists who make the news are drawn from the ranks of the second generation, the so-called "homegrown terrorists." According to a database compiled by Olivier Roy, including information on the persons involved in all the major terrorism attacks in France and Belgium, the typical terrorist is a young, second-generation immigrant or convert.[2] In the U.S., while the 9/11 hijackers were all foreign nationals, Muslim-American terrorism suspects between 2001 and 2009 were mostly American citizens. Half of these acted alone, and many were radicalized through the Internet (Jenkins 2010). Over all, an annual average of 27 Muslim Americans were associated with violent extremism in the 15 years following 9/11 (2001–2016), and over one-third of them were converts to Islam (Kurzman 2017). Despite their relative rarity, in light of a Muslim-American population of about 3 million, these terrorism attempts have garnered tremendous media attention. The unsuccessful car bombing planned by the so-called "Times Square bomber" in 2010, the tragic attacks at the 2013 Boston Marathon, the shootings in San Bernardino, California, in 2015, the Pulse nightclub shooting in Orlando, Florida, in 2016, as well as bombings in New York and New Jersey in 2016, serve to underscore this trend. In the aftermath of these attacks in the U.S., often committed by the second generation, there appears to be an increasing convergence between the European model of so-called "homegrown terrorism" and the American one.

Still, on both sides of the Atlantic, the disproportionate focus on a fringe extremist minority has obscured the experiences of the vast majority of Muslim youth. For instance, while the media is fixated on the UK-born terrorists, there is sometimes a tendency to forget that Sadiq Khan, the mayor of London, whose parents are Pakistani immigrants, also belongs to the second generation. In general, second-generation Muslims have made impressive inroads in holding a wide range of political offices across Europe. Indeed, there are many more Muslim parliamentarians in Western Europe than Muslim legislators and lawmakers in the U.S. The underrepresentation of Muslims in national and local American political offices is mainly attributable to inhospitable attitudes toward this group (Sinno 2008).

Despite an increasingly hostile political environment for Muslims in the Trump era, one cannot help but notice their increasing visibility, especially in popular American culture. A case in point is the comedian of the moment, Aziz Ansari, the South Carolina-born, second-generation son of Indian Muslim immigrants. When he was booked to host the popular TV comedy show "Saturday Night Live" the day after the presidential inauguration, it was widely seen as a rebuke to President Trump's anti-Muslim campaign speeches. More generally, there has been a proliferation of Muslim American standup comedians since 9/11. As Bilici (2012: 33) aptly puts it, "a second-generation phenomenon, Muslim comedy is a symptom of Muslims' Americanization."

As the first substantial generation of native-born Muslim Americans comes of age, allowing for cross-Atlantic comparisons, we need to ask: What does it mean for young people to be both Muslim and American or Muslim and European? How do they reconcile these, at times, conflicting identities in the post-9/11 era? How do they balance the religious cultural norms of their immigrant families with the more liberal ideals of the Western societies that they live in? Finally, and crucially, how do increasingly hostile social and political environments affect their sense of belonging and societal inclusion?

Given the existing state of academic knowledge, we are not yet in a position to answer any of these questions adequately. By convention, the *second generation* refers to native-born children with at least one immigrant (foreign-born) parent (Portes and Rumbaut 2014). The *first generation* refers to immigrants themselves. While there have been at least three large-scale survey research projects on the second generation (the children of immigrants) in the United States, none of them has included any Muslim group (Portes and Rumbaut 2001; Kasinitz et al. 2008; Bean, Brown and Bachmeier 2005; Crul and Mollenkopf 2012). Survey research on the second generation in Europe (i.e., The Integration of the European Second Generation Project [TIES]) has included large Muslim groups such as Turks and Moroccans (Crul, Schneider, and Lelie 2012). There are a number of promising ethnographies of Muslim American youth, but they are often focused on highly specific locations and populations, and hence their findings are not generalizable (see Maira 2009, 2016; Peek 2011). There is, however, a dearth of scholarly research comparing the experiences of Muslim Americans and European Muslims. Through case studies of various trajectories of second-generation Muslims in selected European countries and the United States, this book takes a step toward bridging this gap.

Much of the recent research on the integration of the second generation in Europe is focused almost exclusively on Muslims and the ostensibly unique difficulties they face in attaining full societal membership. Integration is the key concept in European scholarly debates on the subject, whereas assimilation theory dominates the fields of immigration and ethnic and racial studies in the U.S. This is partly because the word "integration" is most often associated with the African American experience in the U.S. In immigration studies, however, integration is defined as "the extent to which immigrants, and especially their children, are able to participate in key mainstream institutions in ways that position them to advance socially and materially" (Alba and Foner 2015: 8). Even Alba and Foner, U.S.-based scholars well-grounded in assimilation theory, opt for using the more broadly applicable concept of integration over assimilation in their comparative book on immigrants in Western Europe and North America. For the same reasons, we choose to use the concept of integration over assimilation in this book as well.

Religion is another integral component of research in Europe. While the effects of religion, and Islam in particular, dominate the scholarly discourse on second-generation integration in Europe, these issues have been under-studied in the U.S. Foner and Alba (2008) argue that religion serves as a "bridge" toward integration in the U.S., whereas it (especially Islam) is a "barrier" in Europe (see also Zolberg and Woon 1999). They maintain that the history of religious pluralism in the United States serves as a platform for integration. Moreover, Americans tend to be more religious than Western Europeans, and are thus less suspicious of immigrant religions. However, this openness is perhaps less applicable to Islam than to other religions. A Pew Research Center survey conducted in 2017 found that Americans gave Muslims the most negative rating out of eight major religious groups (Jews, Catholics, mainline Protestants, evangelical Christians, Buddhists, Hindus, and Mormons), and even rated them slightly lower than atheists (Pew Research Center 2017). According to 25 polls conducted in the decade after 9/11, unfavorable views of Islam steadily increased among Americans (Bail 2015).

In general, sociological research on the second generation in the U.S. has focused far more on social and economic characteristics than on religion (Kasinitz et al. 2008). Even comparative research on the U.S. and Western Europe has addressed socioeconomic issues among immigrant youth (Alba and Waters 2011). Furthermore, to underscore the effects of context, scholars often control for socioeconomic status and compare "low-status" labor migrants in Europe and the U.S., e.g., North Africans in France, Turks in Germany, and Mexicans in the United States (Alba and Foner 2015). Few studies have compared Muslims on both sides of the Atlantic, and those few have focused on the uneasy coexistence of traditional Islam and secular democracies in the West (see Cesari 2014).

To our knowledge, there is a dearth of books, at least in English, on secondgeneration Muslims in Europe and the U.S. To address the social, cultural, and political dimensions of integration, we need empirical studies that allow us to compare and contrast the second-generation Muslim experiences in Europe and the United States. In this volume, we bring together scholars from two different and until now largely separate areas of expertise – the study of the children of immigrants and the study of Muslim minority communities – in an attempt to explore the changing generational nature of Muslim communities in the contemporary western world.

As a background, we present basic data on the population size of Muslims, and their share of the total population, in major immigrant-receiving European countries and in the United States. For the sake of consistency, we rely on the data compiled by a single source at about the same point in time, i.e., the Pew Research Center circa 2010–2011. In 2010, there were about 13 million Muslim immigrants in the European Union. Germany and France had the largest, and roughly the same, Muslim populations (4.8 and 4.7 million, respectively) in Europe, but the percentage of Muslims in relation to the country's total population was higher in France than in Germany (7.5% and 5.8%, respectively). Moreover, Muslims represented a substantial portion (over one-third) of the total share of the first- and the second-generation populations in France in 2009 (Reitz, Simon, and Laxer 2017). With 3 million Muslims, the United Kingdom ranked third, accounting for 4.8% of its total population. The Netherlands ranked sixth with 1 million Muslims, comprising 6% of its total population (Pew Research Center 2016).

In the United States, the Pew Research Center estimated the Muslim population to be 2.75 million in 2011, making up about 0.9% of the total population. While the absolute numbers of Muslims in some European countries (i.e., the United Kingdom) and the United States were comparable, the Muslim share of the total population was much smaller in the U.S. But even more importantly, the immigrant Muslim population in the U.S. is much more diverse than its counterpart in the European countries listed above. Almost two thirds of the Muslim Americans (63%) were of immigrant origin, hailing from a wide range of countries around the world, although mainly from the Middle East (several Arab countries and Iran) and South Asia (Pakistan, Bangladesh, and India). The second generation accounted for 15% of the total Muslim American population (Pew Research Center 2011). Conversely, just a few source countries and regions dominate the Muslim population in each of the largest European countries. The Muslim population in Germany is predominantly Turkish, in France mainly North African (from Algeria, Morocco, and Tunisia), in the United Kingdom mostly South Asian (from Pakistan, Bangladesh, and India), and in the Netherlands predominantly Turkish and Moroccan.

Another major cross-Atlantic difference is the relatively higher socioeconomic status of second-generation Muslim Americans compared to their European counterparts. In terms of education, labor force participation, and income, Muslim Americans compare favorably with the general American population (Pew Research Center 2011). Ultimately, structural factors in the U.S. would lead one to believe that full integration should be much easier for Muslim Americans than for their European counterparts. Such expectations notwithstanding, while second-generation Muslim Americans appear to be doing well socioeconomically, they still seem to lack a sense of belonging and inclusion in American society. We need up-to-date, systematic and generalizable research to gauge this "integration paradox" among Muslim Americans.

Discussing the situation in Europe, Alba and Foner (2015: 120) argue that "there is considerable evidence of socioeconomic disadvantage and even of discrimination experienced by Muslims, including those in the second generation who have grown up in European societies." They present data on low educational attainment of the second generation in various Western European countries to corroborate their argument. This is partly because many second-generation individuals in Europe are the offspring of labor migrants and guest workers (e.g., Turks in Germany). Other research on socioeconomic integration of the second generation in Western Europe has shown that they are disadvantaged in terms of both education and access to labor markets (Heath, Rothon, and Kilpi 2008). Turkish youth were the main second-generation group in each of the ten Western and Northern European countries studied, except for Britain, yet they were among the most disadvantaged. Moroccans in the Netherlands and Belgium, North Africans in France, and Pakistanis in Britain and Norway were likewise disadvantaged educationally and occupationally.

Some second-generation Muslims are developing new forms of religiosity that are markedly different from those of their first-generation parents. In their review article, Voas and Fleischmann (2012) summarize the results of several ethnographic studies of the Muslim youth in both Europe and the U.S. They point to a tendency among the second generation to take an interest in a "pure" Islam, distinct from the often ethnically and culturally inflected religious practice of their immigrant parents. Similarly, Bilici (2012) points out that, in their quest to make Islam an American religion, U.S.-born Muslims often distinguish between the "cultural Islam" of their immigrant parents and their own "true Islam."

In general, Muslim immigrants, like many other groups, often identify in ethnic terms because of their strong attachment to their respective countries of origin. The second generation, however, is more acculturated and hence less likely to identify as strongly with their ethnic heritage. Furthermore, an exclusionary anti-Muslim context can contribute to "reactive religiosity," i.e., the retention of religious identification among the second generation. In the extreme case of the post-9/11 backlash, the "Muslim American" label has become more prevalent (Bozorgmehr, Ong, and Tosh 2016). Maira (2016) has referred to young Muslim Americans as the "9/11 Generation," and has shown how they have come together and mobilized to protect their civil rights.

The internal diversity of young Muslims creates new possibilities in terms of group identity and even religious practice, often with cultural influences from the western societies in which they grow up. For example, the writer Sahar Habib Ghazi notes how during her teens and early twenties, she would meet her Muslim friends for *suhoor*, the predawn meal before fasting during Ramadan, at that most American of locales, the International House of Pancakes, universally known as "IHOP." "It's an all-American ritual," she writes, "I've had suhoor at an IHOP in every United States city where I have lived." She notes the diversity of her young groups of friends, "Arab-Americans, Afghan-Americans, Iranian-Americans and African Americans – some of us born here, some brought here as refugees some who came here to study and others whose great-great grandparents were brought here on slave ships." Yet this happy and decidedly American Muslim rite of passage (for many the "first unsupervised late night out with friends") took on a dark undertone with the 2017 brutal murder of a 17-year-old *hijabi* Muslim girl coming home from a Virginia IHOP on the last weekend of Ramadan, in what police described as a "road rage" incident.[3]

Embracing a shared religious identity is conducive to the development of an ethnically inclusive Muslim community that crosses national lines. This Muslim identity is further reinforced in social spaces such as mosques, Islamic Centers, university campuses, or anywhere else that the second generation congregate. In some notable cases, the second generation may even privilege their religious identity over an ethnic identity, e.g., Bangladeshis in the U.S. and the UK (Kibria 2011).

A hyphenated identity seems to be more problematic in Europe, where second-generation Muslims are often not fully accepted as native. In France, for example, any descendants of immigrants, including Muslims, feel that their Frenchness can be questioned because of their continuing ties to their national origins. The large-scale 2008–09 survey of 22,000 respondents, "Trajectories and Origins: The Diversity of Population in France," showed that French Muslims frequently had a sense of "dual belonging" or "plural allegiances" to French society and their countries of descent. In France, expressing a hyphenated identity is suspiciously regarded as a lack of commitment to French society. Although the vast majority of second-generation respondents (nine out of ten) said that they "feel French," one-quarter reported that they are not perceived as "being French" (Simon 2012). As an immigration country or settler society, the U.S. is overall more accepting of hyphenated identities than European countries (Alba and Foner 2015). Immigrants and their descendants are not forced to choose between a national, ethnic, or religious identity, and all of these identities can coexist.

The chapters in this book cover various aspects of second-generation Muslim life in the U.S. and Europe. In some ways, this experience is similar to that faced by all adult children of immigrants. Like other young people trying to make their way in societies different from those their parents came from, they are both "insiders" and "outsiders," coping with family and community expectations formed in one society while at the same time struggling to integrate into another. They do not completely fit into "mainstream" society, despite the fact that for some, this is the only society that they have ever known. However, second-generation Muslims also face additional challenges in the post-9/11 world. Surrounded by rising nationalism and Islamophobia, they find their right to be a member of the host society questioned. They are confronted with the argument that as Muslims they are fundamentally different from other immigrants, harder to integrate, and perhaps inherently unassimilable. At the same time, within Muslim communities, ideas about what it means to be Muslim in a predominately Christian society are in flux. Indeed, in some cases, the meaning of Islam itself is changing, as young people in the U.S. and in Europe assert their right to be Muslim while creating an Islam often very different from that practiced by their immigrant parents.

Contents of the book

Part I Comparing contexts

In this section, the authors examine the position of second-generation Muslims in various receiving societies, each of which has a distinct history of immigrant integration as well as a different and particular relationship with Islam. Taken as a whole, the chapters reveal both how the situations of Muslims differ across North American and European societies and the ways in which these situations may be converging in the current historical context.

In "Being Muslim in the United States and Western Europe: why is it different?" Nancy Foner and Richard Alba highlight the transatlantic comparison. Looking at the main differences between the social position of Muslims in Western Europe (Britain, France, Germany, and the Netherlands) and the United States, they argue that Islam is a greater "barrier" to integration in Western Europe because of Muslims' strong attachment to religion in what are otherwise largely secular societies. As a result, Islam and Muslims have become the target of right-wing political parties and nationalist movements. The U.S., for all of its troubled history when it comes to racial differences, is a far more religious society as well as one with a long history of religious pluralism. Thus, it has generally been more tolerant of high levels of religiosity and hyphenated identities among ethnic groups. Further, they remind us that there is far more selectivity in the social-class backgrounds of Muslim immigrants to the U.S. than those in Europe. Indeed, they are more likely to arrive well educated and less likely to be refugees. In general, Muslims also make up a far smaller portion of the total immigrant population. In Europe, the fear that nations have lost control of their borders and are being "overrun" by unplanned and unwanted migration is overwhelmingly directed toward Muslims. In the Trump era, one hears similar arguments in the U.S. as well, as the call for "travel bans" directed at Muslims makes clear. Still, anxiety about uncontrolled migrant flows remains largely focused on Latinos.

In "Resilient Islam meets a resistant mainstream: persistent 'barriers' over religious rights for Muslims in European countries," Paul Statham examines tensions between the majority populations and the Muslim minorities over the accommodation of Islam in Western Europe. He finds enduring barriers to Muslim participation in civil society despite generally tolerant attitudes of the Muslims toward the Christian majorities. He argues that strong resistance to even relatively minor accommodations to Muslim practices (e.g., distinctive dress in public settings) may have an enduring effect on the civic integration of the second generation.

In "Religious identities and civic integration: second-generation Muslims in European cities," Karen Phalet, Fanella Fleischmann, and Marc Swyngedouw highlight the role of local (in this case, urban) context in shaping the second-generation Muslim experience. Examining the religious and civic sense of belonging among Turks and Moroccans in Frankfurt, Berlin, Antwerp, Brussels, Rotterdam, Amsterdam, and Stockholm, they show how religious identities vary across these urban contexts, with more strictly observant interpretations of Islam more prevalent in less accommodating cities. Across these cities, local politics and civic participation are more open to second-generation Muslims than is the case at the national level. Their second-generation survey respondents were generally politically well informed and engaged in local issues at levels on par with non-Muslim residents their age. In this regard, it is worth noting that the current mayor of Rotterdam is a Moroccan-born Muslim who immigrated as a teenager. The authors conclude that increasingly diverse cities now play a key role in both the religious life and the civic integration of Europe's Muslims. This could perhaps account for the deepening divisions between relatively cosmopolitan cities and nativist small towns and rural areas, a divide also brought to the fore in the 2016 U.S. election.

In "The integration paradox: second-generation Muslim Americans," Mehdi Bozorgmehr and Eric Ketcham compare the salient characteristics of the foreign- and native-born populations from predominantly-Muslim countries. They argue that the socioeconomic integration progress of second generation Muslim Americans has proceeded relatively quickly. In other ways, however, U.S.-born Muslims are not as integrated or assimilated into American society as one might expect. Their high levels of religiosity are almost exactly the same as those of their immigrant parents and they are only slightly more likely to have non-Muslim friends. Economic success notwithstanding, Muslims across generations see themselves and their religion as distinct from mainstream American culture. In fact, the second generation is actually more sensitive to issues of discrimination and has a keener perception of prejudice than do their parents, which ironically may be a paradoxical form of assimilation in post-civil rights era America. They are also more insistent than their immigrant parents that life has become more difficult for Muslims in the U.S. in the years since 9/11.

Part II Inclusion and belonging

This section addresses the issue of societal membership among Muslim youth in the U.S. and the Netherlands. In "The politics of inclusion: American Muslims and the price of citizenship," Yvonne Haddad provides a historical overview of the place of Islam in America. Early immigrants, she argues, generally sought to integrate into American society, downplaying their religious distinctiveness while seeking inclusion within a broadening vision of American religious pluralism, much as Catholics and Jews had done in the early- to mid-20th century. In the late 1960s, however, the arrival of more observant Muslim college students gave rise to a new, more assertively Islamic and strongly anti-Zionist orientation which was frequently at odds with U.S. foreign policy toward the Islamic world. The rise of the second generation and the post-9/11 backlash further diversified the landscape of Muslim American organizational life. Haddad describes the struggle of today's Muslim Americans to be recognized as full citizens of the United States without having to defend their worthiness, credibility, or loyalty, and without being made to feel that their citizenship is "incomplete" or "qualified." Indeed, she argues that while immigrant Muslims in the U.S. have often attempted to maintain their culture by reinventing it in the Western context, the American-born second generation is in the process of fashioning a new Muslim-American identity, which is reflected in Muslim political participation, social incorporation, and cultural expression, including, among other art forms, rap music and standup comedy.

In "The politics of belonging: religiosity and identification among second-generation Moroccan Dutch," Marieke Slootman and Jan Willem Duyvendak focus on the religious identification and religiosity of adult children of Moroccan immigrants in the Netherlands. They find a strong Muslim identification among the second-generation Moroccan Dutch and attribute it, in part, to an exclusionary Dutch context. "Dutchness," they argue, is increasingly seen in cultural rather than strictly political terms. This creates barriers to the inclusion of culturally different groups. Ironically, this Dutch culture is often identified with a tradition of tolerance, particularly in matters of sexuality and the acceptance of LGBT populations. However, this "tolerance" can become a form of intolerance toward, for example, traditional Muslims, who may object to same-sex relationships. As

"Dutch-ness" is increasingly being defined as progressive and secular, religion (or the lack thereof) is increasingly central to understanding who belongs and who does not. This contrasts with the situation in other countries, such as the United States, where, regardless of one's feelings toward Islam, religion in general is far less contested. It also creates considerable confusion when right-wing anti-Islamic Dutch nationalists such as Geert Wilders, who have sought to forge alliances with conservative anti-Muslim activists in the U.S., are clearly not on the same page as those Americans when it comes to LGBT rights and other social and cultural issues. Indeed, the groups have little in common other than their shared Islamophobia.

Part III Education and integration

This section deals with the role that educational institutions play in the lives of the young second generation. The conclusions in both chapters run counter to conventional wisdom. The authors find that religious education and practices that strengthen transnational connections to parental homelands do not impede and may actually facilitate second-generation integration.

In "Muslim integration in the United States and England: the role of the Islamic schools," Jen'nan Ghazal Read and Serena Hussain argue that public and political debates over faith-based education have resurfaced in recent years due to an increase in Islamic schools in the West and concerns over their potential influence on Muslim youth. The chapter argues that Islamic schools help facilitate the participation of Muslims in mainstream institutions by equipping them with the cultural capital needed to navigate in non-Muslim arenas. To the extent that religion is critical, it often works to strengthen, not weaken, integration by providing administrators and teachers with a legitimate voice to promote student involvement in activities outside of the religious community. Surprisingly, they find that on both sides of the Atlantic, attending Islamic schools does not necessarily translate into greater levels of religiosity among Muslim youth. Indeed, in some cases, it turns them away from religion altogether.

In "Transnational schooling among children of immigrants in Norway: the significance of Islam," Liza Reisel, Anja Bredal, and Hilde Lidén examine the effects of sending children abroad for religious schooling and socialization. Not surprisingly, educators often see this practice as disruptive to children's educational progress and to their integration into Norwegian society. Contrary, however, to the assumption that the more time young people spend in their parents' country of origin, the more influenced they will be by that culture and religion, the authors find that exposure to conditions "there" often brings children closer to Norway and solidifies their Norwegian identity. At the same time, these extended stays abroad allow second-generation students to establish new emotional links to their parents' homelands. Some immigrant parents are sending children "home" to get the traditional Islamic education unavailable in secular Norway. However, there is little evidence that this practice makes children more observant in the end.

Part IV Reconstructed and misconstrued identities

The final section deals with some of the ways in which second-generation Muslims attempt to reconstruct their identities either along racial lines or through shifting boundaries. In spite of these internal nuances, Muslim identity is often misconstrued by the media in stereotypically negative and stigmatizing ways.

In "Strategies of race: second-generation Muslim American advocates and identity," Erik Love argues that identity occupies a central place for civil rights advocates in the United States. He examines the ways in which activists in community-based organizations have developed strategic approaches for navigating American racial politics. He argues that since 2010, second-generation Muslim American advocates have increasingly led efforts to recognize a new racial identity category that would include Arab, Muslim, Sikh, and South Asian Americans. Of course, many traditional leaders of immigrant communities initially found such a category meaningless, if not absurd. Resistance to recognizing such a panethnic and indeed pan-religious category was seen as insurmountable in the 1990s. By 2010, however, such a category increasingly made sense to younger Muslim activists. This is in part a response to a perception of increased hostility from the majority culture and a common linked fate: we are one group because that is how White Americans see us and treat us. Love describes how discussions about racial politics among Muslim American advocates, frequently led by well-educated second-generation activists deeply influenced by the African American civil rights movement, have shaped recent approaches to confront Islamophobia.

By contrast, in "Second-generation Muslims and the making of British Shi'ism," Kathryn Spellman Poots documents the increasing importance of intra-group diversity among Muslims in the UK. More specifically, she examines the ways in which British Shia[4] Muslims, across national-origin backgrounds, create new meanings and strategies to practice Shia traditions in the United Kingdom. Spellman Poots argues that belonging to a Twelver Shia Muslim community, in addition to the wider British Muslim minority and ethno-national diasporic groupings, has become a more salient identity for young Twelver Shia in recent years. She demonstrates how religious boundary formation and practices are informed and configured by sources of authority across a number of transnational spaces as well as in relation to sectarian ideologies and wider geopolitical issues. She further shows how second-generation British Shias are negotiating authority structures, creatively aligning or realigning themselves to Shias from different national-origin backgrounds, and striving to get established as social and political actors in British society.

In "Imagining the 'Muslim terrorist': media narratives of the Boston Marathon bombers," Nazli Kibria, Saher Selod, and Tobias Henry Watson explore the media depictions of the events surrounding the April 15, 2013 Boston Marathon bombings, one of the most significant acts of "homegrown" Muslim terrorism on U.S. soil. They explore how the bombers were depicted as "Muslim terrorists," fundamentally distinct from other young mass murderers responsible for the school shootings and rampages that have tragically become all too common in contemporary America. Their research suggests that when the perpetrator of such violence is a non-Muslim, the media frequently fall into a "school shootings" narrative, blaming the murders on mental illness, family dysfunction, alienation from peers, and exposure to a violent masculine youth culture, as well as on the ready availability of guns in the U.S. While one could just as easily see all of these factors at play in the case of the Boston Marathon bombers, such considerations were quickly overshadowed by a "Muslim terrorist" narrative that explained the acts of violence as expressions of the religious identity and background of the suspects. The findings highlight a discourse in which Muslims, especially young men, are perceived to have a proclivity toward violence, a tendency that is activated by involvement with Islam and Muslim institutions. Indeed, an entire industry has grown up around the dangers of "radicalization" and how to prevent it, despite the fact that many of the perpetrators of terrorist acts like the Tsarnaev brothers have only the most tenuous connections with Islamist or other fundamentalist organizations. In some cases – such as the 2016 Pulse nightclub shooting in Orlando, Florida – such connections seem to exist entirely within the perpetrator's mind. By contrast, when horrific mass violence is committed by non-Muslims, even when there is a clear and clearly articulated ideological motive as was the case in the 1993 Oklahoma City bombing or the 2015 mass shooting in a Charleston, South Carolina, African-American church by a white supremacist, the word "terrorist" is much less readily used.

***

This brings us back to an important point of this book. Of course, terrorism is real and its results are horrific, whether terrorist attacks are carefully planned efforts by international terrorist organizations, "lone wolf" attacks by individuals inspired by such organizations, or the work of deeply troubled young people who, without any real or meaningful connection to Islamist groups, take up their slogans as they play out their murderous fantasies. The danger of the "Muslim terrorist" narrative is that, in deepening the sense of alienation and isolation among second-generation Muslims, it risks exacerbating the problem. The policy attention now given to preventing "radicalization," as if "radicalism" were a disease spread by casual contact and thus requiring the inoculation of vulnerable populations, focuses on a tiny number of young people who might actually commit terrorist violence. As such, it risks losing sight of the long-term dangers of social exclusion among a much larger second-generation Muslim population that now often feels itself under permanent suspicion, closely scrutinized and deeply misunderstood.

This pessimistic view may be only half the story. Many young Muslims growing up in the U.S., and even in Europe, feel deeply conflicted about belonging to a society that, in Moustafa Bayoumi's words, sees them as a "problem" (Bayoumi 2008). After every terrorist attack they are reminded that the only society they have ever known may not want them (see also Maira 2009, 2016). Despite these conflicts, many are making their way and becoming successful on their own terms, seeing the creative potential and even the humor in their situation. Indeed,

Aziz Ansari has become one of America's most popular entertainers in part by talking about these very conflicts. And when Londoners came together to mourn the victims of the attacks on London Bridge and outside the Finsbury Mosque in 2017, it was mayor Sadiq Khan who gave voice to the crowd's defiance of terror by standing up for the ethos of the tolerant city. A year earlier, shortly after his election, Mayor Khan had noted:

> What I think the election showed was that actually there is no clash of civilization between Islam and the West. I am the West, I am a Londoner, I'm British, I'm of Islamic faith, Asian origin, Pakistan heritage, so whether it's [ISIS] or these others who want to destroy our way of life and talk about the West, they're talking about me. What better antidote to the hatred they spew than someone like me being in this position?
>
> (*Time* 2016)

Someday, we hope someday soon, a European or American Muslim will achieve something great and not feel the need to frame this achievement as saying anything about a "clash of civilizations" or terror or ISIS. In the meantime, Mayor Khan speaks for many of his generation who insist that they can be both Muslim and Western, proud of their heritage while deeply committed to the multicultural cities and nations in which they live. It is to them that we dedicate this book.

Notes

1 Patrick Healy and Michael Barbaro, "Donald Trump Calls for Barring Muslims from Entering U.S." *New York Times.* December 8, 2015, A1. Available online at www.nytimes.com/politics/first-draft/2015/12/07/donald-trump-calls-for-banning-muslims-from-entering-u-s/
2 Olivier Roy, "Who are the new jihadis?" *The Guardian.* April 13, 2017.
3 Sahar Habib Ghazi, "Pancakes in a World of Hate." *New York Times.* June 25, 2017, Sunday Review, 7.
4 Shia is the more conventional term for Shi'i.

References

Alba, Richard, and Nancy Foner. 2015. *Strangers No More: Immigration and the Challenges of Integration in North America and Western Europe.* Princeton, NJ: Princeton University Press.
Alba, Richard, and Mary Waters, eds. 2011. *The Next Generation: Immigrant Youth in a Comparative Perspective.* New York: New York University Press.
Bail, Christopher. 2015. *Terrified: How Anti-Muslim Fringe Organizations Became Mainstream.* Princeton, NJ: Princeton University Press.
Bakalian, Anny, and Mehdi Bozorgmehr. 2009. *Backlash 9/11: Middle Eastern and Muslim Americans Respond.* Berkeley, CA: University of California Press.
Banulesco-Bogdan, Natalia, and Meghan Benton. 2017. "In Search of Common Values amid Large-Scale Immigrant Integration Pressures." Brussels: Migration Policy Institute Europe.

Bayoumi, Moustafa. 2008. *How Does It Feel to be a Problem? Being Young and Arab in America.* New York: Penguin.

Bean, Frank, Susan Brown, and James Bachmeier. 2015. *Parents Without Papers: The Progress and Pitfalls of Mexican American Integration.* New York: Russell Sage Foundation.

Bilici, Mucahit. 2012. *Finding Mecca in America: How Islam is Becoming an American Religion.* Chicago: University of Chicago Press.

Bleich, Erik. 2011. "What Is Islamophobia and How Much Is There? Theorizing and Measuring an Emerging Comparative Concept." *American Behavioral Scientist* 55(12): 1581–1600.

Bozorgmehr, Mehdi, Paul Ong, and Sarah Tosh. 2016. "Panethnicity Revisited: Contested Group Formation in the Post-9/11 Era." *Ethnic and Racial Studies* 39(5): 727–745.

Cesari, Jocelyne. 2014. *When Islam and Democracy Meet: Muslims in Europe and in the United States.* New York and Basingstoke: Palgrave Macmillan.

Crul, Maurice, and John Mollenkopf, eds. 2012. *The Changing Face of World Cities: Young Adult Children of Immigrants in Europe and the United States.* New York: Russell Sage Foundation.

Crul, Maurice, Jens Schneider, and Frans Lelie, eds. 2012. *The European Second Generation Compared: Does the Immigration Context Matter?* Amsterdam: Amsterdam University Press.

Foner, Nancy, and Richard Alba. 2008. "Immigrant Religion in the U.S. and Western Europe: Bridge or Barrier to Inclusion?" *International Migration Review* 42(2): 360–392.

Foner, Nancy and Patrick Simon, 2015. *Fear, Anxiety, and National Identity Immigration and Belonging in North America and Western Europe.* New York: Russell Sage Foundation.

Heath, Anthony, F., Catherine Rothon, and Elina Kilpi. 2008. "The Second Generation in Western Europe: Education, Unemployment, and Occupational Attainment." *Annual Review of Sociology* 34(1): 211–235.

Kasinitz, Philip, John Mollenkopf, Mary Waters, and Jennifer Holdaway. 2008. *Inheriting the City: The Children of Immigrants Come of Age.* New York: Russell Sage Foundation.

Kibria, Nazli. 2011. *Muslims in Motion: Islam and National Identity in the Bangladeshi Diaspora.* New Brunswick, NJ and London: Rutgers University Press.

Kurzman, Charles. 2017. "Muslim-American Involvement with Violent Extremism, 2016." Durham, North Carolina: Triangle Center on Terrorism and Homeland Security.

Levin, Brian, and Kevin Grisham. 2016. "Special Status Report: Hate Crime in the United States." San Bernardino, CA: Center for the Study of Hate & Extremism.

Love, Erik. 2017. *Islamophobia and Racism in America.* New York: New York University Press.

Maira, Sunaina Marr. 2009. *Missing: Youth, Citizenship, and Empire after 9/11.* Durham, NC, and London: Duke University Press.

Maira, Sunaina Marr. 2016. *The 9/11 Generation: Youth, Rights, and Solidarity in the War on Terror.* New York: New York University Press.

Marzouki, Nadia. 2017. *Islam: An American Religion.* New York: Columbia University Press.

Papademetrious, Demetrios, Richard Alba, Nancy Foner, and Natalia Banulescu-Bogdan. 2016. "Managing Religious Difference in North America and Europe in an Era of Mass Migration." Washington, DC: Migration Policy Institute.

Peek, Lori. 2011. *Behind the Backlash: Muslim Americans after 9/11.* Philadelphia: Temple University Press.

Pew Research Center. 2011. "Muslim Americans: No Signs of Growth in Alienation or Support for Extremism." Washington, DC: Pew Research Center.

Pew Research Center. 2016. "5 Facts about the Muslim Population in Europe." Washington, DC: Pew Research Center.

Pew Research Center. 2017. "Muslims and Islam: Key Findings in the U.S. and Around the World." Washington, DC: Pew Research Center.

Portes, Alejandro, and Rubén Rumbaut. 2001. *Legacies: The Story of the Immigrant Second Generation.* Berkeley, CA: University of California Press.

Reitz, Jeffrey, Patrick Simon, and Emily Laxer. "Muslims' Social Inclusion and Exclusion in France, Québec, and Canada: Does National Context Matter?" *Journal of Migration and Ethnic Studies* DOI: 10.1080/1369183X.2017.1313105.

Simon, Patrick. 2012. "French National Identity and Integration: Who Belongs to the National Community?" Washington, DC: Migration Policy Institute.

Sinno, Abdulkader, ed. 2008. *Muslims in Western Politics.* Bloomington, IN: Indiana University Press.

Time Magazine. 2016. "Exclusive: London Mayor Sadiq Khan on Religious Extremism, Brexit and Donald Trump." May 9. Available online at http://time.com/4322562/london-mayor-sadiq-khan-donald-trump/

Voas, David, and Fenella Fleischmann. 2012. "Islam Moves West: Religious Change in the First and Second Generations." *Annual Review of Sociology* 38: 525–545.

Witteveen, Dirk. 2017. "The Rise of Mainstream Nationalism and Xenophobia in Dutch Politics," *Journal of Labor and Society* DOI: 10.1111/wusa.12290.

Zolberg, Aristide, and Long Litt Woon. 1999. "Why Islam is Like Spanish: Cultural Incorporation in Europe and the United States." *Politics and Society* 27(1): 5–38.

Part I

Comparing contexts

1 Being Muslim in the United States and Western Europe

Why is it different?

Nancy Foner and Richard Alba

There is no question that being Muslim is a source of stigma for the second generation on both sides of the Atlantic. In the United States, as well as in Western Europe, the children of Muslim immigrants often confront prejudice and discrimination owing to their own and their parents' religion. Yet, to stop here, and emphasize only this similarity, is to give a misleading picture. In fact, Muslim immigrants and their second-generation children have become a greater source of contention and conflict, and Islam has become a more central divide between immigrants and the native (majority) population, in Western European societies than in the United States.

Why this is so is the subject of this chapter. Our basic premise is that a transatlantic comparison can enlarge our appreciation of the experiences of second-generation Muslims in the United States as well as in Western Europe.[1] The comparison can call attention to or bring into sharper focus dynamics that might be taken for granted, missed, or minimized if we just looked at one case. By casting differences into sharper relief, the comparison increases the visibility of processes and structures in one society by highlighting similarities and differences with another.

Beyond revealing transatlantic parallels and contrasts, the comparison also leads us to try to account for them. In this way, we believe, it is useful in broadening our understanding of the kinds of institutions and processes being compared and, especially pertinent to this book, in appreciating how nation-specific institutions and social trends help to shape what it means to be a second-generation Muslim in different societies.

To foreshadow the argument we develop, several factors help to explain why Islam has become a more significant marker of a fundamental social divide between those of immigrant origin and long-established natives in Western Europe than in the United States, and a more common source of conflict with mainstream institutions and practices. For one, demographic characteristics of the U.S. and European Muslim populations, including their relative sizes, are crucial. Also, Western European native majorities have more trouble recognizing claims based on religion because they are, overall, more secular than religiously oriented Americans. Then, too, historically based relations and institutional arrangements between the state and religious groups have made it more difficult to incorporate new religions in Europe. An added element has to do with identities: the position of the United States as a classic settler society, as well as the mid-twentieth century development of more expansive conceptions of American national identity, have led to a greater acceptance of religious and ethnic identities among the children of Muslim immigrants than is the case in Western Europe.

This analysis draws on material from our larger study that examines how European and North American countries are meeting the challenges of integrating immigrants and their second-generation children (Alba and Foner 2015; see also Foner and Alba 2008). On the North American side of the Atlantic, our focus in this chapter is on the United States; in Europe, we look at four countries – France, Great Britain, Germany, and the Netherlands. Together these four are home to sixteen million Muslims or about three-fifths of the Muslims in the European Union (Pew Research Center 2017). All of these Western European societies have experienced large-scale immigration in the decades since the end of the Second World War, and consequently there is a sizable literature available on Muslim immigrants and their children in each of these countries.

What is different?

At first glance, the notion that the United States is more hospitable to second-generation Muslims seems to fly in the face of recent events. After all, there has been a great deal of anti-Muslim sentiment in the United States, which intensified in the wake of mass killings in the past few years by Muslims in Western Europe and, closer to home, in San Bernadino, California, and Orlando, Florida. The last few decades have witnessed many cases of discrimination, bias incidents, and hate crimes, including vandalism of mosques and even occasional violence against Muslims, as well as state surveillance since the attacks of September 11 (Bail 2014; Bakalian and Bozorgmehr 2009; Cainkar 2009; Detroit Arab American Study Team 2009). Controversies have arisen in a number of American towns and cities about the building of mosques; several states have banned judges from considering foreign or religious law, with Sharia law in mind. Writing in response to a *New Yorker* article about the 2015 killing of three Muslim students in his town of Chapel Hill, North Carolina, a physician wrote that "being Hispanic, my wife and I are used to being treated with mistrust." But when they "very naively" went downtown on Halloween night dressed in "traditional Muslim outfits" he received when lecturing in Saudi Arabia, they "were berated with Islamophobic insults and told to go back home . . . [E]ven in our most liberal and intellectual towns we still have a long way to go" (Castillo 2015).

Anti-Muslim discourse is acceptable in American life in a way that no longer is true for anti-black rhetoric, and well-known right-wing talk radio hosts frequently expound, indeed rant, against Muslims. Of particular concern is the extent to which anti-Muslim statements recently have become common in public discourse at the highest levels of society. Republican presidential candidates ramped up anti-Muslim rhetoric in the 2015–16 primary campaign – what the Council on American-Islamic Relations called "the mainstreaming of Islamophobia" – with

Donald Trump calling for banning Muslims from entering the United States, Ben Carson saying a Muslim should not be president, and Jeb Bush arguing that American aid to Syrian refugees should focus on Christians (Blow 2015; Semple 2015). Not long after taking office, Donald Trump issued an executive order banning visitors from several Muslim majority countries, and anti-Muslim hate crimes have spiked during his presidency. Surveys show a substantial proportion of Americans indicating unease or negative feelings toward Muslims. One example: Muslims were on the bottom, with an average rating of only 40, in a 2014 survey asking respondents to rate seven religious groups on a "feeling thermometer," with 0 the coldest and 100 the warmest (Pew Research Center 2014; see also Gallup Center for Muslim Studies 2010; Wuthnow 2005). Interestingly, recent national surveys indicate similar proportions in the United States and Western Europe holding negative views of Muslims. According to a 2016 Pew Research Center survey, 28–35 percent of the population in Britain, France, Germany, and the Netherlands had unfavorable attitudes to Muslims living in their country (Wike, Stokes, and Simons 2016); in a 2016 U.S. national poll, 38 percent expressed unfavorable views of Muslims, although the question referred to Muslims in general, not just those in the United States (Telhami 2016).

Yet despite considerable anti-Muslim hostility on both sides of the Atlantic, it would be wrong to conclude that Islam is the same kind of divide between immigrants and natives in the United States as it is in Western Europe. It is not. The fact is that Islam in Western Europe has become a major cleavage between long-established residents and a large segment of the immigrant-origin population and a frequent subject of public debate about immigrant integration and assimilation in a way that has not happened in the United States. Anti-immigrant sentiment in the United States is, to a significant extent, focused on undocumented Mexican and Central American immigrants, who are overwhelmingly Christian, whereas in Western Europe hostility toward immigrants tends to be closely linked with Muslims, including their European-born children. As Jocelyne Cesari (2013) has put it, immigration debates in the United States have not been Islamicized – or systematically connected with anti-Islamic rhetoric – the way they have been on the other side of the Atlantic.[2]

In the United States, hostility to Islam has to a large degree focused on national security issues and on Islam as an external threat from outside the country, such as the risk of outsiders committing terrorist acts. In Western Europe, security concerns, to be sure, are a component of anxieties about Muslims, but the focus tends to be on *internal* threats from marginalized and radicalized Muslim youth. There is another transatlantic difference, as well. Fears about the threat of Islam to Western Europe's core liberal values, such as free speech, gender equality, and equal rights for previously-stigmatized groups, loom much larger and have become a prominent theme in political discourse and debates. Speaking before the Dutch parliament, Geert Wilders, leader of the populist Party for Freedom, has called "Islam . . . the Trojan Horse in Europe. If we do not stop Islamification now, Eurabia and Netherabia will just be a matter of time. . . . We are heading for the end of European . . . civilization as we know it" (quoted in Alba and Foner 2015: 121). In the 2017 Dutch national election, Wilders campaigned to close all mosques, ban the Quran, and seal the nation's borders to asylum seekers; although his party did less well at the polls than expected, it gained five seats in Parliament as compared to 2012. In France, Marine Le Pen, though suffering a major loss in the 2017 presidential election, appealed to many voters with her anti-Islamic rhetoric, vowing, in her words, to "uncompromisingly fight Islamist fundamentalism which seeks to impose its oppressive rules in our country" (*Newsweek* 2017). Such views are not confined to those on the European political right. The notion that European culture must be defended against Islam is also common among those on the left. For Dutch progressives, for example, Islam "with its . . . ideas on homosexuality or the role of women threatens to overthrow the very gains that progressives fought for in the last century" and their painful wresting free from the strictures of their own religions (Buruma 2010: 5).

The threat of Islam to free speech has inflamed European publics in recent years, from the 2005 Danish cartoon affair, when the *Jyllands-Posten* published twelve Mohammed caricatures, to the January 2015 murders in Paris of staff at the satirical magazine *Charlie Hebdo* by Islamist members of the second generation. Huge marches in Paris and elsewhere were held in response to the murders to support a free press just as a decade earlier leading German, French, and Dutch papers made a point of republishing the Danish cartoons. In the Netherlands, harsh criticism of Islam as a threat to freedom of speech surged in reaction to the 2004 murder of filmmaker Theo van Gogh by a young Dutch Moroccan, who targeted Van Gogh for his anti-Islamic statements and movie, *Submission.*

Nor have cultural practices associated with Muslims, such as ritual animal slaughter for halal meat, aroused the same kind of controversy in the United States as they have in Western Europe. Much of the public criticism in Europe has focused on practices linked to the subordination of women – such as "honor killings" carried out by South Asian and Middle Eastern men against daughters and sisters who have taken partners not approved by their families; arranged marriages, found in some groups like Pakistanis in Britain and Turks in several countries; and, above all, styles of female dress or clothing. Antagonism to these practices has been generalized beyond the small minority of Muslims who may actually adhere to them. The French principle of *laïcité*, or state secularism, is thought to be threatened by female students wearing the headscarf in schools, leading to a 2004 law banning it in French schools; in Germany, half of the 16 states passed laws between 2004 and 2009 prohibiting the Islamic headscarf for public school teachers at work. Everywhere in Europe, the *jilbab*-plus-*niqab*, the black head-to-toe veiling that leaves only slits for the eyes, has been the subject of public debate, with France, once again, banning it in public places.

As for the much greater fears in Western Europe that Muslim young people will become involved in fundamentalist Islam, and that some may commit acts of violence and terrorism on European soil, these fears have escalated with each new brutal assault involving disaffected members of the second generation – including the 2005 London Underground and 2017 Manchester Arena bombings, the November 2015 Paris attacks, and the March 2016 attacks at the Brussels airport and metro station. In the Brussels and Paris attacks, a central role was played by radicalized Belgian nationals who fought in Syria, stoking anxiety about the growing participation of European-raised Muslims in Islamist military groups fighting in the Middle East – who have been far greater in number, it should be noted, than the American Muslims who have gone to join Islamist wars in Iraq and Syria.[3] Although the several thousand from Europe who have fought in the Middle East are only a tiny fraction of the second generation, the jihadist recruits are in a sense the tip of iceberg, reflecting difficulties that affect a much larger number of young European-raised Muslims, who are finding it difficult to feel accepted and fully at home in countries where they should belong.

Along with worries about the allegiances of second-generation Muslims to jihadist causes – and suspicions that they may be an enemy from within – is another pervasive concern in Western Europe: that a strong Muslim (or ethnic) identity competes with (or may even replace) feelings of belonging to the national community. This "either/or" mentality contrasts with that prevalent in the United States, where asserting a religious or ethnic identity goes hand in hand with being American. Public debates in the United States are less focused on national identity issues and fears about cultural fragmentation than in Europe, where anxieties about Muslims' identities are a larger issue (Foner and Simon 2015).

In continental Western Europe in particular, the second generation feels pressure to express an exclusive national identity even though, at the same time, they often are not accepted on the same footing as long-established natives. Combining a Muslim and European identity is quite challenging in the European context (except perhaps in Great Britain). In France, for example, dual identities are disdained, and members of the second generation are expected to be part of the French nation as individuals, not as groups defined by common ethnicity or religion. The problem is that although many children of non-European immigrants say they feel strongly French, they also say they are not viewed by others as French – or as Patrick Simon (2012) has put it, their Frenchness is denied on the basis of their origins (see also Beauchemin et al. 2015). The phrase *Français de souche*, French from the roots, used in popular discourse to refer to long-established French, encapsulates the notion of Muslims as well as people of color as not fully French (Packer 2015).

In the Netherlands, the terms "autochthones," literally those who originate from the soil, for those who are "really" Dutch, and "allochthones," for non-Western immigrants and their children and sometimes even their grandchildren, are not just used in everyday speech but until recently were also official categories in government statistics. Referring to the children of Moroccan and Turkish immigrants born in the Netherlands as "allochthones" or foreigners, Jan Willem Duyvendak argues, is inherently exclusionary and makes it difficult for the second generation to be recognized as "one of us" (Duyvendak 2011; see also Slootman and Duyvendak 2015). Germany, according to a study of second-generation belonging, does not support the idea of hyphenated identities but promotes exclusive ethnonational labels, with notions like Deutschturken (German Turks) only recently gaining some presence in public discourse: "anyone with non-German . . . family roots faces an ambiguous task in defining themselves as German" (Schneider et al. 2012: 215; see also Faist and Ulbricht 2015).

Of the four European countries we are considering, Britain is closest to the United States in recognizing the cultural or ethnic identity of migrants and their children, and, according to polls there, a remarkably high proportion of the children of South Asian immigrants (a great many of whom are Muslim) have a strong identification with and pride in being British (Alba and Foner 2015; see also Meer and Modood 2015). Still, leading British journalists and politicians often portray Muslims as having difficulty feeling British, thereby contributing to a sense among many in Britain that a good many Muslims are outsiders and do not belong (Meer, Uberoi, and Modood 2015).

On the other side of the Atlantic, Americans are more comfortable with extending a national identity to the second generation, including Muslims. Legal permanent residents are treated as Americans-in-the-making; hyphenated identities that combine a national identity with a religious or ethnic label are accepted as normal, expected, and one might even say as the American way. Moreover, it is not just the children of immigrants who may embrace hyphenated identities. So do many long-established natives, at least some of the time. Just as there are Muslim Americans or Chinese Americans, so, too there are millions of Irish, Italian, and Jewish Americans, well established in the mainstream, whose immigrant ancestors go further back. Hyphenated identities, in other words, do not set the second generation apart. And immigrants and their children can easily be American and "ethnic" or Muslim at the same time.

In the United States, there is a long tradition of recognizing and accepting ethnically based religious congregations as part of the American immigrant experience, and of taking for granted that immigrants' religious institutions will not only reproduce and reassert aspects of home-country cultures but also nurture and strengthen a sense of ethnic identity. The main title of the article, "Becoming American by Becoming Hindu," (Kurien 1998) captures the Americanizing dynamic of immigrants' engagement with religion and ethnicity. To what extent asserting a Muslim identity helps immigrants and their children to formulate claims to inclusion in American society is an open question in today's political climate. Yet protests and responses to discrimination among Muslim Americans have reflected an Americanization dynamic, with protesters and leading public figures urging those discriminated against to claim their rights as Americans, thus encouraging them to draw themselves further into the national fold rather than separate from it. Muslims, one sociologist has written, often see their experiences as "another chapter in the American story of the fight for social inclusion that all racial, ethnic, and religious minorities have had to wage" (Cainkar 2009: 265).

Why is being Muslim different?

Demographics

This leads to the question of why being Muslim is a more significant marker of a fundamental social divide for the second generation in Western Europe than in the United States. A major reason is the different demographic landscapes on the two sides of the Atlantic.

For one thing, a much larger proportion of immigrants and their children are Muslim in Western Europe – about 40 percent of all immigrants from outside the European Union (Pew Forum on Religion and Public Life 2012). In the United States, Muslims are a tiny proportion of the immigrant population, an estimated 4–8 percent (about two-thirds of immigrants are Christians). Indeed, in the United States, all Muslims, whether immigrant or native born, are a much smaller percentage of the total population, about one percent (Mohamed 2016). By comparison, 9 percent of the French population is Muslim, as is 7 percent in the Netherlands and 6 percent in Britain as well as Germany (Pew Research Center 2017).

Also important is that Islam in Western Europe is associated with large immigrant groups who are among the most disadvantaged minorities in terms of income, unemployment, and education rates. In Germany, these are Turks (about half of all Muslims in Germany); in Great Britain, Bangladeshis and Pakistanis; in France, Algerians and Moroccans; and in the Netherlands, Moroccans and Turks. In the United States, Mexicans are the largest immigrant group by far, making up more than a quarter of the foreign born; they are also the most problematic immigrant group in terms of legal status and among the most socioeconomically disadvantaged. However, they are overwhelmingly Christian, mainly Catholic. There are hardly any Muslim Latinos (under 1 percent). The Muslim foreign born are diverse in national and regional origin – more so than is the case in the four European countries we consider – with about four in ten from the Middle East or North Africa, more than one in ten from sub-Saharan Africa, and about a quarter from South Asia, including Pakistan, India, and Bangladesh (Pew Research Center 2011). According to a recent estimate, around one out of eight Muslims in the United States is African American, often a convert to Islam (Pew Research Center 2011). Although Islam is making converts among the long-established native population in Europe, Islam there is associated, above all, with recent immigration.

Muslim immigrants in Western Europe have a much lower socioeconomic profile than those in the United States. For the most part, Muslim immigrants in Western Europe arrived with low levels of education, sometimes no formal schooling, and took jobs at the bottom of the labor market; their children have a long way to go to catch up to the majority population. While Muslims in Europe are often stuck in neighborhoods with poor housing conditions and low-paying jobs and stand out for relatively high levels of unemployment, a substantial proportion of Muslim Americans are well educated and middle class. According to a 2011 Pew Research Center study, even at a time when the recession had taken a toll, Muslim immigrants were holding their own compared to the wider U.S. population. Thirty-five percent of foreign-born Muslims had annual household incomes of at least $50,000, with 18 percent over $100,000, about the same as the general public. Foreign-born Muslims were doing better than the general public in educational achievement; nearly a third had graduated from college and a quarter were currently enrolled in college or university classes.

Religiosity of the majority population

A second reason why Islam is a more central dividing line and more pervasive source of conflict between long-term natives and those of immigrant origin in Western Europe has to do with the place of religion in contemporary society. In highly secular Western Europe, those who worship regularly and hold strong religious beliefs, even Christian ones, are a small minority, and social and cultural beliefs and behavioral claims based on religious principles are often viewed as illegitimate. When the religion is Islam, with its particular demands on how followers conduct their lives, these claims often lead to public unease, sometimes disdain and even anger, and, not surprisingly, tensions and conflicts.

Americans are considerably more religious than Western Europeans. Granted, a growing proportion of Americans express no religious preference. Even so, as of 2014, this was only 23 percent (Pew Research Center 2015), and several years earlier, about half of Americans said that religion was very important in their lives, more than twice the proportion in Germany, Britain, or France (Pew Global Attitudes Project 2012). Even if Americans exaggerate the seriousness of their religious beliefs, the very fact that they do, in contrast to the opposite tendency of Europeans, is itself part of the different definitions of the situation.

Because Western Europeans are less religious, they are more likely than Americans to view religious immigrants and their children with discomfort and suspicion. Religion scholar Jose Casanova (2007: 65) refers to the "intolerant tyranny of the secular, liberal majority" in Europe. After centuries of domination by an established and highly restrictive Christian order, many Europeans aggressively support secular values and see Muslims as a threat to them. Europeans often feel that their societies should not tolerate religious practices or cultural customs that conflict with liberal secular norms and widely accepted views on, for example, the equal role of women. At the same time, they expect religious conservatives, Muslim and Christian alike, to tolerate behavior that they consider morally abhorrent, such as open displays of sexuality.

Americans give much more legitimacy to religiously based arguments in the public sphere and in politics than Europeans do. Political demands made on the basis of religion are a common feature of American life, put forward most vocally by evangelical (mostly native white) Christians, who are a substantial proportion (about a quarter) of the U.S. adult population (Pew Research Center 2015) and whose support for banning abortion on religious grounds has been prominent on the American political scene. As the scholarly literature on immigrant religion emphasizes, becoming more religious is a way of becoming American, whereas it is often seen as a problem in Western Europe.

Historical role of religion and institutional arrangements

Then there is the historic role of religion in European and American societies. Historically rooted relations and arrangements between the state and religious groups have created greater difficulties in Europe in accepting new religions than is true for the United States.

Since the early days of the United States, the hard-won and sometimes contested foundational principles of religious freedom and separation of church and state allowed immigrant religions the space to develop their own religious communities, including the construction of houses of worship according to their own ideas, and to claim a sort of parity with the dominant religions (Alba and Foner 2014; 2015). Intertwined with America's legal and constitutional history is its past success in incorporating Judaism and Catholicism into the fabric of mainstream institutions. After all, for much of the country's history, Protestant denominations dominated the public square; Catholicism and Judaism were not just at the periphery but also the subject of deep-seated and virulent prejudice and discrimination. The two religions were associated with disparaged immigrants and seen by nativist observers to be incompatible with mainstream institutions and cultures – not unlike contemporary views in Europe today of Muslims (Alba 2009).

What is key is that Catholics and Jews were eventually incorporated into the system of American pluralism. Because the state was barred from supporting or sponsoring Protestantism, the newer religions were able over time to become part of the American mainstream as the descendants of the immigrants did. By the mid-twentieth century, Americans had come to think of a tripartite perspective – Protestant, Catholic, and Jew – and by the late twentieth and early twenty-first centuries, opponents of multiculturalism were referring to "our Judeo-Christian heritage" in upholding the value of Western civilization.

Although Islam has not become part of the religious mainstream – and it is unclear whether or when it will – Muslim arrivals and their second-generation children have benefited from the religiously more open society that resulted from the earlier incorporation of Jewish and Catholic immigrant groups. Indeed, Islam receives public symbolic recognition in many situations; for example, an imam often has been present on the podium, along with a Protestant minister, Catholic priest, and Jewish rabbi, at public ceremonies in Washington, DC. New York City has recently added two Muslim holidays to the official public school calendar, joining Christian and Jewish ones.

In Western Europe, the ways that Christian religions have been institutionalized, and historically entangled with the state, have made it difficult for Islam to achieve equal treatment. To be sure, European governments have begun to make some accommodations for Muslim religious practices such as granting permission to build mosques and, in a number of countries, permitting ritual animal slaughter. Britain, which has been especially liberal on this score, even allows Islamic Sharia courts to rule in such matters as family disputes as long as there is no conflict with English civil law (Meer and Modood 2015).[4] A number of governments have established local and national "Islam Councils," partly to diminish foreign ties and encourage an Islam that is more compatible with European democratic states. The French Council of the Muslim Faith, for example, which has a mandate to negotiate with the French state over issues affecting Islamic religious practice, represents an attempt by the French government to establish a French Islam rather than merely tolerate Islam in France, thus seeking to imbue it with aspects of French norms and national identity (Laurence 2012; Laurence and Vaisse 2006).

Yet these developments take place in a context in which Islam remains "outside the discourses of national identity and what is socially acceptable" (Cesari 2015). Despite the breaking of many links between church and state and the high degree of secularism, the institutional context continues to favor Christianity in many ways and thus marginalizes Islam. Muslims cannot but be aware of the special privileges accorded to majority denominations and the second-class status of Islam. For example, in Germany, according to the 1949 constitution, the state must be neutral in religious matters, but there are still strong links between church and state. Long-established Protestantism, Catholicism, as well as Judaism – but not Islam, the third largest religion – are recognized as public corporations entitled to federally collected church taxes and the right to run state subsidized religious services and hospitals.

Throughout Europe, magnificent churches and cathedrals dot the landscape, but few mosques can compete in appearance. In France, for instance, where the exclusion of religion from the affairs of state is the official ideology, the 1905 law on the separation of church and state designated all religious buildings built before then as property of the French state; the same law prevents the state from contributing to the construction of new ones. The state therefore owns and maintains most Christian churches and allows them to be used for regular religious services, while most French mosques are makeshift structures in converted rooms in housing projects, garages, or even basements (Laurence and Vaisse 2006).[5] Muslim students in France may not wear headscarves in public high schools, and the far right National Front has opposed allowing non-pork alternatives in school lunches, with former President Sarkozy joining in, calling pork-free lunches a threat to "our tradition, our way of life"; while at the same time some schools serve fish dishes on Friday in keeping with Catholic tradition (Fernando 2015; "French Secularism" 2015; Titley 2014).

Government support for religious schools has created other inequalities in Western Europe between long-established religions and Islam. In Britain and France, the state provides support for religious schools as long as they teach the national secular curriculum. While seemingly fair to all religions, this arrangement favors the established churches. The British government funds more than 6,500 Church of England and Catholic faith schools in England but, as of 2017, only 27 Islamic faith schools in a nation of more than four million Muslims. In France, about 20 percent of French students go to religious schools (mostly Catholic) that receive the bulk of their budgets from the government, but as of 2009 there were only two Muslim schools funded in this way. The majority of children in the Netherlands go to state-supported denominational schools, nearly all Protestant and Catholic, while the country's nearly one million Muslims in 2008 had some 44 of their own publicly funded schools educating about 10,000 pupils. In Germany, Catholic and Protestant students receive regular religious instruction from teachers in the public schools, but Muslim students are taught Islam in only a few places.

Beyond formal institutions, in everyday popular culture in Germany and elsewhere, Muslims cannot help but see the domination of Christianity – and the second-class status of Islam. Public recognition is taken for granted in the case of Christian holidays but denied to even the most important Muslim ones. Christmas dominates public spaces throughout Europe, with *Christkindl* markets taking over town squares in German-speaking countries. In France, the annual public holidays include important Catholic ones but no Jewish or Muslim ones.

The different ways that religion has been institutionalized in the United States and Western Europe have affected the kinds of claims Muslims can make and the conflicts that may result. In the United States, to be sure, problems have arisen in some places over institutional accommodation of Muslim practices such as prayer rooms in public schools, but Muslims, like immigrants with allegiance to other minority religions, have generally sought inclusion in the wider society through public acceptance and recognition of their group. In Europe, equal treatment would require substantial structural change by removing institutionalized arrangements with longer-established religions or, as Muslims have sought, achieving greater support of the sort that the historically based religions already have, including for their own religious schools.

Ethnic, religious, and national identity

If the discourses on national identity contribute to maintaining or even hardening boundaries between Muslims and the majority population in Western Europe, they do not operate the same way in the United States. In the United States, religious and ethnic identities are seen as compatible with national identities and not cast in a competitive or zero-sum situation. History, both distant and closer to the present, explains why this pattern has developed.

For one thing, the United States – unlike the countries of Western Europe – was, from its founding, a settler society, which out of necessity encouraged new arrivals to see themselves as part of the new nation as rapidly as possible. By contrast, in the course of their development as nation states, European countries constructed identities based on histories going back centuries, even millennia, making it more difficult for newcomers and their children to link their origins to these historical roots. These identities are more exclusive in the sense that they pose social and psychological barriers for those who are unable to link their family origins to such historical roots.

More recent developments are perhaps even more significant, especially when it comes to the widespread American acceptance of multiple or hyphenated identities. In the United States, the impact of the twentieth-century incorporation of earlier European immigrants as well as the legacy of the civil rights movement stand out. As we have written elsewhere (Alba and Foner 2015), over the course of the twentieth century, the United States went from being a society that emphasized "100 percent Americanism" and Plymouth Rock (that is, Protestant) roots, to one that saw itself as a nation of immigrants and extolled Ellis Island identities. The integration of once-despised nineteenth- and twentieth-century immigrants and their children not only led to the acceptance of Judaism and Catholicism as American religions but also to the greater acceptance of ethnic identities, either with or without the hyphen. The civil rights movement and legislation of the 1950s and 1960s also contributed to the creation of a more inclusive national identity that acknowledged the experiences of racial and ethnic minorities. Diversity became not just tolerated but also often celebrated as part of America's basic principles, and ethnic hyphenation became a "natural idiom of national belonging" (Jacobson 2006: 10).

What lies ahead?

We have analyzed why religion is more of a barrier to the inclusion of second-generation Muslims in Western Europe than in the United States, but questions inevitably arise about the changes that might lie ahead.

Predicting the future is a risky business. So much, in truth, is unforeseeable, especially given the possibility of unanticipated political events or developments that could intensify prejudices against Muslims in the second as well as first immigrant generation. Nonetheless, it is worthwhile to sketch out factors that may, on the one hand, exacerbate and, on the other, reduce the barriers facing second-generation Muslims.

There are some positive signs on both sides of the Atlantic. In the United States, the historical record provides some optimism that Islam eventually will come to have a more established place. It may have taken more than a century, but America was able to overcome the fear of the "Catholic menace" and widespread views of Catholicism as an anti-modernist religion incompatible with democracy. Perhaps in the decades ahead, as one historian has written, we will be talking about America as an Abrahamic civilization, a phrase joining Muslims with Jews and Christians: "America, at present, is a long way from that formulation of American national identity, but no further than America once was from the Judeo-Christian one" (Gerstle 2015: 50). Moreover, in the context of the American color line – and a society where color-coded racial cleavages are more problematic than divisions based on religion – phenotypically white and very light-skinned members of the Muslim second generation who are economically and educationally successful and culturally assimilated may come to be seen and accepted as part of the dominant white population.

In both the United States and Europe, additional dynamics may operate. It is likely that over time more second-generation Muslims will have routine contact and interactions with long-established Europeans and Americans in a range of social settings, including workplaces, schools, and universities. This kind of intermingling can increase comfort with people of Muslim background, reduce prejudice, and lead to friendships and even intermarriage.

In Western Europe, as the number and proportion of the second and third generations rise, the participation of Muslims in mainstream European political and economic life, including the upper tiers of the occupational ladder, is bound to become more common and increasingly be seen as normal; the 2016 election of Sadiq Khan, a second-generation Pakistani, as the first Muslim mayor of London is one of the latest signs of this development. Those in the European majority population are also likely to grow more accustomed to Islamic religious observance, particularly as Islam becomes more Europeanized, or, given internal divisions within Islam, "European Islams" take root. As members of the second generation in Europe take over in religious associations and institutions, many will strive for a more liberal version of Islam than their parents practiced, one that is focused on integration into Western European society and that is viewed more positively by the wider population. The jury is still out on whether, and to what extent, the children of Muslim immigrants in Europe will become more, or less, religious than their parents, yet it is a good bet that a substantial share of the second generation will come to hold many views in sync with mainstream ideas about the separation of state and religion and gender equality in education and the labor market (see Crul and Mollenkopf 2012; Maliepaard and Alba 2016).[6]

Less happily, there are some dark clouds on the horizon. In the United States, unforeseen issues, events, and controversies may arise that significantly increase hostility to U.S.-born Muslims and political attacks on them. Who, after all, would have predicted the September 11 attacks on the twin towers of New York's World Trade Center, the 2015 San Bernardino killings, or the Orlando shooting? Or Donald Trump's election as president after a campaign in which he and other Republican presidential hopefuls used anti-Muslim rhetoric to rally support? Still, if Muslim Americans' rights to religious freedom are threatened, they have the Constitution, as well as civil liberties advocates and liberal politicians, on their side. Also, the small size of the U.S. Muslim population makes the group seem less threatening, although admittedly, at the same time, this small size can cut the other way in that lack of personal exposure to Muslims could fuel negative sentiments toward them.

In Western Europe, there are many reasons to be concerned. Although the trend of Western European governments to make accommodation for Muslim practices is likely to continue, there is a long way to go before Islam achieves parity with mainstream religions. Then, too, the prospects for relatively high rates of unemployment and stalled social mobility among many second-generation Muslims will provide fodder for "skeptics who will continue to argue that Muslims will never fit in or successfully adjust to European society" (Laurence 2012: 265).

There are other serious worries. While most second-generation Muslims in Western Europe do not support a politicized Islam, a minority do. The aggrieved sense of exclusion felt by some second-generation Muslims has created a pool of potential recruits for fundamentalist doctrines and extremist Islamist groups. This development, along with terrorist incidents by "homegrown" Muslims, could reinforce tensions with long-established Europeans and fuel anti-Muslim hostility and rhetoric. In fact, this has already been happening in the last few years, as several thousand second-generation European Muslims have gone to fight with Islamist groups in the war in Iraq and Syria.

Fears and anxieties about Islam also have been heightened by the violent terrorist attacks involving European-raised Muslims in Paris, Brussels, and elsewhere as well as attacks by Muslim immigrants like the 2016 Bastille Day massacre of Nice specatators.

The recent European refugee crisis, with a massive surge in the number of asylum seekers entering Western Europe, many of them Muslims from Syria, Iraq, and Afghanistan, also has fed into and escalated anti-Muslim sentiment. Indeed, some politicians on the right have played on popular unease about accepting large numbers of refugees by emphasizing the Muslim connection. Speaking in the Dutch parliament, Geert Wilders called the wave of refugees pushing into Europe an "Islamic invasion . . . that threatens our prosperity, our security, our culture and identity" (*Reuters* 2015). In Germany, where more than a million asylum seekers entered in 2015 alone, the far-right Alternative for Germany (AfG) party's opposition to the government's refugee policies and the AfG's increasingly blatant anti-Muslim stance led to gains in its popularity.

To what extent the divisions between the majority population in Western European countries and Muslims will deepen in the near future or become less pronounced over a longer period of time is hard to predict. It does seem likely, however, that second- and indeed third-generation Muslims in Western Europe are poised to continue to experience greater challenges to inclusion owing to their religion than their counterparts in the United States, and the factors that we have put forward to explain the difference will, we would argue, also remain relevant.

Notes

1 In referring to the second generation, we use an expanded definition that includes not only those born in the country of reception – that is, in the United States or Europe – but also those who immigrated as young children and were raised there.

2 As we noted, the 2016 crop of Republican candidates running for the Presidency and the election of Donald Trump have raised the political salience of the Islamic terrorist threat. Whether – and to what extent – these public discussions and Trump's executive order banning visitors from several Muslim majority countries will have enduring consequences on the U.S. political discourse, including on immigration, is not clear.

3 According to a Congressional Research Service (2015) estimate, some 4000 Western European Muslims, including 1200 from France, 600 from Germany, 250 from the Netherlands, and 600 from Britain, were fighting in Iraq and Syria in early 2015 as compared to 150 from the United States.

4 Meer and Modood also note that the laws against religious discrimination in Britain, introduced in 2003 and strengthened in 2007 and 2010, are stronger than in the rest of the European Union. They argue that while Britain is a country in which Christianity is historically established, "it has *also* developed a 'moderate secularism' that is able to accommodate non-Christian faiths without disestablishment by selectively pluralising the Church-State link through constitutional reform, public policy and social services delivery" (Meer and Modood 2015: 530, 534).

5 In recent years, it should be noted, some large mosques have been built in France, and in a number of cases the ban on state support for religion has been circumvented by

using public funds for cultural centers associated with the mosques (Alba and Foner 2015: 136).

6 On one side, some studies indicate a fair amount of stability, and sometimes an increase, in religiosity among native-born as compared to foreign-born Muslims, although we know little about the meaning and impact of religious beliefs and practices in their daily lives (Jacob and Kalter 2013; Lewis and Kashyap 2013; Maliepaard, Lubbers, and Gijsberts 2010; Phalet et al. 2013; Voas and Fleischmann 2012). Other studies suggest that, on average, members of the second generation are becoming less religious and hold many views in sync with mainstream ideas (Connor and Koenig 2013; Diehl and Schnell 2006; Maliepaard and Alba 2016; Van der Bracht, van de Putte, and Verhaeghe 2013).

References

Alba, Richard. 2009. *Blurring the Color Line: The New Chance for a More Integrated America*. Cambridge, MA: Harvard University Press.

Alba, Richard, and Nancy Foner. 2014. "Comparing Immigrant Integration in North America and Western Europe: How Much Do the Grand Narratives Tell Us?" *International Migration Review* 48: S263–S291.

Alba, Richard, and Nancy Foner. 2015. *Strangers No More: Immigration and the Challenges of Integration in North America and Western Europe*. Princeton, NJ: Princeton University Press.

Bail, Christopher. 2014. *Terrified: How Anti-Muslim Fringe Organizations Became Mainstream*. Princeton, NJ: Princeton University Press.

Bakalian, Anny, and Mehdi Bozorgmehr. 2009. *Backlash 9/11: Middle Easterners and Muslim Americans Respond*. Berkeley, CA: University of California Press.

Beauchemin, Cris, Christelle Hamel, and Patrick Simon (eds.). 2015. *Trajectoires et origines: Enquête sur la diversité des populations en France*. Paris: INED.

Blow, Charles. 2015. "Anti-Muslim is Anti-American." *New York Times*, November 23.

Buruma, Ian. 2010. *Taming the Gods: Religion and Democracy on Three Continents*. Princeton, NJ: Princeton University Press.

Cainkar, Louise. 2009. *Homeland Insecurity: The Arab American and Muslim American Experience after 9/11*. New York: Russell Sage Foundation.

Casanova, Jose. 2007. "Immigration and the New Religious Pluralism: A European Union/ United States Comparison." In *Democracy and the New Religious Pluralism*, edited by Thomas Banchoff, pp. 59–84. Oxford: Oxford University Press.

Castillo, Mauricio. 2015. "Islamophobia,." *The New Yorker*, July 27.

Cesari, Jocelyne. 2013. *Why the West Fears Islam*. New York: Palgrave Macmillan.

Cesari, Jocelyne. 2015. "The Lack of Symbolic Integration of Islam in Europe, as Illustrated by the Charlie Hebdo Attacks." *CritCom: A Forum for Research and Commentary on Europe* (Council for European Studies). Available online at http://councilforeuro peanstudies.org/critcom/the-lack-of-symbolic-integration-of-islam-in-europe-as-illustrated-by-the-charlie-hebdo-attacks-2/

Congressional Research Service. 2015. "European Fighters in Syria and Iraq: Assessments, Responses, and Issues for the United States." Available online at www.fas.org/sgp/crs/row/R44003.pdf

Connor, Phillip, and Matthias Koenig. 2013. "Bridges and Barriers: Religion and Occupational Attainment across Integration Contexts." *International Migration Review* 47: 3–38.

Crul, Maurice, and John Mollenkopf. 2012. "Challenges and Opportunities." In *The Changing Face of World Cities: The Second Generation in Western Europe and the United States*, edited by Maurice Crul and John Mollenkopf, pp. 235–259. New York: Russell Sage Foundation.

Detroit Arab American Study Team. 2009. *Citizenship and Crisis: Arab Detroit after 9/11*. New York: Russell Sage Foundation.

Diehl, Claudia, and Rainer Schnell. 2006. "Reactive Ethnicity or Assimilation? Statements, Arguments, and First Empirical Evdience for Labor Migrants in Germany." *International Migration Review* 40: 786–816.

Duyvendak, Jan Willem. 2011. *The Politics of Home: Belonging and Nostalgia in Western Europe and the United States*. Basingstoke, UK: Palgrave Macmillan.

Faist, Thomas, and Christian Ulbricht. 2015. "Constituting National Identity through Transnationality: Categorizations of Inequality in German Integration Debates." In *Fear, Anxiety, and National Identity: Immigration and Belonging in North America and Western Europe*, edited by Nancy Foner and Patrick Simon, pp. 189–212. New York: Russell Sage Foundation.

Fernando, Mayanthi. 2015. "The French Myth of Secularism." *The Conversation*, January 15. Available online at http://theconversation.com/the-french-myth-of-secularism-36227

Foner, Nancy, and Richard Alba. 2008. "Immigrant Religion in the U.S. and Western Europe: Bridge or Barrier to Inclusion?" *International Migration Review* 42: 360–392.

Foner, Nancy, and Patrick Simon (eds.). 2015. *Fear, Anxiety, and National Identity: Immigration and Belonging in North America and Western Europe*. New York: Russell Sage Foundation.

"French Secularism and School Lunch." 2015. Editorial. *New York Times*, October 18.

Gallup Center for Muslim Studies. 2010. "In U.S. Religious Prejudice Stronger against Muslims." January 21.

Gerstle, Gary. 2015. "The Contradictory Character of American Nationality: A Historical Perspective." In *Fear, Anxiety, and National Identity: Immigration and Belonging in North America and Western Europe*, edited by Nancy Foner and Patrick Simon, pp. 33–58. New York: Russell Sage Foundation.

Jacob, Konstanze, and Frank Kalter. 2013. "Intergenerational Change in Religious Salience among Immigrant Families in Four European Countries." *International Migration* 51: 38–56.

Jacobson, Matthew Frye. 2006. *Roots, Too: White Ethnic Revival in Post-Civil Rights America*. Cambridge, MA: Harvard University Press.

Kurien, Prema. 1998. "Becoming American by Becoming Hindu: Indian Americans Take Their Place at the Multicultural Table." In *Gatherings in Diaspora: Religious Communities and the New Immigration*, edited by R. Stephen Warner and Judith G. Wittner, pp. 37–70. Philadelphia: Temple University Press.

Laurence, Jonathan. 2012. *The Emancipation of Europe's Muslims: The State's Role in Minority Integration*. Princeton, NJ: Princeton University Press.

Laurence, Jonathan, and Justin Vaisse. 2006. *Integrating Islam: Political and Religious Challenges in Contemporary France*. Washington, DC: Brookings Institution Press.

Lewis, Valerie, and Ridhi Kashyap. 2013. "Piety in a Secular Society: Migration, Religiosity, and Islam in Britain." *International Migration* 51: 57–66.

Maliepaard, Mieke, and Richard Alba. 2016. "Cultural Integration in the Muslim Second Generation in the Netherlands: The Case of Gender Ideology." *International Migration Review* 50: 70–94.

Maliepaard, Mieke, Marcel Lubbers, and Merove Gijsberts. 2010. "Generational Differences in Ethnic and Religious Attachment and their Interrelation: A Study of Muslim Minorities in the Netherlands." *Ethnic and Racial Studies* 33: 451–71.

Meer, Nasar, and Tariq Modood. 2015. "Religious Pluralism in the United States and Britain: Its Implications for Muslims and Nationhood." *Social Compass* 62: 526–540.

Meer, Nasar, Varun Uberoi, and Tariq Modood. 2015. "Nationhood and Muslims in Britain." In *Fear, Anxiety, and National Identity: Immigration and Belonging in North America and Western Europe*, edited by Nancy Foner and Patrick Simon, pp. 169–188. New York: Russell Sage Foundation.

Mohamed, Besheer. 2016. "A New Estimate of the U.S. Muslim Population." Washington, DC: Pew Research Center.

Newsweek. 2017. "France Has Become a 'University for Jihadists,' Marine Le Pen Claims During a Second Presidential Debate." April 5.

Packer, George. 2015. "The Other France." *The New Yorker* (August 31): 60–73.

Pew Forum on Religion and Public Life. 2012. "Faith on the Move: The Religious Affiliation of International Migrants." Washington, DC: Pew Research Center.

Pew Global Attitudes Project. 2012. "The American-Western European Values Gap." Washington, DC: Pew Research Center.

Pew Research Center. 2011. "Muslim Americans: No Signs of Growth in Alienation or Support for Extremism." Washington, DC: Pew Research Center.

Pew Research Center. 2014. "How Americans Feel About Religious Groups." Washington, DC: Pew Research Center.

Pew Research Center. 2015. "America's Changing Religious Landscape." Washington, DC: Pew Research Center.

Pew Research Center. 2017. "Europe's Growing Muslim Population." Washington, DC: Pew Research Center.

Phalet, Karen, Mieke Maliepaard, Fenella Fleischmann, and Derya Gungor. 2013. "The Making and Unmaking of Religious Boundaries." *Comparative Migration Studies* 1: 123–146.

Reuters. 2015. "Wilders Tells Dutch Parliament Refugee Crisis is 'Islamic Invasion'." September 10.

Schneider, Jens, Leo Chavez, Louis DeSipio, and Mary Waters. 2012. "Belonging." In *The Changing Face of World Cities: The Second Generation in Western Europe and the United States*, edited by Maurice Crul and John Mollenkopf, pp. 206–232. New York: Russell Sage Foundation.

Semple, Kirk. 2015. "'I'm Frightened: After Paris Attacks New York City Muslims Cope With a Backlash." *New York Times*, November 25.

Simon, Patrick. 2012. "French National Identity and Integration: Who Belongs to the National Community?" Washington, DC: Migration Policy Institute.

Slootman, Marieke, and Jan Willem Duyvendak. 2015. "Feeling Dutch: The Culturalization and Emotionalization of Citizenship and Second-Generation Belonging in the Netherlands." In *Fear, Anxiety, and National Identity: Immigration and Belonging in North America and Western* Europe, edited by Nancy Foner and Patrick Simon, pp. 147–168. New York: Russell Sage Foundation.

Telhami, Shibley. 2016. "Measuring the Backlash against the Backlash." Brookings Brief, Brookings Institution, Washington, DC, July 13.

Titley, Gavin. 2014. "Pork is the Latest Front in Europe's Culture Wars." *The Guardian*, April 15.

Tribalat, Michèle. 1998. *Faire France: Une grande enquête sur les immigrés et leurs enfants.* Paris: Éditions La Découverte.

Van der Bracht, Koen, Bart van der Putte, and Pieter-Paul Verhaeghe. 2013. "God Bless Our Children? The Role of Generation, Discrimination, and Religious Context for Migrants in Europe." *International Migration* 51(3): 23–37.

Voas, David, and Fenella Fleischmann. 2012. "Islam Moves West: Religious Change in the First and Second Generations." *Annual Review of Sociology* 38: 525–545.

Wike, Richard, Bruce Stokes, and Katie Simons. 2016. "Europeans Fear Wave of Refugees Means More Terrorism, Fewer Jobs." Washington, DC: Pew Research Center.

Wuthnow, Robert. 2005. *America and the Challenge of Religious Diversity.* Princeton, NJ: Princeton University Press.

2   Resilient Islam meets a resistant mainstream

Persistent "barriers" in public attitudes over religious rights for Muslims in European countries

Paul Statham

In Europe, over the last two decades, the distinction between Muslims and non-Muslims has become the most significant form of demarcation in public debates and policies for minority politics (Koopmans 2013). Questions over whether Islam is compatible with liberal democratic values and societies, and by implication whether a significant presence of Muslim minorities is "problematic" resonate strongly. There are intense discussions over whether the supposed or real cultural/religious characteristics of Muslims impede integration in their own right, independently from socioeconomic factors (Statham and Tillie 2016). Atrocities by perpetrators acting in the name of "Islamic State" are depressingly common across the continent, often committed by second-generation Muslims born in Europe. This has led to increasing political demands for Muslims to identify with their countries of settlement and accept so-called "core" liberal-democratic values in the domains of democracy, separation of church and state, and gender equality. However, barriers to peaceful co-existence and social cohesion also result from a lack of acceptance of cultural/religious differences among significant parts of the majority population. Such majority opposition can range from tacit avoidance of Muslims in everyday life to outright hostility and Islamophobia.

In a volume on how Muslims of immigrant origin and their offspring fare in their societies of settlement, this chapter addresses questions of their acculturation as well as resistance to this from majority populations. We are specifically interested in the strength of "symbolic barriers" between Muslims and majorities that indicate a *socio-cultural distance* between them over the presence of Islam as a minority religion. We think that how Muslims of immigrant origin are perceived by the majority, and how they see themselves as being accepted, or not, will importantly shape their individual life chances, and also their trajectory for social integration as a group in their societies of settlement.

Even in largely secular European societies, resonant public conflicts over cultural/religious difference matter because they mark all Muslims out as a single group and reify their supposed characteristics as a "problem" for liberal societies, regardless of which generation they come from, their family country of origin, and degree of religiosity. Viewed from the perspective of Muslims, however, the expression of Islamic belief is not a "homeland hangover," but increasingly a source of identification for second and third generations, who attempt to find a place between their parents' culture and rejection in their country of birth. Higher religiosity among second-generation Muslims than their peers is not only a revival of faith, but a reaction to the opposition and discrimination they face, i.e., "reactive religiosity" (Connor 2010). Demands by the children of immigrants for religious rights and cultural recognition are stronger than those of their parents' generation. In Europe, research shows that Muslims make most public demands for minority groups rights, and that public debates about groups rights are mostly about the accommodation of Islam (Koopmans et al. 2005).

While Europe's relation to her Muslim immigrants is distinct from the U.S. experience (Alba and Foner 2015), we still consider that the important variations between European countries merit investigation, given that they have different institutional approaches for extending rights to Muslims, based on their specific church-state relations and minority politics (Koopmans et al. 2005). Cross-national variations in the legal and institutional incorporation of Islam in Europe are well established (Fetzer and Soper 2005). The main question is whether religion is a "bridge" or a "barrier" to minority integration (Foner and Alba 2008)? While most scholars see Islam as a barrier in Europe, there are disagreements about the provenance and strength of this barrier. Some argue Islam is a resilient barrier to adaption because European societal institutions and national identities remain significantly anchored in Christianity and do not make equal room for Islam (Zolberg and Woon 1999; Foner and Alba 2008). Against this, Joppke (2009) argues that European liberal nation-states have importantly extended Muslim group rights, precisely because their legal and constitutional institutions uphold liberal norms, often in the face of public opposition. In this view, public sentiments should not be confused with public institutions, which due to the prevalence of liberal norms cannot operate unchallenged on an ethnocentric basis, so that: "religion, particularly Islam, may still be more 'barrier' than 'bridge' to including immigrants in Europe but only as a matter of mentalities, not of institutions." (Joppke and Torpey 2013, 141–142).

So far, however, there has been very little research on these public "mentalities" that build the barriers between Muslims and majorities, and how these relate to state approaches in their respective societies. This study compares Britain, Germany, France, and the Netherlands: countries with the most sizeable Muslim populations of immigrant origin in Western Europe (Buijs and Rath 2002; Alba and Foner 2015) and distinctive policy approaches for Islam (Koenig 2007). We examine public opinions on the place of Islam in state schooling, a field where the outcomes of controversies will clearly shape the socialization processes of the next generations. Our primary analysis is over whether teachers should be allowed to wear (Christian and Islamic) religious symbols in schools, and whether religious classes should be allowed for Christians and Muslims.

Schooling is an important domain in which to examine Muslim inclusion, because this is where the state acts in attempting to socialize the next generations into the values, identities, and ideas of who belongs to the national community (Gellner 1983). Schools are especially important for the children of immigrants, not only because of the importance of educational attainment for achieving upward social mobility, but because this is their first formative lived experience of engagement with the state and how the state addresses issues of minority needs and discrimination in society. For second-generation Muslims, whether or not provisions are made for practicing Islam on the same basis as other minority or majority religions in schools, demonstrates the state's degree of formal inclusion of their faith. However, regardless of the degree of formal inclusion of provisions for Islam within the curriculum, what also matters is whether this is controversial and the degree of opposition that it faces from the majority population, because this will shape the second generation's feelings and experiences of belonging to the community. By examining the strength of barriers to religious rights for Muslims in public attitudes, we gain insight into whether cultural/religious difference is a special additional barrier to integration that confronts Muslims of immigrant origin in Europe.

Multiculturalism and the challenge of Islamic rights to liberal democracies

In contrast to the prevalence of race in the U.S., public controversies over multiculturalism in Europe are dominated by questions over the extension of rights to Muslims. But what is the substance of these claims and counter-claims? The label multiculturalism is often used loosely to refer to any cultural diversity (Koopmans 2013). It is more useful to apply a narrower definition as group specific rights, exemptions and recognition for minorities. Here minority "group rights" exhibit two features: first, if granted, group rights go beyond the set of common civil and political rights of individual citizenship protected in all liberal democracies; second, if realized, group rights constitute the recognition and accommodation by the state of the distinctive identity and cultural needs of the minority (Statham et al. 2005). Examples include policies allowing exemptions from rules and obligations, state support for separate institutions, special facilities in public institutions such as schools and media, representation rights for ethnic/religious organizations, and affirmative action. Of course, group claims are made by a wide range of ethnic, national and racial minorities, but our focus is on those for differential treatment in the name of religion. We use Carol and Koopmans' definition (2013, 166–167):

> Claims about religious rights then contest entitlements regarding the performance (e.g., to be buried according to Islamic prescriptions) or nonperformance (e.g., dispensation from mixed swimming classes) of certain actions for religious reasons, or they are about entitlements that require others to perform (e.g., to create prayer spaces in schools) or refrain from performing (e.g., not to depict the Prophet Mohammed) certain actions for religious reasons.

Regarding the supposed challenge of religious demands by Muslims, a first point is that the idea of a unitary citizenship based on equal individual rights on which liberalism rests is an ideology, not an accurate depiction for most liberal nation-states. Most states already attribute some group rights and privileges in the form of corporatist or federal arrangements, and importantly – as we show shortly – give preferential treatment to specific religions over others.

While some Muslim group demands are for parity with other religious groups, others go further, requesting exceptional treatment. Exceptional demands are not easy to accommodate, when they challenge the very essence of liberal values. For example, Muslims who practice polygamy, female circumcision, or Sharia divorce, are committing acts that contradict most liberal states' legal and moral understandings of individual equality between men and women. How common or representative such practices are is not clear. We suspect they are not very common at all, though when they occur, they gain a disproportionately high resonance from a mainstream media keen to comment on the novelty of this cultural difference of immigrants.

Also, the global Islamic upsurge is not only a political movement, but a revival of commitments with explicitly religious underpinnings (Berger 1999). It involves a restoration of Islamic beliefs and lifestyles based on ideas about religion and the state, women, and the moral codes of everyday behavior, which often contradict the modern ideas of European liberal states. Islam is not just a "homeland hangover" brought by immigrants, but a source of identification for second and third generations, who attempt to find a place between their parents' culture and rejection in their country of birth. Many who wear the dress and accoutrements of Islam are educated professionals, the sons and daughters of assimilated immigrants. This revival of Islam is "Made in Europe" – a combination of the second generation's faith, reactions to difficult integration processes, and perceived hostility.

Although played out through symbols, such as headscarves and minarets, conflicts over Islam are also about the distribution of material resources. Migrants' religious demands in public education or welfare, where the state is responsible for distributing services, challenge a pre-existing institutionalized context in which the majority white population has real stakes too. This is why cultural conflicts often take place in public institutional settings where the state balances its obligations for minority provision against the pressures and possible political backlash of majority demands. A large proportion of the resonance over Islamic group demands actually comes in the form of reactions by representatives of the majority public. While some politicians may be sincere when they uphold what they see as liberal principles, this none the less leads to ethno-nationalist claims, where issues become distorted under emotive rhetoric about assumed national values and identities that "other" Muslims in the public domain.

In sum, religion matters a great deal in understanding European controversies over Muslims. First, although European societies are mostly secular, Christian religions play influential institutional social and political roles, irrespective of the small number of practicing worshippers. These church-state relations define the political environment into which immigrant religions have to negotiate a space for their community. Second, religious identification is a belief system that can shape an individual's core identity and behavior. A religious migrant may consider practicing religion a sacred duty that cannot be compromised. While states consciously try to shape migrants' civic attitudes through integration policies, they do not to the same degree for religious faith, not least because liberal states uphold freedom of religious practice. Third, the nature of the immigrant religion influences how migrants can adapt when faced by the dominant culture. In this respect, the public duties of worship associated with Islam can be more obtrusive within the European societies, than those of immigrant minority religions, such as Hinduism, where worship takes place in a way that is less publicly visible.

Variations in the state accommodation of Islam

The sizable literature on cross-national variations emphasizes how historical resolutions of church-state conflicts have shaped the accommodation of Islam as a minority religion in Europe (Fetzer and Soper 2005; Statham et al. 2005; Koenig 2007; Soper and Fetzer 2007; Laurence 2012). There is considerable agreement on prominent features that define church-state separations. France, the Netherlands, Britain, and Germany represent four distinct institutional types of religious accommodation, here understood as "opportunity structures" (Koopmans and Statham 2000), that importantly influence the degree and form to which Islam has been incorporated through an extension of rights to Muslims. We examine how distinct approaches to the accommodation of religious rights relate to patterns of public attitudes (between Muslim minorities and majorities) by using individual level data. This matters because, so far, there has been little comparative empirical research on whether public attitudes reflect the institutional degree of accommodation of Islam, or not. We present the basic cross-national variations in our countries' traditions for church-state relations, to provide context for the subsequent analyses.

France, under the concept of *laïcité*, is the archetypal secularist case, where there is a strict church-state separation that provides little space for religion in public life and institutions. The French state and public institutions are committed to secularism and even the role of Christian churches is restricted in the public sphere. As a consequence of *laïcité*, the French state has been resistant to the idea of separate institutions, such as schools, for religious groups, and displays of religiosity in public environments. In France there is a broad consensus that civil servants should not display visible markers of religion. In a context where even Catholic institutions, such as schools, receive far less state support and recognition than elsewhere, Islam has faced difficulties in finding an institutional foothold within a restrictive state framework (Laurence 2012).

The Dutch case stands in stark contrast to French *laïcité*. In the Netherlands, church-state relations evolved around the logic of "pillarization" as a consequence of ideological struggles between Catholic, Protestant, and secular groups in the late nineteenth century. Pillarization entails a denominational segregation of society where religious or ideological groups have the right to establish their own social infrastructure with state support. Hence Dutch church-state relations follow a tradition for: non-interference of the state in religious self-governance, which was broadly defined to include religious schools, hospitals, cultural and welfare institutions, and a range of other sectors. The compromise also entailed full state funding – on an equal basis for all denominations – for these sectors (Koopmans 2013). Although actual pillarization died out in the 1960s, its imprint is still influential as a logic embedded in institutional arrangements and law, and serves as a reference point for how to accommodate Muslim rights (Carol and Koopmans 2013). In this context, Muslims and other newcomer religious minorities have found it relatively easy to claim group rights granted to other religious denominations, while the state has traditionally refrained from preventing the expression of minority religions in public institutions.

Britain has an official state Christian church that is privileged over others. The Church of England is led by the Queen, as Head of State, while more than 20 Anglican Bishops sit in the second chamber. In Britain, the privileges that the state grants the Church of England are not automatically extended to other religious groups. Nonetheless, a pragmatic form of accommodation has proceeded, with the state relatively willing to grant rights to newer religions, a process supported in a paternalistic way by the Church of England. As Soper and Fetzer (2007, 936) state: "importantly, the presence of an established church and its close links with politics and public policy in Britain encouraged Muslim groups to look to the state for recognition of their religious rights and public policy needs." Overall, this has provided a considerable degree of parity between religions over time, while elites have been relatively supportive of demands to extend rights to Muslims on an equal basis to other minority religions, though to date full parity has not been achieved (Fetzer and Soper 2005; Statham et al. 2005).

In Germany, state recognition is extended to several Christian (especially Catholic) and Jewish religious denominations as public corporations, a formal status that entails privileges, including to receive Church taxes collected by the government, organize religious education in state schools, and provide social welfare services (Soper and Fetzer 2007). Crucially, the German state has so far not been willing to extend the public corporation status to Islam that it has afforded the Christian and Jewish denominations. This requirement for formal status has proven to be a barrier that has made it relatively difficult for Muslims to gain group rights (Laurence 2012). In addition, a strong imprint of Christianity remains in German liberalism that has been less accommodating than the establishment Church variant in Britain. Joppke (2009, 123) makes this point in his analysis of the legal basis of German headscarf bans:

> This is a case where Muslims are really excluded from a certain 'Christian-occidental' self-definition of the state, simply because one cannot be Christian and Muslim at the same time. This is the identity that transpires in the headscarf laws of the Catholic-conservative Länder.

Another factor in Germany is the difficulty for migrant minorities to gain access to formal citizenship relative to France, Britain, and the Netherlands (Koopmans et al. 2005). Muslims of immigrant origin are less able to demand parity of treatment to others when significant numbers of them remain formally non-nationals and lacking in political leverage.

Comparatively, the Dutch and the British church-state traditions have been more open to accommodating Islam as a new minority religion. In particular, the Dutch form of group-based pluralism inherited from pillarization allows a greater and relatively equal recognition of minority religions and favorable opportunities for Muslims to stake their group claims. Britain's relative openness and accommodating approach is more elite-led and top-down with the aim of avoiding conflict with religious minorities. The Church of England has importantly supported Muslim rights but retains its position at the top of the hierarchy. In Germany, a combination of high formal barriers to state recognition and status and relatively low political influence due to high barriers for migrant populations to gain access to citizenship is not conducive for Muslims. In France, Muslims face very high barriers to religious rights, not least because even Christian churches have historically been denied many privileges and rights within a context of strict state secularism.

There are two important dimensions of variation: the degree to which Muslim group rights are accommodated; and the degree to which Christian religions are privileged over others. First, the Netherlands and Britain have been relatively much more accommodating to Muslim group demands than France and Germany. Second, in Britain and Germany, Christian churches are substantially privileged relative to other religions. By comparison, the Netherlands and France treat religions in a relatively more equal way, notwithstanding that the Dutch are relatively inclusive, and the French exclusive.

Method and data[1]

We use data from an original survey conducted within a EU Framework project *EurIslam* (Statham and Tillie 2016). The data were collected through Computer Assisted Telephone Interviews (CATI) in 2010/2011. The survey oversamples people with a migrant background and includes more than 5,000 respondents. In each country, we interviewed migrant minorities from four important Muslim-origin countries (former-Yugoslavia; Turkey; Pakistan; Morocco). This "Muslim" sample was drawn by onomastic procedure: common family and first names were sampled from the latest electronic phonebooks. Respondents were screened to see if they, or one of their parents, were Muslims, and from our selected countries of origin. Bi-lingual interviewers were used allowing respondents to choose their preferred language. In addition, we collected a Majority (non-Muslim) sample randomly in each country. Efforts were made to ensure gender balance in all samples. Table 2.1 shows the samples.

From the survey, we selected questions relating to an extension of religious rights in state schools: (1) allowing religious symbols on schoolteachers' clothing and (2) the provision of religion in the school curriculum. For both we can compare responses about religious rights for Christianity and Islam.

We compare variations between groups within a country, instead of groups regardless of country. Because our respondents live in distinct national, legal, policy

Table 2.1 Sample of respondents

	Netherlands	Britain	France	Germany
Majority	385	385	385	390
Ex-Yugoslav	151	200	150	255
Turkish	250	350	250	355
Moroccan	250	200	250	256
Pakistani	152	350	150	162
Total (N)	1,188	1,485	1,185	1,418

Source: EurIslam Survey

and interpretative contexts for understanding religious rights, their opinions (for or against religious rights) mean something substantively different dependent on their respective national country context. A respondent living in Britain, whose child goes to a school where a teacher wears a religious headscarf, and is institutionally and legally empowered to do so, is clearly relating to a different interpretive and institutional world than one in France, where this would be inconceivable and legally impossible. The normal in Britain and France is very different precisely because of their distinct state approaches to Islam and Christianity. The scales for agreement/ disagreement in our survey are therefore best employed to measure relative differences between individuals (from majority and minority groups) *within a country*.

We also try to avoid the pitfall of lumping all Muslims together, by allowing for examination of differences between Muslims with backgrounds in four countries of origin (former-Yugoslavia, Pakistan, Morocco, and Turkey).

Allowing teachers to wear religious symbols in schools?

Historically, states use education systems as an important nation-building tool. Schools are important agents for socializing the next generations into the values, identities and ideas of who belongs to a national community (Gellner 1983). This is why schools have regularly been the institutional location for public and legal disputes over the place of religion in society, generally, and specifically over Islam. Conflicts over whether pupils or teachers can wear veils or crucifixes in a state school are common. Teachers perform a special role in schools as public servants acting on behalf of, and as employees of, the state. Hence, whether teachers are banned from wearing religious symbols in their professional role is a good indicator for a state's accommodation of a religion.

Regarding actual situations, we find variations. In 2008, no religious symbols were allowed in French primary and secondary schools. Britain and the Netherlands were more accommodating. Teachers were permitted to wear the Islamic veil, while Christian religious symbols were already accepted in state education. In Germany, Christianity was strongly present in education, while teachers were banned from wearing the veil in some *Länder* (Federal States), although the Federal Court ruled there was no clear legal basis for this in 2003 (ICRI).

We have two questions on teachers' attire and religious symbols: one on Christian symbols and clothing, and one on the Islamic veil. This allows us to compare respondents' opinions over provision for the majority religion and Islam. Our survey asks:

> Several aspects of state-religion relations have recently been under discussion in France/Germany/the Netherlands/the UK. Do you agree or disagree with the following statements?
>
> (a) Teachers in public schools should not be allowed to wear visible Christian symbols such as a cross or a nun's habit.
> (b) Teachers in public schools should not be allowed to wear a veil.
>
> (order of questions randomized)

Tables 2.2a and 2.2b show the main findings.[2] Scores show the adjusted means for a group's responses on a four-point scale after controlling for age, educational level and income. Note that the questions are worded negatively, so agreement indicates an opinion against religious symbols. However, we adjusted the data, so that a mean above 2.5 moving towards 4 indicates increasing disagreement with an extension of religious rights, and below 2.5 towards 1, increasing agreement. The columns show the results within each country. The Majority row gives the adjusted mean score for the non-Muslim sample. The subsequent four rows show adjusted means for the four Muslim groups (ex-Yugoslavian; Pakistani; Moroccan; Turkish), respectively. The * symbol shows when this opinion is highly significantly different from the majority opinion (at **p < .01, ***p < .001). The "Muslim" mean is a score calculated from the means of the four Muslim groups (weighted) per country. Last, the majority/Muslim gap shows the distance between the majority and Muslim means.

Table 2.2a shows findings on teachers wearing symbols associated with the majority Christian religions. First, we see the strong imprint of *laïcité* in the French majority and Muslim minority relative to those in other countries. The French majority respondents have the strongest disagreement with teachers being allowed to wear Christian symbols of all groups and are the only group apart from Moroccan Muslims in France, and former-Yugoslavian Muslims in Britain, who register on the disagreement side of the scale. By contrast, in countries where the state incorporates Christian religions to a greater degree, and allows teachers to wear clothes signifying Christianity, respondents from the majority are clearly against banning Christian symbols. This applies to the Netherlands, but to a greater degree to Germany, and especially Britain, the two countries where the state significantly privileges Christian religions.

Second, turning to Muslim respondents, their overall positions in countries where the state incorporates Christianity, the Netherlands, Britain, and Germany, "agree" with permitting Christian symbols for teachers' attire. This Muslim support for Christian symbols in state schools is most likely because Muslims understand that an expansion of rights for Islam is often best legitimated by a demand for parity with the majority religion. It is harder for liberal states to deny rights to

Table 2.2 Agreement/disagreement with teachers being allowed to wear (a) visible Christian symbols, and (b) (Islamic) veil, by group

2.2a

Christian symbols	Netherlands mean	Britain mean	France mean	Germany mean
Majority	**2.30**	**1.90**	**2.93**	**2.23**
Ex-Yugoslav	2.20	2.69***	2.45***	2.30
Pakistani	2.09	2.01	2.36***	2.06
Moroccan	1.80***	2.05	2.60	2.03
Turkish	2.19	2.40***	2.53**	2.41
"Muslim"	**2.07**	**2.29**	**2.48**	**2.20**
Majority/Muslim gap	**0.23**	**0.39**	**0.45**	**0.03**

2.2b

Islamic veil	Netherlands mean	Britain mean	France mean	Germany mean
Majority	**2.48**	**3.64**	**3.16**	**2.76**
Ex-Yugoslav	2.32	2.52***	2.73**	2.62
Pakistani	2.02***	2.33***	2.35***	1.93***
Moroccan	1.73***	2.14***	2.34***	2.10***
Turkish	2.14***	2.31***	2.37***	2.25***
"Muslim"	**2.05**	**2.33**	**2.45**	**2.23**
Majority/Muslim gap	**0.43**	**1.31**	**0.71**	**0.53**

Notes: Scale 1–4: agree strongly = 1; agree = 2; disagree = 3; disagree strongly = 4
Group significantly different from Majority at $*p < .05$, $**p < .01$, $***p < .001$ – Bonferroni pairwise comparison – shown only for subcategories of "Muslim" by family country of origin.

Source: EurIslam Survey

some that that are already extended to others (Joppke 2009). Even in *laïc* France, the overall Muslim mean is equivalent to neutral, showing neither support nor opposition to Christianity in schools in a context where it is denied. So overall, we witness no Muslim opposition to the actual (or in France possible) state accommodation of Christianity in this form. This goes against the idea of a "Christianity versus Islam" boundary along religious divisions driven and constructed by Muslim minorities. On the contrary, Muslims' relative support for Christian religious rights is indicative of a more pragmatic approach to their own religious accommodation. Regarding the gaps between the majority and Muslim minorities over Christian group rights, it is only in France that Christianity in schools clearly divides the majority and all four resident Muslim minority groups. Here the strong imprint of *laïcité* in the French majority's opinions, who on aggregate "disagree" with teachers wearing Christian symbols in schools, means that former-Yugoslavs, Pakistanis, and Turks are highly significantly different from the majority, while Moroccans just miss significance.

However, when we turn to opinions over teachers wearing the Muslim veil, we see from Table 2.2b that there is a clear dividing line between the majority population and Muslim minorities in all four countries. The opinions of all four groups of Muslim origin in all four countries of settlement are highly significantly different from the majority view, with the exception of former-Yugoslavians in the Netherlands and Germany. Among Muslims, we see that those who most likely came as refugees from the ethno-religious wars that tore Yugoslavia apart, tend to be less in favor of religious rights, than Muslims with origins in Pakistan, Morocco and Turkey.

By comparing Tables 2.2a and 2.2b, we can unpack some important features of the changes in opinion that occur as the question shifts from group rights for Christians to Muslims. First, the overall aggregate Muslim means are remarkably similar for teachers' wearing Christian or Islamic symbols across all countries. This shows that Muslims agree to accommodating religious symbols in state schools for their own and the majority Christian religions to the same degree. Again, we think that this similar level of support for their own minority religion and Christianity comes from the importance of demanding parity with a majority religion for advancing Muslim group rights. However, it demonstrates a second important feature of the significant gap between the majority and Muslims over teachers wearing the veil, namely, that it is produced by a change in the opinions of respondents from the majority populations as the question shifts from Christian to Muslim rights. It is the majority populations' opposition to the veil that drives the relationship and produces the significant gaps. Only in the Netherlands where teachers can wear the Islamic headscarf does the majority remain neutral overall, while in Germany, and especially in France and Britain, the majority agrees strongly with banning teachers from wearing the veil. This may not be a surprise for the France, where the veil is banned for teachers, nor Germany where there is a mixed policy, but where again the veil is banned in some Federal States. However, the British majority's very strong opposition is exceptional in that it goes directly against the country's policies for not banning teachers from wearing the veil.

Here it is worth pointing out that the shift in majority opinions when the question moves from Christian to Muslim rights is largest in Britain, and then Germany, compared to the Netherlands and France. Britain and Germany are the two countries whose church-state accommodations especially privilege Christian religions over other religions, while the Netherlands is relatively more equally accommodating to all religions, and France equally unaccommodating to all. From this, it seems that granting special privileges to Christian religions over others provides legitimacy for majorities to also discriminate in their views and support provision for Christians, but not Muslims. For Britain, the argument is that maintaining the status of a privileged state Church, the Church of England, does more to uphold a sense of Christian privilege in the minds of the majority than the extension of Muslim group rights does undermine it. The British majority clearly agree with teachers being allowed to wear Christian symbols and attire but disagree strongly with an extension of this right to Muslims, even though this is what actually happens. In Germany, where Muslims communities have less of a foothold in society, generally, because of restrictive citizenship, and Christian churches are clearly granted privileges that are not extended to Islam, this discriminating stance of the majority in prioritizing Christian rights is less surprising.

In sum, the British findings are especially striking. The British majority's strong agreement with banning teachers from wearing the veil produces a large gap between Muslims and non-Muslims that is almost twice the size of that in France, where the *laïcité* conditions make teachers wearing a veil an absolute non-starter.

Allowing religious education in schools?

Another query to test opinions on whether group rights should be included within state provision addresses religious education (RE) in state schooling. We replicate the design applied for teachers' clothing and religious symbols and ask questions that allow comparison between provision for Christian and Islamic religions. In part, this is to verify our earlier findings, given that references to the veil might provoke atypical emotive responses from respondents, or that the negative wording of the question might produce distorting effects. Our focus on the place of majority and minority religions in the curriculum of state education goes to the core of questions about the public and institutional incorporation of religion, not least because it is through their education systems that states seek to generate their preferred values and national identities.

With regard to the factual state of affairs facing our respondents, in 2008, Britain, the Netherlands and Germany allowed provision for Christian RE but had not extended this to Islamic RE on an equal basis. In Britain, parents were able to request that local councils on religious education install Islamic classes. This led to some state schools offering Islamic RE in areas with dense Muslim populations. Similarly, in the Netherlands, there is a partial form of acceptance. In Germany, there had been only very few pilot projects for Islamic RE classes by 2008, due to the subordinate position of Islam relative to the Christianity in the state's hierarchy of religious recognition. In France, the exclusion of religious instruction from state schooling meant that provision for Islam was a non-starter (ICRI). The survey asks whether respondents agree or disagree with two statements:

(a) Public schools should offer Christian religious education for those who want it.
(b) Public schools should offer Muslim religious education for those who want it.

(order of questions randomized)

Table 2.3a shows the adjusted means for groups' opinions over Christian RE in state schools. In line with the findings on religious attire, the main dividing line is between *laïque* France and the three countries where state education includes Christian Churches to a greater degree. First, the impact of *laïcité* is clear on the French majority's opinions, they are the only group who on aggregate "disagree" with Christian RE for those who want it. By contrast, all four groups of Muslim origin in France agree with the proposition to a degree that is highly significantly different from the majority. This produces a gap between the French majority and Muslims that is significantly wider than in the Netherlands, Britain, and Germany, where there is a relative majority and Muslim consensus in favor of this right for Christians. Support for Christian religious instruction in schools is especially strong among the German majority. But it is also evident for the British majority, who like their German counterparts live in a country where the state especially privileges Christian religions over others. In the Netherlands, where religious accommodation is relatively more equal across different religions, the Dutch majority on aggregate favors Christian RE, but less decisively. Turning to the Muslim aggregate means, we see that in all countries Muslims broadly "agree" with Christian RE provision. This confirms the earlier finding that Muslims tend to support Christian rights, probably thinking that this is more conducive for a spill over of rights to their own religion. Again, this indicates a pragmatic stance, with no evidence of a sizable Muslim opposition to Christianity simply because it is a different religion. When the question shifts to state provision of RE for Muslims (Table 2.3b), we also find a similar overall pattern to the earlier findings on teachers' wearing religious attire. First, there are clearly divided opinions in all countries between the majority and Muslims. With the exception of former-Yugoslavs in the Netherlands, all groups with Muslim origins in all countries are highly significantly different in their views to the majority, and more in agreement with allowing Islamic RE.

Once more we see that Muslims in the Netherlands, France and Germany, hold similar views on RE provision for Christians and Muslims. It is only in Britain where Muslims shift in their views to be more in agreement with this right for themselves than for Christians. Also, among the Muslims groups, the former-Yugoslavs are relatively less in favor of this Muslim group right than the others, but with the exception of the Netherlands, much closer to the Pakistani, Moroccan and Turkish groups than the majority.

Again, following the pattern that we observed earlier, it is the majority groups' relative shift in opinion against provision for Muslims compared to Christians that leads to important "gaps" between the majority population and Muslims. Also, this shift in majority opinions is greatest in Britain and Germany, the two countries that privilege Christian religions in their state accommodation over other religions. The shift is less pronounced in the Netherlands, where state accommodation generally treats religions more equally, and France, where they are all relatively equally excluded.

The overall findings bear some imprints of the countries' respective forms of church-state accommodation. French majority-supported state *laïcité* leads to a wide majority/Muslim gap (1.01) and few prospects for an extension of religious rights to Muslims. The French majority are unlikely to support rights for Muslims that are denied to Christians. In the Netherlands, where the state treats religions relatively equally and RE for Muslims is partially accommodated, the majority/ Muslim gap (0.37) remains significant but is the smallest of the four countries.

Table 2.3 Agreement/disagreement with schools offering (a) Christian religious education, and (b) Muslim religious education, to those who want it, by group

2.3a

Christian religious education	Netherlands mean	Britain mean	France mean	Germany mean
Majority	**2.32**	**2.15**	**2.80**	**1.57**
Ex-Yugoslav	2.25	2.27	2.30***	1.79
Pakistani	2.01***	1.86***	1.84***	1.67
Moroccan	2.00***	2.01	2.15***	1.85***
Turkish	2.29	2.05	2.07***	1.86***
"Muslim"	**2.14**	**2.05**	**2.09**	**1.79**
Majority/Muslim gap	**0.18**	**0.10**	**0.71**	**0.22**

2.3b

Muslim religious education	Netherlands mean	Britain mean	France mean	Germany mean
Majority	**2.56**	**2.75**	**3.01**	**2.17**
Ex-Yugoslav	2.43	1.96***	2.41***	1.87***
Pakistani	2.07***	1.55***	1.66***	1.50***
Moroccan	2.02***	1.55***	1.84***	1.77***
Turkish	2.25***	1.72***	2.07***	1.70***
"Muslim"	**2.19**	**1.69**	**2.00**	**1.71**
Majority/Muslim gap	**0.37**	**1.06**	**1.01**	**0.46**

Notes: Scale 1–4: agree strongly = 1; agree = 2; disagree = 3; disagree strongly = 4
Group significantly different from Majority at $*p < .05$, $**p < .01$, $***p < .001$ – Bonferroni pairwise
comparison – shown only for subcategories of "Muslim" by family country of origin.

Source: EurIslam Survey

In Germany, state inclusion of (especially) Christian religions but not Islam, leads
to an overall strong majority support for religious provision compared to other
countries, but also a relatively strong reaction by the majority against specific
provision for Muslims (German gap: 0.46). We also see a similarly strong reaction
by the British majority respondents when the question switches from provision for
Christians to Muslims. In the British case, this is supplemented by an assertive-
ness of Muslims for an extension of rights to them relative to Christians.

The British findings are remarkable. For a country with some degree of state
accommodation for religious classes for Muslims, it is striking that the British
majority shows a clear opposition to this policy and makes a very clear distinction in its support for Christian rights and opposition to extending the same rights
for Muslims. Conversely, British Muslims support Christian rights, but advocate
support for their own religious rights to a greater degree, no doubt encouraged to
expect parity from an institutional system that goes a long way to providing it on

many issues. As a consequence, we witness a polarization between the opinions of the majority and Muslims in Britain as the question shifts from Christian to Muslim provision. This results in a striking gap (1.06) along ethno-religious lines between the British Muslims and non-Muslims, driven from both sides. It shows a wide socio-cultural distance in the views of ordinary people and a potential for conflict between the British majority and Muslims over Islamic group rights.

Conclusion and discussion

Overall, regardless of the degree to which states accommodate Islam, we find highly significant "barriers" between majority populations and Muslims over what the provision for religious rights for Muslims should be in all four countries. While earlier comparative studies found that institutional approaches to minority integration and cultural pluralism importantly shape the field of public claims-making mobilized by collective actors and carried by mass media (Koopmans et al. 2005), our key finding shows the relationship holds much less with regard to public attitudes. While findings on the Netherlands, Germany, and France, support "opportunity structure" expectations to some degree, the British findings completely contradict the notion that accommodating policies lead to closer opinions between the majorities and Muslims. Britain is relatively accommodating towards Islam, but this combines with a majority public opinion that strongly opposes Muslim rights and produces the highest "barriers" of socio-cultural distance.

Decades on from the first immigration waves we see relatively few signs of the cultural acceptance of Islam as a minority religion, at least when judged by public attitudes. Religious faith seems to be a particularly resilient form of Muslim identification in Europe, and at the same time, this provokes strong reactions and resistance from largely secular majorities.

Religion matters for majorities even in secular Europe. A striking finding is that majorities' opinions turn against religious rights as the demand shifts from provision for Christians to Muslims. This shift drives the relationship and results in highly significant socio-cultural distances. We also found that the shift in majority opinions for supporting Christian versus Islam provision was greatest in Britain and Germany, the two countries where states clearly prioritize Christian religions above others. The shift was markedly less in Netherlands, which is relatively more accommodating across religions, and France that is restrictive to all. This is not to suggest that people in Britain and Germany see themselves as more Christian, but that they find greater legitimacy for placing Christianity over Islam and in doing so they repeat the discrimination within their country's approach to religious accommodation. For Britain, it seems that maintaining the status of a privileged state church, the Church of England, does more to uphold a sense of Christian privilege in the minds of the majority than the extension of Muslim group rights does to undermine it. Overall, majority opinions matter a great deal in determining the potential for controversy over Muslim religious rights.

The strength of British majority opposition to Muslim group rights is exceptional. This large gap between supportive policies and oppositional majority public attitudes raises a number of issues. It underlines that a liberal state's institutional approach towards Islam is clearly distinct from public sentiments about Islam. The two should not be conflated, because relatively liberal policies can be out of synch with oppositional public attitudes. This occurs when liberal states place obligations for protecting the cultural needs of (permanent) minorities over the popular majority view. It supports the view of Joppke and Torpey (2013) mentioned in the introduction. However, Joppke and Torpey underestimate the degree to which a state's ability to do this over the long term is restricted by majoritarian politics. What we see in the UK is a significant opposition to Muslim religious rights that also constitutes a potential for politicians to seek votes by mobilizing populist anti-Muslim sentiments. A rise of ethno-nationalist populist politics that targets Islam, not only impacts negatively on (all, not just religious) Muslims by stigmatization, but it also politically challenges the ability of a liberal state to live up to its ideals and support extensions of group rights to a minority religion.

From the majority side, the difference of Islam as a religion and associated assumptions about cultural characteristics of Muslims have become an interpretive masterframe in the public domain for "explaining" problems of social integration. Such cultural "explanations" that simply lump all Muslims together as the same, regardless of immigration type, country of origin, faith, and degree of individual religiosity, etc., build a strong "barrier" that must be hard for individuals to break out from in the social world. Populist politicians reinforce these barriers, when they "explain" complex social integration problems by the "unwillingness of Muslims to assimilate" or "incompatibility of Islam and liberal democracy." The power of populism is that it provides simple answers for complex social issues by blaming the cultural characteristics of an outgroup.

Religious faith clearly matters for Muslims. However, our findings point towards Muslims making religious demands on a pragmatic and not a religious anti-Christian basis. Muslims supported religious rights for Christians within state education too. It seems that they see better opportunities to advance Islamic rights through a context that supports all religious rights.

Most evidence indicates religiosity has not decreased among the second generation. But the Islam that remains resilient in Europe is different from that which came with the first immigration waves. It is "Made in Europe" and generated by living with rejection, while being stimulated by a global Islamic revival of commitments that have explicitly religious underpinnings. According to our findings, second-generation Muslims in Europe face at best a lack of support and at worst outright opposition from the majority over practising their faith requirements. In some cases, the state has accommodated such practices, perhaps in the face of a lack of tolerance from the majority population. However, controversies in important socializing public institutions, such as state schools, must have had an impact on the second generation and their acculturation trajectory. The strong symbolic "barrier" that demarcates non-Muslims from Muslims in the social world marks them all out as "culturally different," irrespective of their individual trajectories of social integration in higher education or the labour market. In this sense, culture and religion matters a great deal in shaping life chances for Muslims, even in European societies that are largely secular. This is also a situation that against the linear expectations of classic assimilation theories the passage of time does not seem to erode but reinforce. The "barriers" are strong, persistent, and enduring.

Acknowledgements

Funding support from the European Commission is gratefully acknowledged, reference: SSH-2007-3.1.1 grant 215863.

Notes

1 The analysis draws from Statham (2016).
2 We conducted five (group: native; ex-Yugoslavian; Moroccan; Turkish; Pakistani) × two (gender: male; female) two-way analyses of covariance (ANCOVA), controlling for age, educational level and income, for each country. We include age, education, and income as covariates, and gender as an independent variable, to see whether our findings hold, regardless of age, whether people are better educated or not, or how much they earn, plus we examine whether gender matters. In ANCOVA the test of whether groups' means are the same is represented by the F-ratio and an associated significance value. A first general finding is that gender does not affect results, while group belonging matters a great deal in explaining variance. For this reason, we focus on group differences within the four countries, respectively. Our tables show the means adjusted for the effects of covariates and level of significance of Bonferonni-corrected pairwise comparisons of these means.

References

Alba, Richard, and Nancy Foner. 2015. *Strangers No More: Immigration and the Challenges of Integration in North America and Western Europe*. Princeton, NJ: Princeton University Press.
Berger, Peter L. (ed.). 1999. *The Desecularization of the World: Resurgent Religion and World Politics*. Grand Rapids, MI: Eerdmans.
Buijs, Frank, and Jan Rath. 2002. "Muslims in Europe. The State of Research." New York: Russell Sage Foundation.
Carol, Sarah, and Ruud Koopmans. 2013. "Dynamics of Contestation over Islamic Religious Rights in Western Europe." *Ethnicities* 13(2): 165–190.
Connor, Phillip. 2010. "Contexts of immigrant receptivity and immigrant religious outcomes: the case of Muslims in Western Europe." *Ethnic and Racial Studies* 33(3): 376–403.
Fetzer, Joel S., and J. Christopher Soper. 2005. *Muslims and the State in Britain, France, and Germany*. Cambridge: Cambridge University Press.
Foner, Nancy, and Richard Alba. 2008. "Immigrant Religion in the US and Western Europe: Bridge or Barrier to Inclusion?" *International Migration Review* 42(2): 360–392.
Gellner, Ernest. 1983. *Nations and Nationalism*. Oxford: Blackwell.
"Immigration Citizenship Rights Indicators (ICRI) Project Accessible online from Wissenschaftszentrum Berlin (WZB)." Available online at www.wzb
Joppke, Christian 2009. *Veil: Mirror of Identity*. Cambridge: Polity.
Joppke, Christian, and John Torpey. 2013. *Legal Integration of Islam: A Transatlantic Comparison*. Cambridge, MA: Harvard University Press.

Koenig, Matthias 2007. "Europeanising the Governance of Religious Diversity: An Institutionalist Account of Muslim Struggles for Public Recognition." *Journal of Ethnic and Migration Studies* 33(6): 911–932.

Koopmans, Ruud. 2013. "Multiculturalism and Immigration: A Contested Field in Cross-National Comparison." *Annual Review of Sociology* 39: 147–169.

Koopmans, Ruud, and Paul Statham. 2000. "Migration and Ethnic Relations as a Field of Political Contention: An Opportunity Structure Approach." In *Challenging Immigration and Ethnic Relations Politics*, edited by Ruud Koopmans and Paul Statham, pp. 13–56. Oxford: Oxford University Press.

Koopmans, Ruud, Paul Statham, Marco Giugni, and Florence Passy. 2005. *Contested Citizenship: Immigration and Cultural Diversity in Europe*. Minneapolis, MN: University of Minnesota Press.

Laurence, Jonathan 2012. *The Emancipation of Europe's Muslims: The State's Role in Minority Integration*. Princeton, NJ: Princeton University Press.

Soper, J. Christopher, and Joel S. Fetzer. 2007. "Religious Institutions, Church-State History and Muslim Mobilisation in Britain, France and Germany." *Journal of Ethnic and Migration Studies* 33(6): 933–944.

Statham, Paul. 2016. "How Ordinary People View Muslim Group Rights in Britain, the Netherlands, France and Germany: Significant 'Gaps' Between Majorities and Muslims?" *Journal of Ethnic and Migration Studies* 42(2): 217–236.

Statham, Paul, and Jean Tillie. 2016. "Muslims in their European Societies of Settlement: A Comparative Agenda for Empirical Research on Socio-Cultural Integration across Countries and Groups." *Journal of Ethnic and Migration Studies* 42(2): 177–196.

Statham, Paul, Ruud Koopmans, Marco Giugni, and Florence Passy. 2005. "Resilient or Adaptable Islam? Multiculturalism, Religion and Migrants' Claims-Making for Group Demands in Britain, the Netherlands and France." *Ethnicities* 5(4): 427–459.

Zolberg, Aristide, and Long Litt Woon. 1999. "Why Islam is like Spanish: Cultural Incorporation in Europe and the United States." *Politics and Society* 27(1): 5–38.

3 Religious identities and civic integration

Second-generation Muslims in European cities

*Karen Phalet, Fenella Fleischmann and
Marc Swyngedouw*

Comparing the challenges of immigrant integration on both sides of the Atlantic, Alba and Foner (2015) conclude that Western Europeans are less likely than North Americans to include newcomers into the nation. Whereas immigration was at the origin of nation formation in North American history, Europeans tend to see their national identities as derived from an alleged pre-migration cultural heritage with a historical claim on the national territory. In particular, European national identities are historically grounded in a Christian religious tradition, which is now being mobilized in opposition to the increasing presence of Islamic faith traditions (Kunovich 2006). In public debates over immigrant integration across Europe, the accommodation of religious diversity is a salient and often divisive issue (Cesari 2004). Public acceptance of Islam and Muslims in Europe has long been hampered by secularist attitudes, which represent religion in general as backward and oppressive (Voas and Fleischmann 2012). Specifically, Islam is commonly seen as incompatible with European values such as religious tolerance, liberal democracy and gender equality (Minkenberg 2008). The contested position of Islam in Europe is further undermined by its securitization in the wake of recent terrorist attacks implicating European-born Muslims. On both sides of the Atlantic, prejudice and discrimination against Muslims have been on the rise since 9/11 (Bakalian and Bozorgmehr 2009), as national security threats are conflated with issues of immigration and integration (Foner and Simon 2015). Against this backdrop of increased public hostility toward Islam and Muslims, this chapter examines the religious identities and civic integration of native-born Muslims in European cities.

European-born Muslims make up a major portion of the second generation of immigrant origin in European cities. European-born Muslims make up a major portion of the second generation of immigrant origin in European cities. Their parents came from majority Muslim Mediterranean, Middle Eastern or African, West Asian, and Southeast Asian sending regions as immigrant workers (e.g., Turks in Belgium, the Netherlands, and Germany), post-colonial immigrants (e.g., Moroccans in France, Pakistanis, and Bangladeshis in Britain), and increasingly also as refugees and asylum seekers (e.g., Syrians in Sweden and Germany). The second generation are currently either enrolled in schools or entering the labor market, and most of them have been granted citizenship or at least local voting rights.

In spite of persistent claims of "Muslim disadvantage" overall (Heath, Rothon, and Kilpi 2008), second-generation attainment varies considerably across countries (Crul, Schneider, and Lelie 2012) and urban areas (Fleischmann et al. 2013). Within European cities, Muslim immigrants have developed vibrant religious communities which pass on Islamic religious ties and traditions to the next generation (Güngör, Fleischmann, and Phalet 2011; Phalet, Fleischmann, and Stojčić 2012). As Muslim citizens, the second generation face public prejudice and institutional racism in all European cities, yet cities also differ in their openness to religious diversity. This chapter focuses more specifically on the religious and civic belonging of the second-generation Muslims in different urban contexts: Frankfurt, Berlin, Antwerp, Brussels, Rotterdam, Amsterdam, and Stockholm.

Ethnic exclusionism – anti-immigrant attitudes in general (Fasel, Green, and Sarrasin 2013) and especially anti-Muslim attitudes (Pew Research Center 2013) – is well-documented in European societies. Such exclusive claims by the national majority population are less obvious, however, in cities, which are more demographically diverse. As primary settlement areas for immigrants, cities show much higher levels of migration-related diversity than the peripheries. Cities are also less clearly defined by prevailing public discourse and canonized national history than are nation states. Moreover, urban economies incorporate a highly diverse workforce both at the bottom and at the top of the stratification system. Finally, urban politics and civic life are also more permeable for immigrants than national politics, as is evident in the political salience of ethnic minorities in multicultural cities across the Atlantic (Kasinitz et al. 2009; Morales and Giugni 2011). For all of these reasons, city identities are not totally governed by the majority nationals, and hence leave more room for cultural as well as religious diversity. From their perspective, immigrant minorities stake ownership of their cities as local residents when they convene in urban spaces in ways that include their diverse ethnic ties, cultures, or religious creeds. This chapter focuses on cities as local contexts for religious community building and civic integration of Muslim minorities. We address two broad questions about cities as local integration contexts: (1) How do native-born Muslims construct their religious identities, and how do they combine religious and civic identities in the different cities? (2) How do they engage as citizens in the political life of their cities? To empirically examine both questions, we make use of the civic integration module in the Belgian national TIES (The Integration of the European Second Generation) survey of the Turkish and Moroccan second generation (ages 18 to 35) in the cities of Brussels and Antwerp (Swyngedouw et al. 2008). For comparative purposes, we draw on the religion and social integration modules in the international TIES surveys in Germany (Berlin and Frankfurt), the Netherlands (Rotterdam and Amsterdam), and Sweden (Stockholm) (Crul, Schneider, and Lelie 2012).

Religious and civic identities of Muslim minorities

Across Europe, self-identified Muslims are often strongly attached to, and actively involved in, the religious life of their communities (Voas and Fleischmann 2012).

As a rule, the first generation of Muslim immigrants transmits their distinct faith traditions to the next generation. Religious transmission is a central part of the more general heritage cultural transmission across immigrant generations through family socialization and religious community building (Güngör, Fleischmann, and Phalet 2011). Looking beyond generally sustained religiosity over time and generations (Diehl and Koenig 2009; Maliepaard, Gijsberts, and Lubbers 2012), qualitative studies of Muslim immigrant communities and youth in Europe and Britain document multiple "religious identity options" (Hopkins and Greenwood 2013). Along those lines, this chapter explores different ways of being Muslim for the second generation, with various European cities as local contexts of reception for religious identity construction and community building. Cities differ in the ways they define and organize religious groups and intergroup relations with varying degrees of religious accommodation and social disadvantage of local Muslim communities. Viewing religion as a symbolic boundary, we ask whether more accommodation and/or less disadvantage enable less rigid religious group boundaries in some European cities. As an indication of boundary blurring, we examine the prevalence of less strict, more selective, or more private ways of being Muslim and how they relate to civic belonging across the cities. How do city contexts shape the religious attachment and practices of native-born Muslims? Are religious identities compatible or in conflict with civic identities in the different cities? Empirically, we draw on comparative measures of religious attachment and practice for local and national self-identification across the above-mentioned cities (Fleischmann and Phalet 2016; Phalet, Fleischmann, and Stojčić 2012).

Cities and religious diversity

Muslim communities make up significant portions of immigrant-origin population in different European cities (Crul, Schneider, and Lelie 2012). Specifically, for the Turkish and Moroccan second generation in our research, their rough share in the total same-age population varies, with rates above 10% in Amsterdam (15%), Rotterdam (14%), and Frankfurt (13%) and below 10% in Berlin (9%) and Stockholm (2%). While the Turkish second generation predominates in Berlin, Frankfurt, Sweden, and Rotterdam, they are outnumbered by Moroccan Muslims in Amsterdam, Antwerp, and Brussels. In absolute numbers within the same age range, Berlin counts most local-born Turkish Muslims (over 35,000) and Brussels most Moroccan and Turkish Muslims by far (together around 80,000), followed by Amsterdam and Rotterdam (around 15,000), and finally Frankfurt, Antwerp, and Stockholm (all over 5000). Religious group boundaries can be salient and rigidly defined – or alternatively more fluid and negotiable – for second-generation Muslims in different European cities. The ways that cities, as local integration contexts for Muslim minorities, represent and organize religious diversity can make or unmake religious group boundaries (Phalet, Fleischmann, and Stojčić 2012). Below we briefly review country and city differences in terms of institutional rigidities, social inequalities, and religious discrimination experiences, which set the stage for different ways of being Muslim among the second generation.

European countries differ in the scope and timing of institutional accommodation (Fetzer and Soper 2005). Thus, the incorporation of Islam in the Netherlands builds on its historical legacy as a multi-faith society of formally equal and largely autonomous religious communities. Dutch Muslims have made the most of this unique opportunity structure to establish densely networked mosque associations as well as state-sponsored Islamic schools and media. In contrast, Germany's Christian churches are established as corporations of public law, a privileged status which has been denied to Islamic communities in the absence of a single religious authority. Without formal recognition, German Islamic organizations remain marginalized relative to their Christian counterparts. Sweden, like the Netherlands, has formally recognized Islam on an equal footing with other religions. Due to the historical quasi-monopoly of the Swedish Lutheran Church, however, Islamic institutions are less complete in Sweden than in the Netherlands. In Belgium, early formal recognition of Islam has only recently been fully implemented due to the late establishment of a representative body of all Belgian Muslims as required by the Belgian state. The recent implementation of equal status implies that Islamic institutions in Belgium too are less fully developed.

Zooming in on local contexts of religious community building, cities also differ in the degree to which religion overlaps with restricted access to socioeconomic resources. Comparing Turkish Muslim minorities in Europe, the first generation were typically recruited as guest workers with very limited human capital in the late 1960s and early 1970s, and significant social disadvantage persists into the next generation (Heath, Rothon, and Kilpi 2008). At the same time, socioeconomic disparities vary between cities (Crul, Schneider, and Lelie 2012). In part, immigrant parents were differentially selected into different cities so that some cities, most notably Brussels, attracted greater shares of qualified immigrants (Phalet and Heath 2011). Real selection effects do not fully account, however, for marked city differences in second-generation attainment as evident from their access to higher education and better occupations (Crul, Schneider, and Lelie 2012). For instance, second-generation attainment was highest for Turkish Muslims in Stockholm (where 36% accessed higher education) and least in Berlin and Frankfurt (only 6% in higher education) – with intermediate attainment levels in Belgian and Dutch cities (around 20% in higher education).

Varying degrees of religious accommodation and related Muslim disadvantage across cities are also reflected in self-reported experiences of discrimination by the second generation (Phalet, Fleischmann, and Stojčić 2012). Focusing on personal experiences of religious discrimination specifically, most discrimination on religious grounds was reported by Turkish Muslims in Frankfurt (42% one or more personal experiences) and Berlin (37%) and least in Stockholm (6%), with Belgian and Dutch cities in between (around 20%). Interestingly, experiences of religious discrimination were less frequent in countries where religious accommodation is more advanced. This suggests that more fully developed religious communities and organizations may better protect the next generation from discrimination.

To sum up, cities as local integration contexts differ in the institutional environments, socioeconomic resources, and lived experiences of local Muslim minorities. These urban differences amount to "bright" vs. "blurred" religious group boundaries, which in turn shape religious identity options for local-born Muslims. Applying boundary dynamics to religious differences in today's European cities, we expect more blurred group boundaries and hence more individualized ways of being Muslim in cities where Islam is more fully accommodated, less overlapping with social disadvantage, and more protected from discrimination.

Ways of being Muslim

Distinct ways of being Muslim were inductively derived from the patterns of religious attachments and practices among the Turkish second generation in each city separately (Phalet, Fleischmann, and Stojčić 2012). For this purpose, various measures of the religiosity of self-defined Muslims were entered into parallel cluster analyses.[1] Very similar clusters in all comparison cities indicated three distinct patterns of religious identity, which were labelled "strict," "selective," and "private ways of being Muslim" (see Table 3.1). A strict variant of Muslim identity combined strong religious attachments with devout adherence to ritual and dietary practices. In contrast, a private variant of being Muslim retains significant religious attachments which are largely decoupled from religious practice. Finally, selective Muslims combine strong religious attachments with selective practice as they mostly retain dietary practices, such as fasting during Ramadan and eating halal food, without regular ritual practice, such as saying prayers or visiting a mosque.

Comparing ways of being Muslim among the second generation across cities, we found that distinct identity options are more or less prevalent in different cities (see Table 3.1). Strict ways were most prevalent among native-born Turkish Muslims in German cities where Islam is least accommodated, upward mobility most restricted, and religious discrimination most pervasive. In contrast, private religiosity prevailed in Stockholm, where Islam is formally recognized on a par with the Swedish church, upward mobility is most evident and religious discrimination least frequent. In the lowlands, Turkish Muslims in Brussels and Amsterdam were more selective and less strict than Muslims in Antwerp and Rotterdam. Different ways of being Muslim within the same countries can be due, in part, to the selectivity of Muslim immigrants into different destination cities: Brussels and (to a lesser extent) Amsterdam have attracted more "human-capital immigrants" than Antwerp and Rotterdam. In addition, these cities also represent different local contexts of integration for the second generation: Both world ports (Antwerp and Rotterdam) are historically social-democrat strongholds with record levels of unionization. Moreover, they are currently home to new Radical Right parties capitalizing on anti-immigrant votes from disenchanted majority electorates. The more numerous strict Muslims in Antwerp and Rotterdam suggest religious reaction formation in response to a divisive local political climate. We will come back to city politics and civic life when we discuss the civic integration of Muslim minorities in the next section.

Table 3.1 Private, selective, and strict ways of being Muslim: religious identities of Turkish Muslims in seven European cities

	Berlin %	Frankfurt %	Antwerp %	Rotterdam %	Amsterdam %	Brussels %	Stockholm %
Private	16.7	15.1	21.6	25.7	20.5	24.8	52.9
Selective	33.3	43.8	33.4	32.3	50.0	47.6	24.5
Strict	50.0	41.1	45.0	42.0	29.5	22.7	22.6
Total	100	100	100	100	100	100	100

Note: Only self-identified Muslims were included in cluster analysis, excluding (very few) secular and Christian Turkish minorities.

Source: TIES 2007–2008 Germany, Belgium, Netherlands, Sweden

Conflict or compatibility with civic identities?

Looking beyond religious identity proper, Muslim minorities combine ethno-religious membership in immigrant communities with civic membership in the wider society. As noted above, from a majority viewpoint, Islamic values and ways of life are commonly represented as incompatible with civic values in European societies (Minkenberg 2008). From a minority perspective, however, recurrent experiences of being denied civic belonging on account of a distinct religious creed can undermine the perceived compatibility of dual identities as Muslims and citizens (Wiley and Deaux 2010). Accordingly, minorities in general, and Muslim minorities in particular, appear less strongly committed to the national identity than the majority population. At the same time, Muslim youth were found to challenge restrictive majority definitions of citizenship and to promote more inclusive understandings of civic belonging, for instance by simultaneously asserting their religious and national identities (Hopkins and Greenwood 2013).

This chapter focuses on city identities as less researched sites of civic membership which local minorities share with majority residents, and which may be more inclusive of ethnic and religious diversity than national identities. For instance, being a Berliner, Amsterdammer or Bruxellois may mean being both a Muslim and a fellow citizen, whereas being German, Dutch, or Belgian may not. Accordingly, we ask how the second generation combines their religious and civic identities, and how different cities as local integration contexts attenuate or exacerbate identity conflict. In cities like Berlin, for instance, where religious accommodation is less complete and upward mobility more restricted, religious attachment negatively affects the social integration of the second generation in mainstream society (Fleischmann and Phalet 2012). In contrast, the second generation in more accommodating cities like Amsterdam was less pressured to sever their religious ties in order to fully participate in mainstream society.

To address our questions about the compatibility of religious and city identities, we draw on comparative findings about the identification patterns of both the Turkish and the Moroccan second generation in five cities in Belgium, Netherlands, and Sweden (Fleischmann and Phalet 2016). As can be seen from Table 3.2,

Table 3.2 Religious, city, and national identifications: Muslim minorities in Antwerp, Brussels, Rotterdam, Amsterdam, and Stockholm

	Turk Antw	Moroc Antw	Turk Brus	Moroc Brus	Turk R'dam	Moroc R'dam	Turk A'dam	Moroc A'dam	Turk S'holm
Religious identity	4.06 (1.39)	4.18 (1.33)	3.16 (1.92)	4.12 (1.46)	4.22 (1.17)	4.27 (1.04)	4.02 (1.23)	4.18 (1.15)	3.75 (1.46)
City identity	2.95 (1.79)	3.17 (1.73)	2.91 (1.88)	3.28 (1.63)	3.69 (1.21)	3.96 (1.07)	3.74 (1.17)	3.90 (1.00)	3.70 (1.34)
National identity	2.37 (1.90)	2.80 (1.84)	2.98 (1.71)	2.94 (1.78)	3.02 (1.21)	3.24 (1.14)	3.19 (1.17)	3.27 (1.23)	3.01 (1.36)

Note: The means range from 0 to 5. The standard deviations are in parentheses.

Source: TIES 2007–2008 Belgium, Netherlands, and Sweden

both national and local civic identities of the second generation were psychologically significant (above the scale midpoint) against the background of strong and sustained religious identification. However, city identification was significantly and consistently stronger than national identification (except for Turks in Brussels). Furthermore, city differences in strength of religious identification were rather small – with second-generation Moroccan Muslims in Rotterdam being most strongly identified and second-generation Turkish Muslims in Brussels and Stockholm most weakly identified. The civic identities of the second generation were stronger in the Netherlands and Sweden than in Belgium – in line with delayed and hence less complete religious accommodation in Belgium.

Not only were city identities more strongly claimed by the second generation, they were also more compatible with religion than related national identities (Fleischmann and Phalet 2016). Specifically, compatible religious and city identities contrast with more frequent conflict between religious and national identities across cities. In addition, cities also differed so that religious and national identities were either compatible or in conflict depending on local integration contexts. Across cities, however, and in line with reactive religiosity, second-generation Muslims who reported more discrimination were more strongly committed to their religious identity and at the same time more weakly identified with their countries and cities of residence. The resulting identity conflict among second-generation Muslims was largely explained by their experiences of discrimination (Fleischmann and Phalet 2016).

Civic integration of Muslim minorities

As citizens, Muslim minorities participate in the political life of their cities and countries of residence. Looking beyond feelings of belonging, the second part of this chapter examines the political participation of Muslim minorities as a critical touchstone of their civic integration (Heath et al. 2013). Minorities' national identification reliably predicts political participation, so that more strongly identified minorities show more political interest, trust and engagement in voluntary associations at the national level (Fleischmann, Phalet, and Swyngedouw 2013). Similarly, minorities' commitment to the city identity – as an alternate civic identity shared with majority residents of the same city – might motivate their political participation at the local level. Indeed, if city identities are more open to cultural and religious diversity, this should lower the threshold for minorities to become politically engaged. From their side, political parties and leaders in multicultural cities are increasingly seeking to recruit minority candidates and to attract votes from numerically significant minority electorates (Jacobs and Tillie 2004). Zooming in on a less well-studied local level of participation, we ask: To what extent do Muslim minorities participate in the political life of their cities? And how do distinct city contexts shape their political participation? To address these questions, we use comparative findings from the Turkish and Moroccan second generation in two cities in Belgium as distinct local integration contexts (Fleischmann, Phalet, and Swyngedouw 2013; Swyngedouw et al. 2010).

Cities play a key role in the civic integration of citizens in general, and for immigrant minorities in particular. In spite of critical voices questioning the explanatory value of national models or philosophies of integration, earlier comparative studies of the incorporation of Islam and Muslim minorities in Western Europe have focused mainly on national institutions and policies (Fetzer and Soper 2005). National institutional arrangements and integration policies set the scene for local community building and political voice, yet cities are historically and demographically more multicultural than their peripheries, and hence politically more open to minority influence. As political parties in multicultural cities are seeking to attract votes from numerically significant minority electorates, they are increasingly catering to the needs of minority voters and recruiting minority candidates (Morales and Giugni 2011). Looking beyond electoral motives proper, city administrations intervene most directly in the social life of their citizens due to local competences such as social services and welfare, schools and education, urban planning and public facilities, and the police. Cities also routinely sponsor social activities and cultural festivities in which minority communities can participate or even take the lead. Turning to religion, cities are important partners for community leaders seeking to protect or promote religious minority interests or rights. Examples of religious issues which are politically contested and negotiated at the local level are Islamic prayer spaces or mosques in urban neighborhoods, headscarf bans by city schools, and city regulations of ritual slaughtering (Cesari 2004). Finally, minority representatives are not only key interlocutors of local decision makers, in time they also become part of city administrations in most multicultural cities (Kortmann and Rosenow-Williams 2013).

To make the case for the civic integration of Muslim minorities at the city level, we draw on the political module of the Belgian TIES surveys among the Turkish and Moroccan second generation, and majority reference samples in Antwerp and Brussels (Swyngedouw et al. 2008). Specifically, we asked participants about their voting behavior in the last local elections, political interest in local news, and trust in local institutions as indicators of their civic integration in the cities. We compared the civic integration of second-generation Muslims with (same-age and same-neighborhood) local reference groups of majority Belgians in both cities. In view of multiple civic membership, we also compared the political interest and trust of second-generation Muslims at the local level (cities) with national (Belgian) and transnational levels (Turkey or Morocco). Under the heading of civic integration, we explored the following questions: Do second-generation Muslims differ from majority populations in their civic engagement – as measured by voting behavior, political interest, and trust? How does the civic engagement of second-generation Muslims at the city level relate to their engagement at the national and transnational level? And do the cities of Antwerp and Brussels as local integration contexts make a difference in the civic integration of second-generation Muslims?

Antwerp and Brussels as comparative cases

The cities of Antwerp and Brussels present interesting comparative cases to study the civic integration of Muslim communities, as they exemplify distinct types of urban integration contexts in Europe. As a world port, Antwerp represents an industrial economy with a large working class. The city continues to attract immigrant workers in spite of its shrinking industrial sector. Politically, Antwerp boasts strong trade unions and a long line of social-democrat mayors. At the same time, the city has long been a hotbed of Flemish nationalism and its new mayor is the Flemish nationalist party leader. Since the early 1990s, the electoral success of the new Radical Right in Antwerp has fueled anti-immigrant and anti-Muslim public sentiments among the local majority population. As a triple regional, national, and European capital city, Brussels represents an urban service economy which attracts large numbers of highly qualified professionals as well as unskilled workers from diverse backgrounds. The intricate multi-layered structure of governance of this binational and multiethnic city provides multiple entries for minority political voice. At the same time, the city lacks a unified civic life or discursive space where minorities can connect and engage with political issues. In both cities, second-generation Muslims are dramatically over-represented among the early school leavers and the unemployed; and they experience pervasive prejudice and discrimination, for instance in encounters with the local police (Alanya et al. 2015). On a cautionary note, comparative evidence on the local civic integration of the second generation from the TIES surveys in Antwerp and Brussels precedes most recent strains on inter-religious relations between Muslim minorities and majority groups in Europe in the wake of new terrorist attacks implicating local-born Muslims in cities like Paris and Brussels.

Minority voters and candidates

One indicator of civic integration is minority voter turnout in municipal elections. Another indicator is the election of minority candidates into municipal councils. Voting is the main form of conventional political participation, and Muslim minorities constitute numerically significant urban electorates in many European cities. In order to win the "ethnic vote" of Muslim minorities, most political parties in Belgium make sure to recruit one or more minority candidates, especially in cities and in local elections (Jacobs and Tillie 2004). The democratic (under)representation of minority populations in political decision-making is the normative counterpart of their civic membership in the country of residence. In the Belgian political context, the vast majority of Turkish and Moroccan Muslims not only have local voting rights, but as citizens they also have the obligation to vote under the Belgian law. The TIES samples in Belgium allow us to compare the Turkish and Moroccan second generation in Antwerp and Brussels (aged 18 to 35) with comparison samples of (same-age) majority Belgian inhabitants of the same urban neighborhoods (N = 1,626 eligible voters, not counting 84 neligible participants). There were no significant differences in turnout rates between Muslim minorities and a majority reference group in either city. Rather, minority turnout reflects known city differences in the compliance of majority voters with their civic obligation to vote. In Antwerp, over 95% of majorities and minorities alike cast their vote; in Brussels turnout rates were just over 75% across groups. While turnout rates of local-born Muslims mirror majority participation levels in the same city, Muslims in both cities participated in large numbers.

Muslim minority voters were also distinctive. Not only were they more left-leaning on average than otherwise similar majority voters in both cities, they also reported relatively large shares of preferential votes for ethnic minority candidates.[2] Specifically, of the Moroccan second generation in Belgium, 34% in Antwerp and 55% in Brussels voted for a Moroccan candidate; of the Turkish second generation, 67% in Antwerp and 64% in Brussels voted for a Turkish candidate; yet the most "ethnic" electorate by far were majority voters, whose preferential votes went to majority candidates only. Furthermore, more frequent voting along ethno-religious lines among Turkish than among Moroccan minorities in both cities is in line with existing evidence of cohesive ethnic and religious community building by Turkish (vs. Moroccan) immigrants, as evident in higher levels of ethnic language retention, associational life, and media use, for instance (Phalet and Heath 2011). In addition, preferential votes were also gendered. More women than men voted for female candidates. One out of two Moroccan or Turkish women (51% and 50%, respectively) and two out of three Belgian women (66%) gave a preferential vote to a female candidate (as against 34%, 40%, and 41% of men of Moroccan, Turkish, and Belgian origin who voted for female candidates). Challenging common stereotypes of Muslims as less accepting of women in public office, support for female candidates differed mainly by gender and much less between Muslim minorities and the Belgian majority.

Political interest

Another aspect of civic integration is civic competence, which refers broadly to political interest as well as political knowledge and skills in citizenship behavior. To assess political interest, social surveys ask questions about general media use and national politics in the surveyed country. Citizenship is a multi-layered construct, however, and minorities in particular can define their (formal and/or informal) civic membership in multiple ways. Therefore, the Belgian TIES surveys inquired into participants' political interest at the local, national, and transnational level. Specifically, participants were asked how frequently (from 1 = never to 5 = frequently) they followed local news about the cities of Antwerp and Brussels (all), national news in Belgium (all), as well as transnational news from Turkey or Morocco (only minority participants).

As can be seen from Table 3.3, the Turkish and Moroccan second generation did not differ consistently from Belgian majority inhabitants of both cities. Compared to majority Belgians, both Muslim minorities were at least as interested in city politics, with less than 10% never following local news and up to 40% frequently following the news. Comparing across local, national and transnational levels, the interest of the second generation in local news was as high (in Brussels) or higher (in Antwerp) than their interest in national news about Belgium or transnational news from their homelands. Furthermore, ethnic differences between the Turkish and the Moroccan second generation were mostly restricted to homeland politics: Roughly one in two Moroccan participants never followed homeland news and very few were frequent users of Moroccan media, but only one in five Turkish participants never followed homeland news, and one in ten were frequent users. Again, this pattern reflects known community differences in ethnic associations and media use between Turkish and Moroccan Muslim populations (Phalet and Heath 2011).

Last but not least, clear differences in political interest emerged between the cities of Antwerp and Brussels. In accordance with lower overall voter turnout in Brussels, interest in local news was also much lower. While this reflects in part the status of Brussels as the national (and European) capital city, national political interest was also lower in Brussels than in Antwerp. Apparently, city differences in local political interest spill over into national politics.[3] To conclude, political interest among second-generation Muslim minorities is roughly on par with that of local

Table 3.3 Interest in local, national, and transnational news: Muslim minorities and majorities in Antwerp and Brussels

	Turkish Muslims Antwerp %	*Moroccan Muslims Antwerp* %	*Belgian majority Antwerp* %	*Turkish Muslims Brussels* %	*Moroccan Muslims Brussels* %	*Belgian majority Brussels* %
Local news	31	42	30	11	14	8
National news	15	23	22	9	13	16
Transnational news (Turkey, Morocco)	12	1	N/A	11	3	N/A

Notes: Percent frequent users
    N/A = not applicable.

Source: TIES 2008 Belgium

majorities in major Belgian cities; and cities as local integration contexts make the difference between the civic engagement or disengagement of Muslim citizens.

Political trust

One last aspect of civic integration is institutional trust: To what extent do Muslim minorities trust the political institutions that regulate and legitimize state authority in their country of residence? While institutional trust has been advanced as the oxygen of democratic governance, researchers disagree about the question of how trust relates to varying degrees and patterns of migration-related diversity in society (Kesler and Bloemraad 2010). A recent body of comparative work zooms in on the local aspect of multicultural cities (Morales and Giugni 2011). Looking beyond ethnic composition (ethnic categories and counts), this research relates political trust to more fine-grained measures of the quality of ethnic relations within and across immigrant minorities and majorities. In sum, dense ethnic networks of immigrant associations (Jacobs and Tillie 2004), as well as positive contact with the majority society, were reliably associated with enhanced political trust among minorities (Schildkraut 2015). Conversely, we found preliminary evidence relating negative interethnic contact, as indicated by personal experiences of discrimination, to reduce political trust among Muslim minorities (Fleischmann, Phalet, and Swyngedouw 2013).

Against this background, we draw on the Belgian TIES surveys to explore the political trust of the second generation in state authorities (from 1 = no trust at all to 5 = complete trust). We distinguished between local, national and transnational state authorities respectively at the city level (municipal administrations), in Belgium (national government), and in the homelands (Turkish or Moroccan government). Since trust in the national parliaments or heads of state (king or president) has evinced roughly similar patterns across cities and groups, we focus here on most comparable executive political power across local and national levels. In comparison with majority Belgians as a local reference group, the second generation reported rather similar levels of local political trust in Antwerp and even slightly higher trust in Brussels (see Table 3.4). Across the cities, political trust in local authorities was higher overall than trust in the national government. Again, ethnic differences within the second generation were mostly restricted to homeland politics, with Moroccan Muslims showing least political trust in homeland authorities. Trust in Turkish politics was assessed here preceding president Erdogan's most recent and dramatic authoritarian turn. In the April 2017 referendum, about one third of the Turkish Belgian electorate voted in support of Erdogan. Finally, political trust among the second generation was remarkably similar in both cities, in spite of distinctively low levels of trust among majority Belgians in Brussels only. To conclude, relatively high (as compared to majorities) and very similar levels of political trust (across cities) for Muslim minorities in Belgium challenge supposedly general associations of high ethnic diversity or ethnic tension in today's multicultural societies with low political trust and more generally, with endemic threat to the viability of liberal democracy.

Table 3.4 Local, national, and transnational political trust

	Turkish Muslims Antwerp %	Moroccan Muslims Antwerp %	Belgian majority Antwerp %	Turkish Muslims Brussels %	Moroccan Muslims Brussels %	Belgian majority Brussels %
Municipal administration	86	78	83	79	81	69
National government	66	59	72	60	56	42
Turkish/Moroccan government	67	36	N/A	57	44	N/A

Notes: Percent high trust
  N/A = not applicable.

Source: TIES 2008 Belgium

Religion and civic integration: some comparative lessons

Large portions of the second generation coming of age in European cities are Muslims, and most local-born Muslims are actively involved in the religious life of their communities. At the same time, they are also participating as fellow citizens in the wider society and in the civic life of their cities in particular. This chapter drew on comparative data on the integration of the second generation across Belgian, Dutch, German, and Swedish cities to explore how different cities afford distinct forms of religious and civic belonging among the second generation.

The first section of this chapter addressed the question of how Muslim minorities define their religious and civic identities, and how these identities are shaped by cities as local integration contexts. Comparative findings cover seven cities in four countries which received large numbers of Muslim immigrants from Turkey and/or Morocco. In spite of institutional barriers, restricted human capital and widespread public prejudice across European cities, most local Muslim minorities have built resilient religious communities which support the continued religious involvement of the second generation. Cities also differ, however, in the way they define religious group boundaries so that some cities (like Stockholm or Amsterdam) are more accommodating or less unequal along religious lines than others (like Antwerp or Frankfurt). In a nutshell, two strands of evidence highlight the importance of cities as local contexts for religious identity formation among the second generation. First of all, strict, selective, and private ways of being Muslim represent distinct identity options which are available in all cities for second-generation Muslims. Yet, different identity options were prevalent in different cities. In less accommodating German cities, for instance, religious attachment was most often coupled with strict conformity to religious rites and rules. Conversely, religious attachment more often allowed for selective or irregular practice in more accommodating city contexts, such as Amsterdam or Stockholm. Relatedly, cities also differed in the levels of religious discrimination that second-generation Muslims reported. When discriminated against, the participants in our survey experienced their religious and civic identities as more conflicting (negative correlations). Importantly, local city identities were never conflicting with the religious identities of the second generation, suggesting that multicultural cities uniquely afford identity multiplicity. We conclude that identity conflict is not inherent in the nature of Islamic values or ways of life, as it is commonly assumed in public debates. Rather, religion can reinforce civic identification, especially at the local level of multicultural cities and when religious disadvantage and discrimination are less pervasive. In other words, when European countries accommodate Islam and include Muslims, the Islam of the second generation will further evolve into a "civic religion" which is politically attuned to public life in European cities.

The chapter also addressed the question of how Muslim minorities participate in the political life of their cities of residence. Our comparative analysis of Turkish and Moroccan Muslim communities in two cities speaks to the strategic role of cities as local integration contexts. In particular, three findings extend the evidence for local integration contexts to the domain of civic integration. First, comparing minority and majority groups, Muslim minorities showed generally similar levels of political participation, interest, and trust to those of local majority inhabitants of the same cities and urban neighborhoods. Second, local majority groups differed markedly, with generally less (conventional) political participation, interest, and trust in the capital city of Brussels than in Antwerp. As a consequence, the political behaviors and attitudes of second-generation Muslims in Antwerp were rather more similar to those of majority Belgians in the same city than to the behaviors and attitudes of fellow Muslims in Brussels. The double comparison across communities and cities supports the conclusion that Muslim minorities integrate politically into the distinct local socio-political contexts in both cities. Moreover, comparing across local, national, and transnational levels, Muslims reported significant political engagement at the local level in Antwerp in particular, which seems to spill over into national politics as well. Lastly, city differences in the political behaviors and attitudes of Turkish and Moroccan Muslims were also more important than ethnic differences between the communities, with the exception of a distinctively Turkish involvement in homeland politics. To conclude, threefold comparisons of the Turkish and Moroccan second generation across communities, cities, and levels of governance suggest that Muslim minorities integrate politically into the local civic life of their cities of residence. How current trends towards political polarization in Europe and overseas will affect Muslims' civic involvement is as yet an open question. In Antwerp, for instance, the current nationalist mayor is antagonizing local Muslim communities by publicly stating that their religious fervor stands in the way of civic loyalty. Our findings suggest that the European second generation will not likely withdraw from the political arena, but will continue to be a political force that European cities will have to reckon with.

Acknowledgements

The authors are grateful to the Advanced Research Collaborative and the Sociology Department at the CUNY Graduate Center for supporting their work on this chapter. The authors would like to thank Richard Alba and Nancy Foner for contributing a transatlantic perspective, and Kay Deaux for her comments on earlier versions of this chapter.

Notes

1 We ran K-means cluster analysis of the TIES religiosity measures in each city to empirically derive a typology of Muslim identification and practice, and to assign each participant to the type (or 'cluster') that was closest to their individual response pattern.
2 The Belgian electoral system allows for one or more preferential votes for individual candidates.
3 It should be acknowledged that Antwerp had a social-democrat mayor at the time of this survey. Hence, we do not know whether Muslim civic integration is sustained under the current nationalist mayor.

References

Alanya, Ahu, Karen Phalet, Marc Swyngedouw, and Veronique Vandezande. 2017. "Close Encounters: Minority and Majority Perspectives on Discrimination and Intergroup Relations in Antwerp, Belgium." *International Migration Review* 51(1): 191–217.
Alba, Richard, and Nancy Foner. 2015. *Strangers No More: Immigration and the Challenges of Integration in North America and Western Europe.* Princeton, NJ: Princeton University Press.
Bakalian, Anny, and Mehdi Borzorgmehr. 2009. *Backlash 9/11: Middle Easterners and Muslim Americans Respond.* Berkeley, CA: University of California Press.
Cesari, Jocelyne. 2004. *When Islam and Democracy Meet: Muslims in Europe and in the United States.* New York and Basingstoke: Palgrave Macmillan.
Crul, Maurice, Jens Schneider, and Frans Lelie. 2012. *The European Second Generation Compared: Does the Integration Context Matter?* Amsterdam: Amsterdam University Press.
Diehl, Claudia and Matthias Koenig. 2009. "Religiosität Türkischer Migranten im Generationenverlauf." *Zeitschrift für Soziologie* 38(4): 300–319.
Fasel, Nicole, Eva Green, and Oriane Sarrasin. 2013. "Facing Cultural Diversity: Anti-Immigrant Attitudes in Europe." *European Psychologist* 18(4): 253–262.
Fetzer, Joel S. and Christopher J. Soper. 2005. *Muslims and the State in Britain, France and Germany.* Cambridge: Cambridge University Press.
Fleischmann, Fenella, and Karen Phalet. 2012. "Integration and Religiosity Among the Turkish Second Generation in Europe: A Comparative Analysis Across Four Capital Cities." *Ethnic and Racial Studies* 35(2): 320–341.
Fleischmann, Fenella and Karen Phalet. 2016. "Identity Conflict or Compatibility: A Comparison of Muslim Minorities in Five European Cities." *Political Psychology* 37(4): 445–577.
Fleischmann, Fenella, Karen Phalet, and Marc Swyngedouw. 2013. "Dual Identity Under Threat: When and How Do Turkish and Moroccan Minorities Engage in Politics?" *Zeitschrift für Psychologie* 22(4): 214–222.
Fleischmann, Fenella, Patrick Deboosere, Karel Neels, and Karen Phalet. 2013. "How Family and Co-Ethnic Neighborhood Resources Affect Second-Generation Attainment in Belgium." *European Sociological Review* 29(6): 1239–1250.

Foner, Nancy, and Patrick Simon, eds. 2015. *Fear, Anxiety, and National Identity: Immigration and Belonging in North America and Western Europe.* New York: Russell Sage Foundation.

Güngör, Derya, Fenella Fleischmann, and Karen Phalet. 2011. "Religious Identification, Beliefs, and Practices among Turkish Belgian and Moroccan Belgian Muslims: Intergenerational Continuity and Acculturative Change." *Journal of Cross-Cultural Psychology* 42(8): 1356–1374.

Heath, Anthony, Catherine Rothon, and Elina Kilpi. 2008. "The Second Generation in Western Europe: Education, Employment and Occupational Attainment." *Annual Review of Sociology* 34(1): 211–235.

Heath, Anthony, Stephen Fisher, Gemma Rosenblatt, David Sanders, and Maria Sobolewska. 2013. *The Political Integration of Ethnic Minorities in Britain.* Oxford: Oxford University Press.

Hopkins, Nick, and Ronni Michelle Greenwood. 2013. "Hijab, Visibility and the Performance of Identity." *European Journal of Social Psychology* 43(5): 438–447.

Jacobs, Dirk, and Jean Tillie. 2004. "Social Capital and Political Integration of Migrants." *Journal of Ethnic and Migration Studies* 30(3): 419–427.

Kasinitz, Philip, Mary Waters, John Mollenkopf, and Jennifer Holdaway. 2009. *Inheriting the City: The Children of Immigrants Come of Age.* New York: Russell Sage Foundation.

Kesler, Christel, and Irene Bloemraad. 2010. "Does Immigration Erode Social Capital? The 3 Conditional Effects of Immigration-Generated Diversity on Trust, Membership and Participation across 19 Countries." *Canadian Journal of Political Science* 43(2): 319–347.

Kortmann, Matthias, and Krestin Rosenow-Williams. 2013. *Islamic Organizations in Europe and the USA: Multidisciplinary Perspectives.* Basingstoke, UK: Palgrave Macmillan.

Kunovich, Robert M. 2006. "An Exploration of the Salience of Christianity for National Identity in Europe." *Sociological Perspectives* 49(4): 435–460.

Maliepaard, Mieke, Mérove Gijsberts, and Marcel Lubbers. 2012. "Reaching the Limits of Secularization? Turkish- and Moroccan-Dutch Muslims in the Netherlands 1998–2006." *Journal for the Scientific Study of Religion* 51(2): 359–367.

Maxwell, Rashaan. 2006. "Muslims, South Asians and the British Mainstream: A National Identity Crisis?" *West European Politics* 29(4): 736–756.

Minkenberg, Michael. 2008. *The Radical Right in Europe: An Overview.* Verlag Bertelsmann Stiftung.

Morales, Laura, and Marco Giugni. 2011. "Political Opportunities, Social Capital and the Political Inclusion of Immigrants in European Cities." In *Social Capital, Political Participation and Migration in Europe: Making Multicultural Democracy Work,* edited by Laura Morales and Marco Giugni, pp. 1–18. Basingstoke, UK: Palgrave Macmillan.

Pew Research Center. 2013. "The World's Muslims: Religion, Politics and Society." Washington, DC: Pew Research Center.

Phalet, Karen, and Anthony Heath. 2011. "Ethnic Community, Urban Economy and Second-Generation Attainment: Turkish Disadvantage in Belgium." In *The Next Generation: Immigrant Youth in Comparative Perspective,* edited by Richard Alba and Mary Waters, pp. 135–165. New York: New York University Press.

Phalet, Karen, Fenella Fleischmann, and Snezana Stojčić. 2012. "Ways of 'Being Muslim': Religious Identities of Second-Generation Turks." In *The European Second Generation Compared. Does the Integration Context Matter?*, edited by Maurice Crul, Jens Schneider, and Frans Lelie, pp. 341–373. Amsterdam: Amsterdam University Press.

Schildkraut, Deborah J. 2015. "Does Becoming American Create a Better American? How Identity Attachments and Perceptions of Discrimination Affect Trust and Obligation." In *Fear, Anxiety, and National Identity*, edited by Nancy Foner and Patrick Simon, pp. 83–114. New York: Russell Sage Foundation.

Swyngedouw, Marc, Fenella Fleischmann, Karen Phalet, and Gülseli Baysu. 2010. *Politieke Participatie van Turkse en Marokkaanse Belgen in Antwerpen en Brussel*. KU Leuven: CeSo/CSCP Research Report.

Swyngedouw, Marc, Karen Phalet, Gülseli Baysu, Veronique Vandezande, and Fenella Fleischmann. 2008. *Technical Report TIES 2008*. KU Leuven: CeSo/CSCP Research Report.

Voas, David, and Fenella Fleischmann. 2012. "Islam Moves West: Religious Change in the First and Second Generations." *Annual Review of Sociology* 38: 525–545.

Wiley, Shaun, and Kay Deaux. 2010. "The Bicultural Identity Performance of Immigrants." In *Identity and Participation in Culturally Diverse Societies,* edited by Assaad Azzi, Xenia Chryssochoou, Bert Klandermans, and Bernd Simon, pp. 49–68. Malden, MA: Wiley-Blackwell.

4 The integration paradox

Second-generation Muslims in the United States

Mehdi Bozorgmehr and Eric Ketcham

> Donald J. Trump is calling for a total and complete shutdown of Muslims entering the United States until our country's representatives can figure out what the hell is going on.
>
> (Donald Trump, December 7, 2015)

The election of Donald Trump to the U.S. Presidency was a traumatic moment for the nation's Muslim residents and citizens. The Trump campaign crystalized much of the anti-Muslim sentiment that had been growing since the terrorist attacks of 9/11, leaving many Muslims feeling deeply misunderstood and politically vulnerable. While the Trump administration eventually retreated from a clearly unconstitutional travel ban based solely on religion, the rewritten versions of the ban targeting specific nations were widely perceived as an attack on Muslims in general, including the growing number of Muslims born and raised in the US.

It was not always this way. Until fairly recently, anti-immigrant sentiment in the U.S. was largely targeted at Latinos. In contrast to Europe, America's Muslim population is relatively small, generally well educated and largely middle class. The U.S. lacks the deep colonial entanglements with the Islamic world that have shaped relations with immigrant communities in France and the United Kingdom. Nor does it have a long history of border conflicts with a feared Islamic "other." To be sure, the American support of Israel and the Iranian hostage crisis have stoked hostility between Americans and some Muslim groups. But rarely was this directed towards Muslims in general prior to 1990s.

Even in immediate aftermath of the 9/11 attacks, many American observers took solace in the fact that the 9/11 hijackers were foreign nationals. Whatever hatreds had stirred U.S. enemies in the Islamic world abroad, "home grown" terrorism was largely a European problem, or so Americans liked to think. And it is true that U.S.-born Muslims are in many ways better integrated, in terms of both educational attainment and labor force participation, than their European counterparts. Yet it now seems that this faith in the assimilative powers of American culture may have been overly optimistic. In many ways, second-generation Muslims in the United States appear increasingly alienated from the American mainstream. Indeed, in recent years U.S. terrorism suspects have increasingly included long-term residents, children of immigrants, and native-born converts to Islam (Kurzman, Schanzer, and Moosa 2011). The San Bernardino, California, shootings as well as the attacks at the 2013 Boston Marathon, the Orlando nightclub shooting, and the unsuccessful attempts by the Times Square bomber in 2010 serve to underscore this trend.

Of course, the media focus on acts of terrorism by a tiny number of extremists should not be allowed to obscure the experiences of the vast majority of Muslim American youth. Yet surprisingly little is known about this group. The major research efforts on the children of immigrants have largely excluded the Muslim American experience. Although there have been at least three large-scale survey research projects on the second generation in the United States, none of them has included any Muslim group (Crul and Mollenkopf 2012; Kasinitz et al. 2008; Portes and Rumbaut 2001). And while there have been numerous studies of Muslims in the U.S. since 9/11, they have almost exclusively focused on immigrants, not on their U.S. born children (Bakalian and Bozorgmehr 2009). Therefore, there is a need for research that examines social, cultural, economic, and political dimensions of the second-generation Muslim experience in the United States. As the first substantial generation of native-born Muslim Americans comes of age, we need to know what it means for these young people to be both Muslim and American. How do they reconcile these identities in post-9/11 America?

This chapter examines the socioeconomic progress and cultural integration of second-generation Muslims in the United States.[1] Two major datasets are used to gauge integration of the second generation relative to Muslim immigrants. The socioeconomic aspects of integration are examined through an analysis of data from the U.S. Census Bureau's American Community Survey (ACS). The cultural and political dimensions of integration are examined using the Pew Muslim American Survey.

Background

According to the Pew population estimates, there are about three million Muslims in the United States, making up slightly less than 1% of the U.S. population. They are, however, one of the fastest growing religious groups in America (Pew Research Center 2015). This population is very diverse and complex, hailing from countries from all over the world, though mainly from the Middle East, North Africa, Sub-Saharan Africa, South Asia, and Southeast Asia. While far smaller than the European Muslim population, the U.S. Muslim population is more ethnically diverse than that of most European countries.

The focus of this chapter is on second-generation integration and how the second generation compares with their immigrant parents. It should be noted, however, that a considerable portion of the U.S. Muslim population are people whose forebears have been in the U.S. for many generations. Most of these Muslims are African Americans, but journalistic accounts suggest an increasing number of Latino and White Americans in this population as well (Dooley 2002). Estimates of the number of these longtime American Muslims vary, but the general consensus is that they make up about 25% of the American Muslim population (Pew Research Center 2015). This group includes many of the most well-known and visible Muslims in the U.S. including the athletes Muhammad Ali and Kareem Abdul-Jabbar, the actor and musician Yasiin Bey (formerly known as Mos Def) and U.S. Representative Keith Ellison, currently the only Muslim in Congress. While these longtime American Muslims are often referred to in the literature as "converts," many are in fact Muslims by birth, born into families who have practiced Islam for two or even three generations. How much contact they have with immigrant-descended Muslims and how their practice of Islam differs from that of immigrant-origin Muslims is a topic that clearly merits further investigation.

We should also be cautious that in using a religious label we do not imply that all American Muslims are devout or particularly "observant." In fact, many of the people who are considered "Muslims" in the United States are thoroughly secular, cultural, or even nominal Muslims, and identify more strongly with their national origin than with their religion (Bozorgmehr, Ong, and Tosh 2015).

The complexity of the Muslim population of immigrant stock in the United States calls for a brief background on Middle Easterners, North Africans, sub-Saharan Africans, South Asians, and Southeast Asians. Middle Eastern and North African immigrants to the United States are particularly diverse, representing many nationalities, ethnicities, and religions. In 2015, the U.S. Census Bureau tested the addition of a "Middle Eastern or North African," or "MENA" racial category. The results showed that the inclusion of the MENA category enabled respondents to choose this option over "White" or "Some Other Race." Accordingly the Census Bureau recommended that a separate MENA option be added to the race categories available on the 2020 U.S. census, however this proposal was not ultimately adopted.

In addition to immigrants of MENA origins, South Asians from almost exclusively Muslim countries often identify along religious lines (i.e., Afghans, Bangladeshis and Pakistanis). While Asian Indians make up the largest segment of the South Asian American population, the relatively small Muslim component of this population identifies with the other Muslim countries in the region (Kibria 2006; Leonard 1997). Muslim South Asian immigrants from Afghanistan, Bangladesh, Pakistan, and India are officially classified under the Asian American category by the U.S. Census, but have more in common culturally (e.g., religion, language, food, and music) with Middle Easterners than with East Asians (Leonard 1997). Furthermore, both Middle Eastern and South Asian Americans have experienced substantial post-9/11 backlash, and the protracted wars in Afghanistan and Iraq have further aggravated the situation, feeding stereotypes, prejudice, and discrimination against these groups (Bakalian and Bozorgmehr 2009; Maira 2009; Abraham, Howell, and Shryock 2011).

Given that the vast majority of contemporary immigrants from predominantly Muslim countries are part of the new wave (post-1965), their offspring can largely be considered the new second generation, or individuals who are currently coming of age in America. Unfortunately, since the American Community Survey does not gather data on parental nativity of the adult population, the second generation cannot be directly identified. However, it is reasonable to assume that the majority

Table 4.1 Population estimates, percent foreign born, and year of immigration for foreign born

Country, territory, or ancestry	Total population (Est.)	% Foreign born	% Immigrated 1995–2014
Afghanistan	100,061	66.7	46.0
Albania	183,176	61.0	76.4
Algeria	25,409	76.2	65.3
Azerbaijan	19,540	98.0	64.7
Bangladesh	250,992	78.2	71.9
Egypt	243,860	69.1	59.6
Gambia	8,047	95.8	73.9
Guinea	13,334	96.6	82.3
Indonesia	134,014	75.9	57.1
Iran	510,393	73.2	41.5
Iraq	210,988	87.1	70.7
Jordan	96,019	69.7	48.4
Kazakhstan	25,838	95.5	85.4
Kurdish	6,136	9.0	53.2
Kuwait	27,857	93.3	63.4
Lebanon	126,266	94.1	36.5
Libya	8,690	72.8	63.0
Malaysia	79,557	88.5	54.8
Morocco	106,344	64.0	69.9
Pakistan	528,018	67.2	61.5
Palestinian Territories	77,643	31.6	37.0
Saudi Arabia	81,908	85.8	91.2
Senegal	27,629	80.0	69.6
Somalia	145,328	67.3	89.3
Sudan	60,183	71.5	82.7
Syria	76,643	96.2	49.9
Turkey	195,654	61.2	63.1
Turkmenistan	3,890	71.3	95.7
United Arab Emirates	10,897	88.9	88.5
Uzbekistan	58,923	93.9	76.8
Yemen	68,019	63.5	70.6
Total	3,511,256	72.9	61.4

Note: The population sizes of the Lebanese and Syrians are small because we do not use Lebanese or Syrian ancestry in the construction of our subsample in order to exclude the older wave of immigration.

Source: 2010–2014 American Community Survey 5-year estimates of native-born individuals who identify their primary or secondary ancestry as a predominantly Muslim country have at least one foreign-born parent, and thereby fit the conventional definition of the Muslim second generation (see Table 4.1).

The Immigration and Nationality Act of 1965 abolished the restrictive national-origins quotas enacted in 1924 and established a seven-category preference system based on family reunification and skills. A per-country limit of 20,000 persons annually was set for the Eastern Hemisphere, and for the first time a cap on immigration from the Western Hemisphere was imposed (amended in 1976). These changes facilitated a second major wave of migration, including newcomers from the MENA countries, Asia, and Africa. However, the impetus to emigrate has also come from disruptive political developments in the region, such as the Iranian Revolution, Arab nationalist movements, and civil wars.

The oil boom, which enriched oil-exporting countries and brought about massive social change, further triggered Middle Eastern immigration to the United States after the 1970s. Given the limited number and capacity of institutions of higher education in the region at the time, the Middle East became the number one exporter of foreign students to the United States. Citizens of Saudi Arabia, Kuwait, the Emirates, Iran and other oil-producing countries benefited directly from generous government subsidies or indirectly through personal wealth to study abroad. Kuwaitis, Saudis, and Algerians came to the U.S. mostly after the 1980s. In addition, Arab and Muslim expatriates who worked in the Gulf economy after the 1970s earned high salaries that financed their children's American education.

The new South Asian immigration consists of many doctors, engineers, and other professionals. In the 1980s and 1990s, they came on the H-1B visa which granted highly-skilled migrants work permits for several years. Family reunification visas and the 1990 Diversity Visa Lottery or "Green Card Lottery" allowed for more varied immigration patterns based on national origin and socioeconomic status. Among the newcomers were Bangladeshis, 40 percent of whom entered the country through the visa lottery (Kibria 2006). Afghans are also among the relative newcomers (Gold and Bozorgmehr 2007).

The Yearbook of Immigration Statistics provides additional information on the types of immigrants admitted by their "selected class of admission." Many Middle Eastern and South Asian immigrants were admitted under "employment-based preferences," indicating a skilled and educated crop of newcomers. Egyptians, Iranians, Bangladeshis, and Pakistanis ranked particularly high in terms of employment preferences. At the same time, many came either as refugees or asylee adjustments, mainly from Iran, Iraq, and Afghanistan. Others were admitted under the U.S. Diversity Program, which primarily benefited immigrants from Egypt, Morocco, Turkey, Bangladesh, and Pakistan. However, by far the largest number entered under family-sponsored preferences and as immediate relatives of U.S. citizens.

In order to make sense of the experiences of first and second-generation Muslims, it is important to take into account the way in which immediate post-9/11 U.S. governmental policies and initiatives affected this population. Directly after the terrorist attacks that took place on September 11, 2011, government initiatives targeted immigrants from Arab and predominantly Muslim countries specifically.

For example, soon after the attacks, 5,000 young men from countries where Al Qaeda had a presence were called in by the Attorney General for "voluntary" interviews. At the same time, the visa granting process for men from Arab and Muslim countries was slowed down. However, two government initiatives targeted non-Arab Muslims as well: the National Security Entry-Exit Registration System (NSEERS) and the required special registration with the former Immigration and Naturalization Service (INS), renamed after 9/11 as Department of Homeland Security (DHS). The NSEERS dragnet included non-Arab, predominantly Muslim countries such as Afghanistan, Eritrea, Indonesia, Iran, and Pakistan. Similarly, while the INS special registration program originally targeted Arab and Muslim men, it was eventually extended to include Iranians (Bakalian and Bozorgmehr 2009).

In the years since 9/11, "homegrown terrorism" and the radicalization of Muslim youth have become major policy preoccupations in the U.S. There has been a major shift in local and federal government policies and initiatives, as a focus on Muslim immigrants has expanded to a more all-encompassing dragnet of Muslim communities, including the native-born. This was perhaps best exemplified by the New York Police Departments' Muslim Mapping (Demographics) Unit, which was recently disbanded due to heavy pressure from the civil rights community. However, the NYPD and other law enforcement agencies across the country continue to routinely monitor and surveil mosques and other Muslim gathering centers, using undercover informants and other techniques (Apuzzo and Goldstein 2014). At the federal level, in 2011 Representative Peter King (Republican, New York) led a series of five congressional hearings to investigate radicalization in the American Muslim community, which were subjected to broad spectrum push back but also enjoyed significant support (CAIR 2013). This policy shift – to profiling Muslim citizens as well as non-citizens – has only furthered the alienation of Muslim communities in the U.S., both native-born and foreign-born alike.

We do not address the Trump era policies in our analyses since the 2011 Pew Muslim American Survey precedes it, but clearly the anti-Muslim rhetoric and the so-called Muslim travel ban have exacerbated the predicament of Muslim Americans. Indeed, according to the Pew Research Center's analysis of the 2017 Muslim American Survey (not available for public use, as of the writing of this chapter), 68% of U.S. Muslims reported feeling "worried" by Donald Trump and 75% reported feeling that Trump is "unfriendly" towards Muslims (Pew Research Center 2017). Perhaps unsurprisingly, the percentage of U.S. Muslims who report being satisfied with the direction of the country has shifted from 56% in 2011 to only 29% in 2017 (Pew Research Center 2017). On the other hand, Pew's recent findings indicate that the vast majority of U.S. Muslims report they are "proud to be American" (92%), and 80% report being satisfied with the direction of their own lives. Pew concludes, from these indicators among many others, that "Muslims in the United States perceive a lot of discrimination against their religious group, are leery of Trump and think their fellow Americans do not see Islam as part of mainstream U.S. society. At the same time, however, Muslim Americans express a persistent streak of optimism and positive feelings" (Pew Research Center 2017: 5).

Our findings, which consider specifically the immigrant origin Muslim American population, are similar, in that most indicators point to a paradoxical mix of outcomes and emotions among Muslim immigrants and their children. Socioeconomic indicators such as education and income show considerable progress from the first to the second generation and suggest successful integration into U.S. society. However, sociocultural indicators show experiences of discrimination and isolation from the U.S. mainstream, putting findings from these two fields of integration at odds with each other.

Methods

Federal law forbids mandatory questions on religion by government agencies including the Census Bureau. In light of this limitation, we turned to two underutilized data sources for this chapter, namely the Pew American Muslim Survey and the American Community Survey (ACS). Although the ACS data, collected by the U.S. Census, does not have any information on religion, it has a wealth of data on the ethnic and racial groups who trace their ancestry and ethnic origin to predominantly Muslim countries in the Middle East and North Africa (MENA) and sub-Saharan Africa as well as South Asia and Southeast Asia.

Most of this population are relatively recent immigrants. Overall, only 3.1% of the total foreign-born sample entered the U.S. before 1965. Indeed, nearly two-thirds (61.4%) entered during 1995–2014. Thus, while the ACS does not collect information on parental nativity, it is reasonable to assume that U.S.-born respondents reporting "ancestry" in one of the predominantly Muslim countries, and at least one foreign-born parent, are in fact "second generation" with only a few very young third generation respondents.

The respondents were identified in the 2010–2014 ACS 5-year Public Use Microdata Sample (PUMS) dataset (United States Census Bureau 2014). Respondents were subsequently divided by nativity into foreign-born (first generation) and native born (second generation). Altogether, 148,060 Muslims made up the total sample. U.S.-born Muslims made up 27.1% of the sample, and the foreign-born 72.9%. Descriptive statistics were prepared with frequencies, percentages, and valid percentages, where applicable. Sampling weights were used for population estimates only. We include ACS respondents who reported place of birth, first- or second-ancestry, or race from a country or territory with a Muslim majority population (50% or higher), using a 2011 Pew report to identify these countries (Pew Research Center 2011a). Specifically, we included the following places of birth, ancestry, or race: Afghanistan, Albania, Algeria, Azerbaijan, Bangladesh, Egypt, Gambia, Guinea, Indonesia, Iran, Iraq, Jordan, Kazakhstan, Kuwait, Lebanon, Libya, Malaysia, Morocco, Pakistan, Palestinian Territories, Saudi Arabia, Senegal, Somalia, Sudan, Syria, Turkey, Turkmenistan, United Arab Emirates, Uzbekistan, and Yemen, as well as Kurdish ancestry. Note that for ancestry, we exclude respondents reporting Syrian or Lebanese to avoid inclusion of an older, mostly Christian, wave of migration to the U.S., however we do include foreign-born Syrian and Lebanese respondents to include more recent, mostly Muslim, immigrants from these countries. For race, the ACS includes separate categories for Bangladeshi, Pakistani, and Indonesian, which we include in our subsample.

Following Alba and Foner, we use the notion of "integration" to mean "the extent to which immigrants, and especially their children, are able to participate in key mainstream institutions in ways that position them to advance socially and materially" (Alba and Foner 2015: 8). Integration involves successful participation and representation in the labor market, schools, housing, and politics, as well as equal life chances with the native-born population (Alba and Foner 2015; Alba, Reitz and Simon 2012). Although socioeconomic integration (educational and occupational attainment) is widely considered to be the most important dimension, the cultural aspects (e.g., identity, ethnic attachment, religion) of immigrants and their descendants are also critical. This multidimensional conceptualization further allows for the possibility that cultural retention can unfold independent of socioeconomic integration. Indicators of "belonging" for the second generation include labels used for self-identification, ethnic language use and maintenance, religious identity, and transnational connections (Schneider et al. 2012).

For data on cultural and political dimensions of integration (e.g., religiosity, religious networks, and discrimination), we turn to the 2011 Pew Muslim American Survey (Pew Research Center 2014), the most recent publicly available data. The Pew Muslim American Survey uses a national probability sample of 1,033 Muslims in the United States. Although Pew contains rich data by generation, and Pew reports include analysis of certain Muslim American Survey questions by generation, to our knowledge no one has previously analyzed the data for second-generation Muslims (Pew Research Center 2017; Pew Research Center 2011b). Respondents were categorized as foreign-born or native-born based on country of birth and country of parents' birth. Those born in the U.S., whose parents were also born in the U.S. (3rd generation and higher) (162 respondents), were excluded from the sample, since this subsample largely represents long time American Muslims rather than third-generation immigrants. Of those remaining, 744 (85.4%) constitute the first generation, and 127 (14.6%) constitute the second generation.

Socioeconomic integration

Table 4.1 presents the estimated population sizes of predominantly Muslim ancestry and racial groups by nativity (foreign-born and native-born) using the ACS 2010–2014 five-year estimates. Over half of these groups are from the Middle East and North Africa (54.6% of the native-born and 54.5% of the foreign-born sample). South Asians are the next largest group, making up 27.6% of the native-born and 24.1% of the foreign-born sample. Pakistanis constitute the largest single group from a predominantly Muslim country (18.3% of the native-born and 13.9% of the foreign-born sample), followed by Iranians with 15.6% of the native-born and 15.6% of the foreign-born sample. The sizable Pakistani share of the total Muslim population is particularly noteworthy, in light of their recent influx. It must be pointed out that not all persons who report an ancestry or race from a predominantly Muslim country are Muslim due to migrant selectivity by religion. This is particularly the case among political refugees, exiles and asylees, who could include members of religious minorities. For instance, in the wake of the Iranian Revolution of 1978–79 and the subsequent establishment of the Islamic Republic of Iran, this predominantly exile/refugee group includes members of religious minorities (Bahais, Christians, Jews and Zoroastrians). Even so, Muslims make up the largest segment of the Iranian-American population. Christians from Iran often report Armenian and Assyrian ancestries and are enumerated separately in the ACS data (Bozorgmehr 1997), and hence are not counted as having Iranian ancestry. However, this is less of a problem with other Muslim groups, such as Pakistanis, who come from countries that are much more homogeneous in terms of religion. Furthermore, many other Muslim groups are mostly economic migrants rather than political refugees, and therefore religious minorities are less likely to be substantial enough to affect the estimates.

California is the most popular state of residence for the Muslim population in the U.S., with 24.4% of the foreign-born population and 19.5% of the native-born. This suggests some geographical dispersion for the second generation. The top eight states of residence for the Muslim American population are California, New York, the District of Columbia (including Maryland and Virginia), Texas, New Jersey, Michigan, Florida and Illinois, in that order.

Not surprisingly, the second-generation population is much younger than the immigrants, with a mean age of only 19.5 in contrast to mean age of 43.0 for the foreign-born. Nearly three-quarters of the U.S.-born population is under age 25, while over three-quarters of the foreign-born population is over the age of 25. The foreign-born population has a slightly imbalanced sex ratio (52.5% male, 47.5% female). This discrepancy is reduced in the native-born population, with 51.3% male and 48.7% female. Given their relatively high levels of educational and occupational attainment, and in some cases, refugee/exile status (see Portes and Rumbaut 2014), it is not surprising that most of the foreign-born Muslim immigrants hold U.S. citizenship (61.7%).

Migrants from MENA countries are generally classified as "White" in the U.S. racial scheme. Yet, only slightly more than half of the native- and foreign-born population identify as "White alone" (58.9% native-born, 57.4% foreign-born). There is also a slight increase in the proportion of respondents identifying as two or more races (9.2% native-born, 7.6% foreign-born), indicating a possible mixing of populations. The proportion of those identifying as "Asian alone" has decreased from 28.7% for the foreign-born to 25.2% for the native-born. This may point to a differential in the birth rates of various racial groups, or it may indicate a larger proportion of Asian Muslims having multi-racial children. This may change if proposed "Middle Eastern or North African" (MENA) racial category is included on the 2020 U.S. Census.

A majority of the Muslim immigrant population speaks English very well or well (82.0%). Not surprisingly, this increased to 96.0% in the native-born population. However, English is not the only language spoken in most households. Among the foreign-born population, only about one out of ten (10.8%)

households speak "English only." Nearly half (47.9%) of households speak "English only" among the native-born population. While this indicates a generational shift towards English, this relatively high proportion of the native-born that report using a language other than English at home may indicate a highly transnational population in which the parents actively seek to pass on linguistic capital to their children, as has been found previously for Iranians (Bozorgmehr and Moeini Meybodi 2016). However, one must be cautious in interpreting these results, given the young average age of the native-born and the likelihood that many are still living with their immigrant parents.

Reflecting the youth of the native-born population, 62.3% are enrolled in public or private school, while only 37.7% have not attended school in the last three months before the survey. By the same token, 79.8% of the foreign-born population have not attended school in the last three months, which reflects the older age structure of this segment. Overall, for the population over 25 years old, the native-born population is more highly educated than the foreign-born population (see Table 4.2). Notably, the proportion of females with less than a high-school education dramatically drops from 18.2% of the foreign-born to 5.8% of the native-born population. There is also a surprisingly large increase of the proportion of females with bachelor's degrees and even advanced degrees from 25.9% and 16.6%, respectively, among the foreign-born. These figures increase to 30.9% and 25.9%, respectively, among the native-born. We distinguished between the "bachelor's degree" and "advanced degree" categories for this relatively highly-educated population. For males, there is an increase in the proportion with bachelor's degrees (26.6% of foreign-born and 29.8% of native-born), but a decrease in the proportion with advanced degrees (25.6% of foreign-born and 22.7% of native-born). Furthermore, there is a large increase in the proportion of males with some college (19.3% for the foreign-born to 26.2% for the native-born). This could indicate that many native-born males are stopping short of a bachelor's degree or that they are taking longer to graduate than their female counterparts, although, again, we should be cautious in reaching conclusions given the youth of the sample. The larger proportion of females than males holding bachelor's or higher degrees may also reflect the educational attainment patterns of the U.S. population as a whole (Kasinitz et al. 2008; Rumbaut 2008). These educational outcomes speak to the universal and egalitarian availability of education in the U.S., as compared to some of the countries of origin of Muslim immigrants. While the data indicate that both male and female native-born Muslim immigrants are highly educated, the reduction in the proportion of males with advanced degrees could also reflect the high qualifications of skilled immigrants from predominantly Muslim countries. At the same time, the number of second-generation women with advanced degrees may imply a shift in gender roles and greater educational opportunities than were available to their immigrant mothers.

There is also a reduction in the proportion of females aged 25 to 64 who are not in the labor force (41.9% of the foreign-born respondents to only 26.5% of the native-born). This suggests that the observed paradox between high educational attainment and low labor force participation of Middle Eastern female immigrants (Read and Oselin 2008; Bozorgmehr and Douglas 2011) is diminishing among the U.S. born. On the other hand, there is an increase in the proportion of males who are not in the labor force (13.1% of the foreign-born to 17.3% of the native-born).

Some MENA groups are among the most entrepreneurial immigrant populations in America (Gold and Bozorgmehr 2007). Studies report that the self-employment rate generally declines between the first and second generations, though they do not generally make a gender distinction (Gold, Light, and Johnston 2006; Min 2008; Kasinitz et al. 2008). Among males, a smaller proportion of native-born respondents are self-employed, compared to foreign-born respondents, while females report approximately the same self-employment rate. Of those who have worked within the previous five years, for the foreign-born population 20.6% of males and 10.7% of females report self-employment, compared to 14.3% of native-born males and 9.0% of native-born females, respectively (see Table 4.2). While the second-generation self-employment rate is relatively lower than that of the first (11.9% compared to 16.0% respectively), it is still higher than the native-born U.S. population as a whole (10.5%).

There are also marked differences in occupational patterns between foreign- and native-born respondents, calculated for respondents between the ages of 25 and 64, who are currently employed. There is a sizeable decline in the percentage of males in the fields of architecture and engineering (see Table 4.2) as well as in food services, transportation, and material moving. This reflects a movement away from typical high- and low-skill immigrant occupations among the native-born population. Furthermore, there are also large increases in the percentage of native-born male respondents who report occupations in management, law, and arts and entertainment. For females, there is a reduction in occupations such as food services and sales, along with an increase in management and law.

Among both males and females, who are 25 to 64 years old and currently employed, the U.S.- born earn more (see Table 4.2). Most notably, there is a large reduction in the proportion of females who earned less than $30,000 (in constant 2014 dollars), from nearly half of foreign-born to just under one-third of the native-born respondents. However, there is still a much larger proportion of females who fall into this low-earning category than males. About one-third of foreign-born and about one-quarter of native-born males earned less than $30,000. Overall, among native-born males, there is a small increase in the proportion making $50,000 or more compared to foreign-born males; females show a similar small increase in the proportion making $30,000 or more compared to foreign-born females. Male earnings are less skewed towards the lower categories than those of females. For males, median earnings rose from $46,100 for the foreign born to $60,200 for the native born. For females, median income also rose, from $31,100 to $43,600. Notably, while higher proportions of native-born females have bachelors and advanced degrees than native-born males, females have lower median incomes. In sum, uniform increases by gender in educational

Table 4.2 Socioeconomic characteristics by generation and gender

	Foreign born		Native born		% Total
	% Male	% Female	% Male	% Female	
Educational attainment[a]					
Less than High School	11.9	18.2	6.3	5.8	13.9
High School or equivalent	16.6	19.0	15.0	14.6	17.4
Some college	19.3	20.3	26.2	22.8	20.3
Bachelor's	26.6	25.9	29.8	30.9	26.7
Advanced degree	25.6	16.6	22.7	25.9	21.7
Class of worker[b]					
Wage and salary	78.5	86.8	85.0	89.8	82.5
Self-employed	20.6	10.7	14.3	9.0	16.0
Unemployed/Not in labor force	0.9	2.5	0.7	1.1	1.5
Occupation[c]					
Management, business, science & arts	13.5	8.8	15.8	11.6	12.1
Computer and mathematical	6.2	2.3	6.9	2.2	4.8
Architecture and engineering	5.5	1.6	4.0	0.9	3.9
Legal	0.6	1.1	2.9	4.3	1.2
Education, training, and library	4.1	10.8	4.4	12.6	6.8
Arts, design, entertainment, sports, and media	1.7	2.1	3.0	3.4	2.0
Healthcare practitioners and technical	6.7	11.2	8.0	12.4	8.6
Food preparation and serving	5.2	5.0	2.6	3.2	4.8
Sales and related	16.5	13.0	14.1	10.4	14.9
Office and administrative support	5.3	14.2	6.5	14.5	8.8
Transportation and material moving	10.4	1.5	5.0	0.9	6.6
All other	24.3	28.4	26.8	23.6	25.5
Earnings[d]					
<$30k	33.1	48.0	23.4	32.3	37.1
$30–$50k	19.5	20.2	18.4	25.0	20.0
$50–$100k	25.7	21.6	31.9	29.5	25.0
$100k+	21.7	10.3	26.4	13.2	17.9
Mean	$74,500	$47,600	$86,900	$60,100	$66,000
Median	$46,100	$31,100	$60,200	$43,600	$41,600

Notes: [a] Respondents 25 years old and older.
[b] Respondents 25 to 64 years old. Does not include individuals who have not worked in the last 5 years or who have never worked.
[c] Employed respondents 25 to 64 years old.
[d] Employed respondents 25 to 64 years old. Dollars adjusted to 2014 constant collars.

Source: 2010–2014 American Community Survey 5-year estimates attainment and earnings suggest socioeconomic progress from the first to the second generation among Muslim Americans. Indeed, native-born Muslim immigrants seem to be a relatively highly educated and high-income group, successful as measured by a variety of socioeconomic measures.

Cultural integration

By and large, the socioeconomic data on Muslim American migrants and their children tell a story of rapid and generally successful integration into the U.S. mainstream. Muslim immigrants started out more positively selected than many of their European counterparts, and their children have generally been upwardly mobile, in terms of both educational and economic achievement. The second generation's occupational profile is more diverse than that of their parents and their female labor force participation has increased, making them more like other middle-class Americans.

However, the data on cultural integration tell a very different story. Despite near universal English fluency, residential integration and occupational upward mobility, in many respects, the post-9/11 second generation is as culturally isolated from U.S. society as are their immigrant parents. Indeed, given their educational success and economic mobility, they show a startling degree of alienation as well as less cultural assimilation than might be expected. In this respect, they seem increasingly similar to their European cousins.

Time in the U.S. has clearly not made American Muslims more secular. Overall, the role of religion in everyday life has not changed between generations. About two-thirds of respondents of the foreign-born and second generation reported that religion was "very important" in their everyday lives (see Table 4.3). Observation of daily prayers (praying five times a day) do not vary much across generations (see Table 4.3); nearly half of the foreign-born and two-fifths of the native-born sample report observing all daily prayers. Approximately another fifth of both generations report occasionally praying, while only around 20% of both generations report praying only on *Eid* (Muslim holiday) or never. These results indicate a consistently high degree of religiosity across generations for Muslim Americans.

While there is some movement away from having exclusively or mostly Muslim friendship networks, there is not much of a difference between the foreign-born and native-born generations in terms of friendship religious composition (see Table 4.3). Less than 10% of foreign-born respondents report having only Muslim friends, while under 5% of the second-generation respondents report the same. Less than one out of ten foreign-born respondents report that "hardly any" or "none" of their friends are Muslim, while nearly one in five of the second generation reports the same. These patterns suggest strong ties within the Muslim American community, though it would be interesting to know the extent to which these networks are oriented toward co-ethnics (e.g., fellow Pakistanis) as opposed to co-religionists (i.e., fellow Muslims), by generation.

Table 4.3 Sociocultural characteristics and experiences by generation

	% First generation	% Second generation	% Total
Religiosity			
Very important	68.4	64.6	67.9
Somewhat important	21.2	30.7	22.6
Not very important/not at all	9.0	4.7	8.4
Don't know/refused	1.3	0.0	1.2
Religious observance			
All	47.5	40.2	46.4
Some	18.6	18.1	18.5
Occasionally	16.1	23.6	17.2
Eid only	6.9	10.2	7.4
Never	9.5	7.1	9.2
Don't know/refused	1.5	0.8	1.4
Coreligionist friendship networks			
All	8.1	4.7	7.6
Most	42.9	38.6	42.3
Some	39.0	40.2	39.2
Hardly any	8.3	15.0	9.3
None	0.9	1.6	1.0
Don't know/refused	0.8	0.0	0.7
Experiences of discrimination (% reporting)			
Called offensive names	13.0	29.1	16.7
Singled out by airport security	20.8	29.9	20.8
Singled out by law enforcement	6.6	11.8	9.0
Physically threatened or attacked	3.1	7.1	4.0
Post-9/11 experiences in the U.S.			
More difficult	49.9	69.3	52.7
Not much changed	42.2	28.4	40.2
Became easier	1.1	1.6	1.2
Moved to U.S. afterward	3.5	0.0	3.0
Don't know	3.4	0.8	3.0
Primary identity			
American	27.0	38.6	28.7
Muslim	44.9	43.3	44.7
Both	19.8	13.4	18.8
Neither	2.6	2.3	2.5
Other	1.5	1.6	1.5
Don't know	4.3	0.8	3.8

Source: 2011 Pew Muslim American Survey

Kurzman (2013) empirically documents that terrorist arrests have steadily and substantially declined in the U.S. since 9/11 from 88 in 2001 to only 6 in 2012. Islamic terrorists accounted for a negligible percentage (0.0002) of all murders in the U.S. since 9/11. In spite of the fact that Americans have less reason to fear Islam on their soil, negative attitudes toward Islam and Muslims have increased in recent years (Bail 2015). A variety of recent surveys and polls, gauging both attitudinal and objective measures, consistently report that Muslims are the targets of the highest levels of prejudice and discrimination, compared to other major religious groups in the United States. For instance, according to Gallup (2010a), 43% of Americans report feeling at least a little prejudice against Muslims, more than the percentage reporting prejudice against both Christians and Jews. In a 2014 survey by Pew, respondents were asked to rate their feelings of "warmth" towards various religious groups on a scale of 0 to 100. The mean rating for Muslims was 40, lower than for all other religious groups, even including atheists. Not surprisingly, Muslims are also more likely to report having experienced racial or religious discrimination in the past year than other religious groups, and are on par with Hispanics and African Americans, two highly stigmatized groups in the United States (Gallup 2010b).

Regarding experiences of discrimination, a *higher* proportion of the U.S.-born population report instances of discrimination compared to the foreign-born (see Table 4.3): 29.1% of native-born respondents indicated that they have been called offensive names, compared to 13.0% of the foreign-born. Similarly, 29.9% of native-born respondents indicate having been singled out by airport security, compared to 20.8% of the foreign-born. It could be that second-generation respondents have in fact experienced higher levels of discrimination due to social mobility, geographic dispersion, and subsequent exposure to Islamophobia in the American society and workplace. It could also be that the second generation is more aware of such discrimination and is more likely to speak out. U.S. citizens by birth, they may feel a citizen's entitlement to fair treatment. Whatever the cause, it is notable that nearly 70% of second-generation respondents report that life in the United States has gotten more difficult after 9/11, compared to half of foreign-born respondents (see Table 4.3). Similarly, just over 70% of the second generation report believing that the U.S. government's anti-terrorism policies single out Muslims, compared to about two-fifths of the foreign-born sample. Moreover, nearly 72% of the second generation believes that American media coverage of Islam and Muslims is unfair, compared to nearly 55% of the foreign-born Pew sample. Together, these data indicate that the second generation is much more sensitive to issues of discrimination and has a keener perception of prejudice than do their immigrant parents.

In spite of this, but perhaps not surprisingly, a larger proportion of second-generation respondents identify themselves primarily as "American" as opposed to "Muslim" (38.6% of the second generation compared to 27.0% of the foreign-born) (see Table 4.3), though a large proportion (approx. 45%) of both groups report

"Muslim" as their primary identity. Religion clearly plays a large role in identity formation across generations, however there is evidence of a slow generational shift away from religion-based identity. Interestingly, nearly three-fifths of both foreign-born and second-generation respondents report believing that most Muslims want to adopt American customs and ways of life. The remainder are more or less evenly split between reporting that Muslims want to be distinct and that Muslims want some middle ground between the two. Similarly, a sizeable majority (more than 70%) of both foreign-born and second-generation respondents believe there is no conflict between being a devout Muslim and modern society. Together, these data suggest that immigrant Muslims across generations see themselves and their religion as distinct from mainstream American culture as evidenced by a plurality of immigrant Muslims identifying primarily with their religion over identifying as American or some other identity. However, despite this prioritization of religious identity and despite widespread experiences and perceptions of discrimination, a majority indicate believing that most Muslims want to acculturate and that there is no conflict between practicing Islam and being a part of modern society.

Conclusion

Given the increasingly negative context of reception for Muslims in the United States, it is important to understand how this growing population is integrating. The preliminary findings suggest a pattern of uneven incorporation in which the second generation is experiencing socioeconomic progress without the commensurate cultural and social integration. Given the socioeconomic success of the second generation, it would be expected that this population is also increasingly woven into the mainstream. Surprising, the sociocultural evidence is to the contrary. Second-generation Muslim immigrants, even more so than their first-generation counterparts, report experiences of discrimination and increased difficulty living in the United States after 9/11. And while friendship networks are somewhat less religiously homogenous among the second generation than the first, approximately two out of five Muslim immigrants report that "most" or "all" of their friends are also Muslim. Paradoxically, even though the second-generation is largely achieving the American dream of upward mobility, more second-generation Muslim Americans identify primarily as Muslim as compared to those that identify primarily as American. There is little reason to believe that immigrant Muslim Americans will feel more accepted by the general American public in the near future given the current political climate. In comparison with the European context, first- and second-generation Muslim Americans are more economically integrated and upwardly mobile. However, their feelings of social exclusion paradoxically mirror those of their European counterparts. For this growing population, sociocultural and socioeconomic integration has a complex relationship that will require further research to disentangle.

Note

1 By sociological convention, "second generation" refers to native-born children with at least one immigrant (foreign-born) parent (Portes and Rumbaut 2014). "First generation" refers to immigrants.

References

Abraham, Nabeel, Sally Howell, and Andrew Shryock (eds.). 2011. *Arab Detroit 9/11: Life in the Terror Decade.* Detroit: Wayne State University Press.

Alba, Richard, and Nancy Foner. 2015. *Strangers No More: Immigration and the Challenges of Integration in North America and Western Europe.* Princeton, NJ: Princeton University Press.

Alba, Richard, Jeffrey Reitz, and Patrick Simon. 2012. "National Conceptions of Assimilation, Integration, and Cohesion." In *The Changing Face of World Cities: Young Adult Children of Immigrants in Europe and the United States,* edited by Maurice Crul and John Mollenkopf, pp. 44–61. New York: Russell Sage Foundation.

Apuzzo, Matt, and Joseph Goldstein. 2014. "New York Drops Unit that Spied on Muslims." *New York Times,* April 16, A1.

Arab American Institute. 2015. "Demographics." Available online at www.aaiusa.org/demographics (accessed September 14, 2015).

Bail, Christopher. 2015. *Terrified: How Anti-Muslim Fringe Organizations Became Mainstream.* Princeton, NJ: Princeton University Press.

Bakalian, Anny, and Mehdi Bozorgmehr. 2009. *Backlash 9/11: Middle Eastern and Muslim Americans Respond.* Berkeley, CA: University of California Press.

Bozorgmehr, Mehdi. 1997. "Internal Ethnicity: Iranians in Los Angeles." *Sociological Perspectives* 40(3): 387–408.

Bozorgmehr, Mehdi, and Daniel Douglas. 2011. "Success(ion): Second-Generation Iranian Americans." *Iranian Studies* 44(1): 3–24.

Bozorgmehr, Mehdi, and Maryam Moeini Meybodi. 2016. "The Persian Paradox: Language Use and Maintenance among Iranian Americans. *International Journal of the Sociology of Language* 2016(237): 99–118.

Bozorgmehr, Mehdi, Paul Ong, and Sarah Tosh. 2015. "Panethnicity Revisited: Contested Group Boundaries in the Post-9/11 Era." *Ethnic and Racial Studies* 39(5): 727–745.

CAIR (Council on American Islamic Relations). 2013. *Legislating Fear: Islamophobia and its Impact in the United States.* Washington, DC. Available online at www.cair.com/islamophobia/legislating-fear-2013-report.html

Crul, Maurice, and John Mollenkopf (eds.). 2012. *The Changing Face of World Cities: Young Adult Children of Immigrants in Europe and the United States.* New York: Russell Sage Foundation.

Dooley, Tara. 2002. "Muslims gain Hispanic converts." *Houston Chronicle,* Saturday, September 28.

Foner, Nancy, and Patrick Simon (eds.). 2015. *Fear, Anxiety, and National Identity Immigration and Belonging in North America and Western Europe.* New York: Russell Sage Foundation.

Gallup. 2010a. "In U.S., Religious Prejudice Stronger Against Muslims." Available online at www.gallup.com/poll/125312/religious-prejudice-stronger-against-muslims.aspx (accessed October 16, 2015).

Gallup. 2010b. "Islamophobia: Understanding Anti-Muslim Sentiment in the West." Available online at www.gallup.com/poll/157082/islamophobia-understanding-anti-muslim-sentiment-west.aspx (accessed October 16, 2015).

Gold, Steven, and Mehdi Bozorgmehr. 2008. "Middle East and North Africa." In *The New Americans,* edited by Mary Waters, Reed Ueda, and Helen Marro, pp. 518–533. Cambridge, MA: Harvard University Press.

Gold, Steven, Ivan Light, and Francis Johnston. 2006. "The Second Generation and Self-Employment." *Migration Information Source.* Washington, DC: MPI.

Kasinitz, Philip, John Mollenkopf, Mary Waters, and Jennifer Holdaway. 2008. *Inheriting the City: The Children of Immigrants Come of Age.* New York: Russell Sage Foundation.

Kibria, Nazli. 2005. "South Asian Americans." In *Asian Americans: Contemporary Trends and Issues,* edited by Pyong Gap Min, pp. 206–227. Beverly Hills, CA: Sage Publications.

Kurzman, Charles. 2013. "Muslim-American Terrorism: Declining Further." Triangle Center on Terrorism and Homeland Security report. Available online at http://sites.duke.edu/tcths/files /2013/06/Kurzman_Muslim-American_Terrorism_February_1_2013.pdf

Kurzman, Charles, David Schanzer, and Ebrahim Moosa. 2011. "Muslim American Terrorism Since 9/11: Why So Rare?" *The Muslim World* 101 (3): 464–483.

Leonard, Karen. 1997. "Changing South Asian Identities in the United States." In *Beyond Black and White: New Faces and Voices in U.S. Schools,* edited by Maxine S. Seller and Lois Weis, pp. 165–179. Albany, NY: State University of New York Press.

Maira, Sunaina Marr. 2009. *Youth, Citizenship, and Empire after 9/11.* Durham, NC: Duke University Press.

Min, Pyong Gap. 2008. *Ethnic Solidarity for Economic Survival: Korean Greengrocers in New York City.* New York: Russell Sage Foundation.

Pew Research Center. "2011 Dataset." *Muslim American Survey.* 29 September 2014. Available online at www.people-press.org/2011/08/30/2011-muslim-american-survey/

Pew Research Center. 2011a. "The Future of the Global Muslim Population: Projections for 2010–2030." Available online at www.pewforum.org/2011/01/27/the-future-of-the-global-muslim-population/ (accessed October 16, 2015).

Pew Research Center. 2011b. "Muslim Americans: No Signs of Growth in Alienation or Support for Extremism." August 30, Washington, DC: Pew Research Center. Available online at www.people-press.org/2011/08/30/muslim-americans-no-signs-of-growth-in-alienation-or-support-for-extremism/ (accessed September 14, 2015).

Pew Research Center. 2014. "How Americans Feel About Religious Groups." Accessed October 16, 2015. Available online at www.pewforum.org/files/2014/07/Views-of-Religious-Groups-full-PDF-for-web.pdf (accessed October 16, 2015).

Pew Research Center. 2015. "America's Changing Religious Landscape." Available online at www.pewforum.org/files/2015/05/RLS-08-26-full-report.pdf (accessed November 18, 2015).

Pew Research Center. 2017. "U.S. Muslims Concerned About Their Place in Society, but Continue to Believe in the American Dream." Available online at http://assets.pewresearch.org/wp-content/uploads/sites/11/2017/07/25171611/U.S.-MUSLIMS-FULL-REPORT.pdf (accessed September 20, 2017).

Portes, Alejandro, and Rubén Rumbaut. 2001. *Legacies: The Story of the Immigrant Second Generation.* Berkeley, CA: University of California Press.

Portes, Alejandro, and Rubén Rumbaut. 2014. *Immigrant America: A Portrait* (4th ed.). Berkeley, CA: University of California Press.

Read, Jen'nan Ghazal, and Sharon Oselin. 2008. "Gender and the Education-Employment Paradox in Ethnic and Religious Contexts: The Case of Arab Americans." *American Sociological Review* 73: 296–313.

Rumbaut, Rubén. 2008. "The Coming of the Second Generation: Immigration and Ethnic Mobility in Southern California." *Annals American Academy of Political and Social Science* 620(1): 196–236.

Schneider, Jens, Leo Chavez, Louis DeSipio, and Mary Waters. "Belonging." In *The Changing Face of World Cities: Young Adult Children of Immigrants in Europe and the United States*, edited by Maurice Crul and John Mollenkop, pp. 206–232. New York: Russell Sage Foundation.

Tehranian, John. 2009. *Whitewashed: America's Invisible Middle Eastern Minority.* New York: New York University Press.

United States Census Bureau. "Summary File."*2010–2014 American Community Survey 5-year Public Use Mictrodata Samples (PUMS).* U.S. Census Bureau's American Community Survey Office, 2015.

Part II
Inclusion and belonging

5 The politics of inclusion

American Muslims and the price of citizenship

Yvonne Yazbeck Haddad

During the 2008 presidential campaign, a Lakeville, Minnesota, supporter of Republican nominee Senator John McCain expressed concern about Barack Obama's eligibility for the presidency of the United States by stating, "Obama is an Arab." McCain corrected her. "No, ma'am. He is a decent man. He is a citizen." Was McCain implying that an Arab might not be a decent person, or that an Arab might even be unfit to be a "citizen"? When Colin Powell was subsequently questioned about McCain's answer, he replied,

> But the really right answer is, what if he is? Is there anything wrong with being a Muslim in this country? The answer is no, that's not America. Is there something wrong with some seven-year-old Muslim American kid believing that he or she could be president?
>
> (Iftikhar 2012: 39)

The candidacy of Barack Obama, who had a Muslim father, once again raised the question of whether Muslims can be considered "real Americans." These exchanges reflect ongoing debates on citizenship, focused not only on who is worthy of being granted American citizenship, but also on which citizens are considered deficient or lacking in qualifications (since they are not one of "us"), and thus should not be afforded the full rights available to a "true citizen." These questions are not unique to Muslim Americans, but rather have surfaced throughout the history of the Republic whenever Americans deem a group to be different from the image they have of themselves as "true Americans." They are also raised every time Americans feel threatened by new immigrants who do not share the same ethnic and/or religious heritage of the founders, particularly during periods in which the U.S. is engaged in foreign wars. The U.S. Constitution and immigration laws recognize two avenues to citizenship: naturalization and birthright. Periodically throughout the history of the Republic, however, certain American citizens, individuals, and communities have been considered "un-American." Their loyalty and allegiance to the United States have been questioned, and sometimes they have been denied the full guarantees of the Constitution.

This chapter will attempt to describe the struggle of Muslim Americans to be recognized as full citizens of the United States with no questions raised about their worthiness, credibility, or loyalty. While they have been granted citizenship (albeit at times reluctantly), carry American passports, have served in all branches of the military, and died defending American freedom, many continue to feel that their citizenship is somewhat "incomplete" or "qualified," as each new generation has had to face particular obstacles which emphasize their "otherness" or attempt to prove that they are not "real Americans." A brief review of the various ways in which Muslims in the United States have been perceived as unqualified for full rights of citizenship shows how this disqualification has been variously based on the particular factors of race, politics, and religion. While all three categories appear to apply throughout history in the U.S., Helen Samhan (1987) has identified three phases in which one of the categories has risen to paramount importance. When this has happened, Muslim immigrants have needed to make adjustments in order to "fit" the changing criteria so as to be accepted without suspicion. The pre-1967 criteria were largely based on race; post-1967 on politics; and post-2011 on religious identification. The chapter will also explore particular moments in American history where it seems that Arab and Muslim American identities are intertwined with U.S. attitudes towards race and people of color. These moments often occur during periods of military engagement overseas or when the religious identity of the nation is noticeably evolving.

The price of becoming a "real American" citizen

The concept of American citizenship is not essential or immutable but rather has been constructed by different generations of Americans as they have attempted to incorporate various immigrants into the body politic. Karen Cerulo (1997: 387) argues that American citizenship "is a social artifact – an entity remodeled, refabricated and mobilized in accord with reigning cultural scripts and centers of power." Various generations of Arabs and Muslims in the U.S. have attempted to accommodate to the dominant ideals and discourse as well as to the values and evolving expectations of American citizenship. While it is hard to generalize about all Arab and Muslim Americans, this chapter will highlight the principal kinds of activities they engage in during their quest to gain full recognition as "real Americans," with specific reference to the apparent changes in the focus of their leadership and the position of the second generation coming of age in America.

The religious factor

One of the great stories of the founding of America is that the early colonists came seeking religious freedom. What they defined as freedom, however, allowed little, if any, room for dissent. Intolerant of divergent beliefs, their newfound bastions of orthodoxy often proved just as exclusionary as the Old World they had left behind. The New England colonies, for example, imposed Puritanism on their residents. Over the next two centuries, American ideas about religious freedom focused on the freedom to practice different forms of Christianity. Indeed, as late as the 1960s John F. Kennedy's Catholicism still raised doubts in the minds of some, as did President Ronald Reagan's recognition of the Vatican as a state 20 years later.

American exceptionalism is the foundational narrative of the United States, which proclaims its divine destiny as a light unto the nations. As John Winthrop put it, America is a "City upon a hill" that will dictate its values to the world (Winthrop 1867: 19). Exceptionalism includes the idea of a covenant with God, who will guard and guide the nation. Should its citizens veer from the right path, by implication God would withdraw his support.

The impetus to incorporate new immigrants into the body politic not surprisingly came from "outsiders" seeking a place in a redefined "America." With the immigration of Jews and Catholics from the mid-nineteenth to the early twentieth century, a new definition of America began to emerge. Israel Zangwill was a British Jew who promoted the idea of America as a melting pot where immigrants from various nations and of many ethnicities are fused together and become American. In his play entitled *The Melting Pot*, he referred to Syrians, at the time the identity favored by immigrants from the Middle East, but he did not specifically mention Muslims. In the 1950s, a new paradigm of inclusiveness was floated. Will Herberg (1955) promoted the idea of the triple melting pot, where identity is grounded not in ethnicity, culture, or race, but in one's religious affiliation (Protestant, Catholic, or Jewish).

The opening of the gates of immigration after 1965 brought large numbers of new immigrants who adhered to other religions. By the 1990s, two paradigms competed for the definition of American society. The first sought to define the United States as a "Judeo-Christian" nation. Broadening the earlier idea of the U.S. as a "Christian" (read Protestant) nation, this notion nonetheless maintained a hard boundary between Christians (now including Catholics and Orthodox Christians) and Jews and the members of other faiths: Muslims, Hindus, Buddhists, Jains, etc. By contrast, a second, more liberal paradigm promotes the United States as a nation committed to religious pluralism, and indeed to the celebration of many different faiths, traditions, and cultures. Still, this more tolerant approach has its limitations. The United States has never had a strong secularist movement, and its population is far more likely to practice a religion than is the case in Western Europe. Religion plays a prominent role in American life. National leaders, even those with highly secular lifestyles such as President Trump, are still expected to profess faith and worship publicly. Ronald Reagan famously argued that the constitution guaranteed "freedom of religion, not freedom from religion."

Thus, the American attitude toward s religion and religious minorities is something of a paradox. We lack a national religion, but we celebrate and, in many contexts, require religiosity. And, of course, the increase in the numbers of members of non Judeo-Christian religions since the resumption of mass immigration in the late 1960s further complicates matters. Yet, while the pluralist vision of religion in American life has increasingly begun to embrace Buddhism and even polytheistic Hinduism and Sikhism, Islam remains largely outside of this tolerant consensus, representing, for many Americans, an unassimilable "other." Despite the more or less successful integration of many Muslims into American economic life, Islam remains a marked category fundamentally outside even the pluralist vision of the national community.

The rise of "Islamic exceptionalism"

Perhaps the most successful transition from ethno-religious outsiders to insiders was that made by American Jews in the mid-twentieth century. Indeed, the very notion of a "Judeo-Christian" nation – something unthinkable for many nineteenth-century Americans – illustrates how much this ethno-religious boundary has moved. In part, this was due to Jewish upward mobility, and in part, to the non-zero sum mobility that allowed many of the children of the pre-1924 immigrants to partake in the rising tide of American prosperity in the 1950s and 1960s (Alba 2012). However, it is also true that in the wake of the Holocaust, anti-Semitism became inextricably linked to Nazism and genocide in the American imagination. Thus, for the first time in American life, excluding Jews came to be seen as profoundly un-American, at least among American liberals.

Starting in the 1960s, many Muslims looked for a similar entrée into American society. As newly naturalized citizens, they saw that their choice was between two models: what they saw as the "Mennonite" option, forging a distinct and isolated community with its own social, economic, religious, and cultural values and living as an implant in the American body politic, or the "Jewish" option of engaging as a full partner in American society while maintaining a religious identity distinct from, yet compatible with participating in mainstream American life. Most chose the Jewish option.

The timing seemed right. America was in the early days of a transition away from traditional White Anglo-Saxon Power (WASP). Scholars of religion noted that many Americans were rejecting the bedrock of their faith. Increasingly American intellectuals on the East and West coasts were defining the United States as a religiously pluralist nation. Muslim leadership in the U.S. set out to create a place for Islam in the American mainstream, establishing organizations that parallel those of the other religions and waiting for the day when America would define itself as "Christian-Jewish-Muslim."

Post-1965 Muslim immigrants came to a nation that was in the throes of racial turmoil. It was a society that had achieved world dominance, but at the same time was undergoing social and religious upheaval at home. Islamic exceptionalism developed in the context of contesting exceptionalisms in the United States that were challenging the traditional WASP power structure. It was the period in American history when various groups left out of the WASP model clamored for recognition. African Americans argued for Black Power and grounded their claims as a counter to the society that had long suppressed them and relegated them to the fringes. Other claimants included feminists, gay rights groups, and First Nations peoples.

In the U.S., a new vision of a Muslim community began to flourish as foreign college students living away from the oppressive regimes of their home countries experienced a new atmosphere of freedom. On January 1, 1963, they established the Muslim Students Association (MSA). This group was a counter to the Arab Student Association, then thriving on American campuses, whose members adhered to generally secular Arab nationalism and socialism. By the end of the year, the MSA had branches on 20 American campuses.

The Muslim Students Association's members were convinced that they had a better option to offer American youth – a different avenue for salvation – than contemporary American culture could provide. At the same time, they were also disillusioned with the secularism and socialism propagated in the Arab world. In the attempt to fashion a new *umma* (community), the MSA members began to separate themselves from the Islamic modernism preached in the nations they left behind and sought to create a modern Islamic culture centered on a distinctive Islamic identity. While the early immigrants saw Islam simply as a religion that could take its modest place in the public square, the new immigrants conceptualized a unique and distinctive Islamic culture, which they promoted as a way of life.

This core group of the leadership of the MSA, whose proclivity was toward the Muslim Brotherhood of Egypt and *Jamaat-i Islami* of Pakistan, tended to look askance at those Muslims who had come before 1965 and integrated into the American fabric and identified with American culture and society. Many of them had Anglicized their names and emulated American patterns of religious institution building. They had served in the American military and had also negotiated between the two cultures to create a small niche for Muslim prayer and community organizations. The task the new immigrants faced was more difficult, as they began to represent more nationalities and cultures. They found the "American Islam" of the early arrivals to be alien to their goals, and believed that in order to "fit in," the early immigrants had accepted an inferior status and lost their self-esteem.

Meanwhile, in order to confront the anti-Arab and anti-Palestinian diatribe that filled the American airwaves after the 1967 Arab-Israeli war, secular Muslims and Arab Christians were forming such organizations as The Arab American University Graduates (AAUG) and the American-Arab Anti-Discrimination Committee (ADC). When their scholarly writings on the Arab world were rejected, they published their own magazines and established their own printing presses. They struggled to provide a more accurate view of the reality of the Arab world. Although alienated from American foreign policy in the Middle East, they generally believed in American fairness and set out to produce information about the Arab world, in the belief that anti-Arab and anti-Muslim sentiments in America are due to ignorance and can be rectified by accurate information (Haddad 2011; Suleiman 1999).

By 1982, two major events overseas brought more focused attention on Arabs and, particularly, Muslims living in the U.S.: The Iranian Revolution of 1978–1979 and the Israeli invasion of Lebanon in 1982. Many Muslim students had decided to settle in the U.S., and their attention turned to creating American Islamic institutions. They formed the Islamic Society of North America (ISNA), which promoted a more moderate Islamic identity anchored in the U.S. They advised the Muslims in diaspora to abandon the concept that divided the world into *dar al-Islam* (abode of Islam) and *dar al-harb* (abode of war). They saw the role of Muslims in America as disseminating the virtues and values of Islam in the West. Muslims were urged to propagate the faith and participate in the public affairs of their adopted country, emphasizing the pluralistic nature of Islam and its amity with the other "Abrahamic" faiths: Christianity and Judaism.

Islamic exceptionalism also utilized American values in defining itself, and emulated other distinctive groups celebrated as monuments of American pluralism. In the later decades of the twentieth century, the phrase *E pluribus unum* signified a model Muslim community to be created out of all the nationalities, ethnicities, and ideological and sectarian groups represented in the U.S. The ideology emerged at an opportune time, as it fit into the foreign policy goals of the U.S. in combatting communism during the Cold War. For two decades, Islam had been perceived by various American administrations as a potential bulwark against the spread of communism and socialism. President Reagan, who helped in financing and arming the Afghan Mujahideen, celebrated their prowess in defeating the Soviet Union. This idea ran parallel with the American Muslim discourse as the leaders struggled to elaborate a model Islamic community.

With the collapse of the Soviet empire, the neoconservative quest for a new evil to be vanquished did not take too long to find. America had been enraged at Shia Islam as espoused by Ayatollah Khomeini and Iranian revolutionaries that took American hostages and held them for 444 days in Iran. As promoted by neoconservatives, Islam or "Radical Islamic Terrorism" replaced communism as the enemy of freedom, godliness, civilization, and all that is good. Francis Fukuyama (1992) and Samuel Huntington (1996) alerted Muslims that the U.S. was looking for a new enemy and they could be the target. The 1991 Gulf War led to the isolation of the Muslims in the U.S. as Gulf nations stopped their financial support. New American Muslim organizations were formed that were particularly geared to engage Muslims in American society.

The 1995 Oklahoma City bombing was a major wake up call for Muslims. Despite the fact that the perpetrators were Evangelical Christians, Muslims were initially blamed and targeted. Congress passed the Anti-Terrorism Act, which allowed the government to try Muslims using secret evidence. Muslims began to be more active in seeking to participate in American politics and taking advantage of the privilege of voting and having a say in American society.

One downside to Islamic exceptionalism was that it had entailed a self-imposed alienation from the dominant culture, which it saw as wayward and sinful. It also objected to the religious cultural identity that is not part of the Judeo-Christian ideal. This became a major problem since Islam was now held not only as un-American, but viewed in an even more sinister light, as its adherents were accused of sharing the hatred that terrorists harbored for Americans. The religion itself once again became a threat and its very name became an epithet hurled at Muslims.

The American-born children of post-1965 Muslim immigrants – the second generation – are citizens by birthright who, unlike their parents or grandparents, have not grown up overseas. Most have come of age in a bicultural environment, learning to negotiate a hyphenated American identity. While they cross daily between the two, they are aware of the lines of demarcation that spell out "us and them," proper and improper, *halal* (acceptable) and *haram* (forbidden), and for those whose parents happen to be more doctrinaire, the distinction between Muslim and *kufr* (unbeliever).

The aftermath of 9/11

Upon hearing of the airplane hitting the World Trade Center, Alia Malek wrote:

> I quickly recited the very Arab American prayer (which now has a Muslim American version as well) that we say in moments like these, moments when anything goes boom and all of a sudden an entire people are called to task for the acts of individuals: "Lord, please don't let it be Arabs."
>
> (Malek 2011: 15)

The attacks of 9/11 aggravated the fear the general American public already had of Muslims. Every government warning of an impending security breach, raising the color code of the terror threat from yellow to orange to red, raised the level of apprehension of the American public. Propaganda supporting the war on terrorism in Afghanistan and Iraq tapped into a long heritage of Western fear and demonization of Islam. The attacks of 9/11 ended any pretense of political correctness toward Muslims and gave way to diatribe against Islam, its prophet, and its adherents. As a consequence of 9/11, the "Americanness" of Muslims and in particular the foundations of their faith began to be attacked as a threat to the U.S. Newt Gingrich, the former Speaker of the House, argued that the primary threat to America was not terrorism but Sharia law.

Following the attacks of 9/11, attorney General John Ashcroft contemplated establishing internment camps to hold Muslim citizens deemed enemy combatants. This method of maintaining security during periods of fear has a precedent in American history in the internment of German Americans during WWI and Japanese Americans during WWII (Bakalian and Bozorgmehr 2009; Krammer 1997). Some even perceived echoes of 1950s McCarthyism and its campaign against communists, noting that the Red Scare had been replaced by the Green menace. Ashcroft's plan for incarceration, as it turned out, was rendered unnecessary because of advances in technology. Thus, while Muslims were not confined to a physical camp, they were placed in virtual internment – identified, scrutinized, and watched, their civil liberties and human rights constrained in the name of security (Hagopian 2004; Cole and Dempsy 2006).

During the 2000 presidential election, Republican George W. Bush reached out to the Muslim community and even questioned parts of the Anti-Terrorism Law stripping them of their rights. In the immediate aftermath of September 11, Bush, then President, condemned attacks against Muslims, making it clear that terrorism does not represent Islam or the views of American Muslim citizens. Yet specific policies, including the passing of the USA PATRIOT Act and the decision to invade Afghanistan and Iraq, caused many Muslims to shift allegiance from the Republican Party. Arab-American and South Asian-American Muslims, who had supported Bush in 2000, switched their support in 2004 overwhelmingly to the Democratic candidate, John Kerry.

By associating Muslims with an ideology promoting the destruction of America and its values, Americans began to place new demands on Muslim citizens. In the imagination of many Americans, Muslims had been transformed from aliens to enemy combatants. Muslim denunciation of the perpetrators was not sufficient; it became necessary to incarnate a new consciousness and a new identity. The former "self" that identified with Islamic exceptionalism had to be excised as it no longer fit the demands of "unqualified" American citizenship. In a very important way, Muslims were being asked to pay a new price for belonging, namely the abandonment of an identity that had been fostered and promoted for over two decades. Islamic distinctiveness had to be suppressed if not eradicated. The order of the day was to create a "moderate Islam," appropriating American exceptionalism as the essential core of Islamic values (Haddad 2004).

The Bush administration made it clear also that it expected moderate Islamic governments overseas to implement certain measures to assure American interests. These included curbing "inflammatory" speech directed against American or Israeli policies. President Bush, in his address after the attack, posited a bifurcated world reaffirming the neoconservative tendency to see the world in polarities: a world in which there are contending forces of good and evil, civilized and uncivilized, democratic and despotic, free and hostage (Mamdani 2004). He challenged the world by saying "You are either with us or against us," allowing no wiggle room in the public square for pluralism that celebrates difference. Since 9/11 the United States government under the aegis of the Department of Homeland Security has been involved in an effort to reformulate a mainstream, acceptable form of being a Muslim American. This project was quickly classified as a matter of national security. Thus both American Muslims and the American government were working toward a similar goal of transforming Muslims living in the United States into Muslim Americans (Haddad 2011).

American policies adopted since 9/11 are seen by many Muslims in the U.S. and overseas as a declaration of war not only on terrorism but on Islam itself. These include the USA PATRIOT Act, which legitimized the singling out of Muslims for profiling, arrest, and incarceration without evidence or access to legal counsel; raiding of homes and offices of U.S. Islamic leadership by federal agencies; and freezing the assets of Muslim charities. Arrest, seizure, and deportation were enacted. Implementation of the USA PATRIOT Act made it clear that Constitutional guarantees can no longer provide a protective shield that insulates Muslim citizens from profiling and entrapment, seizure and search, arrest and deportation (Bakalian and Bozorgmehr 2009). Republican legislators convened congressional hearings to investigate whether Islam is a religion, and proposals were made in more than 22 states to legally ban Sharia law – all of which led to Muslims feeling ostracized in their own country.

Fashioning a new Muslim-American identity

Post-9/11 events made clear the need for a new American Muslim leadership to emerge, one that would call for engagement with American society and take to heart the government's demand for a "moderate Islam." The emphasis shifted to a more robust civic engagement necessitating a better knowledge of the American political system. Building upon greater civic literacy, this new approach would call for participation in the political process, respect for the founding principles of the Republic, and active commitment to the common good. Thus, the younger generation has moved beyond flirting with the political system in the way that their parents had gingerly and reluctantly tested in 2000 when they endorsed George Bush for president, only to see two of his most ardent Muslim supporters sentenced to jail during his administration for their support of Islamic causes. The second generation is now eager to be part of the system. A few have overcome their parent's reluctance to engage in politics, having learned that it is not enough to sit on the sidelines. They must be engaged in the daily rough and tumble of politics in order to make a difference and to be taken seriously. They have organized voter registration drives and worked for candidates of their choice.

Among Muslims, particularly second-generation youth, 9/11 was a defining moment that sometimes even led to an increase in religiosity. However, rather than a re-Islamization, or a return to a former level of religious adherence, Muslim identity in America has been transformed in specifically creative and assertive ways. Core religious observance is increasingly civil-rights oriented and concerned with egalitarianism and justice. Efforts include initiation through the Council on American-Islamic Relations (CAIR), Muslim Public Affairs Council (MPAC), and Muslim Students Association (MSA) projects as well as government internship programs featuring engagement in mainstream American society, politics, and culture to secure the right of religious freedom granted by the Constitution and the Bill of Rights. Thus, for the majority of the American-born generation, post-9/11 demonization did not lead to concealment of their faith but rather to an effort to publicize it and to educate non-Muslims and Muslims alike about the uniquely democratic, pluralistic, and modern nature of Islam. The main project became integrating American Muslims in the name of religious pluralism and diversity through such means as networking, the blogoverse, work on college campuses, and conferences and seminars around the country (Wuthnow 2007).

While the major Muslim umbrella organizations, as well as the majority of Muslim American youth, are seeking to affirm their American roots and loyalty to the U.S., there persist some small pockets of believers that hold on to the ideal of Islamic exceptionalism. *Wahhabis*, a few *Salafis*, *Tablighi Jamaat*, and *Hizb ut-Tahrir* groups persist in teaching that the West is *bilad kufr* (an infidel nation) needing to be converted to Islam and that Muslims should emphasize their opposition to American social, political, and economic policies which have targeted Islam and Muslims overseas. They insist that the Muslim community must maintain itself as a unique entity and not as a transplant, a living organism that adjusts to its environment to survive and is open to being altered in an alien soil. Muslims, they warn, must beware of the possibility of contamination by a corrupt and corrupting culture; they must maintain a barrier to ensure the wholeness, difference, and distinction of Islam.

Some Muslims are vocal in their disapproval of the steps taken by Muslim organizations to integrate Muslims into the larger American institutions. Kaukab Siddique, publisher of *New Trend Magazine*, which has some appeal among a tiny fringe of African American Muslims in Baltimore, Maryland, and North Carolina, has condemned the Islamic Society of North America (ISNA) and other Islamic organizations that have been leading the way into integrating Muslims into the fabric of American life. He believes that Islam is unique and supersedes Christianity and Judaism. Collaborating with the American government, he argues, is against Islamic interests, and forming coalitions with Jewish and Christian organizations and interfaith activities is tantamount to acting like an unbeliever, or kafir. "ISNA is very friendly and cooperative with the White House, the Pentagon, American Jews, and Rabbis supporting Israel and the Zionist myth and the Zionist media. ISNA's president, a real stooge of the Zionists, has even visited Auschwitz" (Siddique 2012). He also criticizes Muslims for participating in interfaith activities, which he deems unacceptable in Islam. Siddique accused mainline organizations such as CAIR, ICNA, and ISNA of voting in a *kufr* structure, of collaborating with a government that bombed Iraq, Afghanistan, and Pakistan.

> These groups have consistently supported the government and are still doing it. No shame even when the marines urinated on dead Muslims. No *haya* (shame) when the Quran is desecrated. Surely these four letter organizations know on which side their bread is buttered.
>
> (Siddique 2012)

Siddique's ideas have been rejected by the majority of Muslims who seek to be accepted as "real Americans." While his shrill voice is ignored by most Muslims, he provides endless fodder for those right-wing organizations who wish to criticize all Muslims.

With the fall of the World Trade Center Towers and the security measures instituted by the government, the old leadership made room for new leaders to step forward. Major changes appeared, specifically transformation in the role of women and of youth. Women were elected as presidents of the major Islamic organizations: Ingrid Mattsen of the Islamic Society of North America and Hadia Mubarak of the Muslim Student Association. The mainline organizations issued new directives to incorporate women in the mosque. The media vilification of women in Islam became an impetus for Muslim women to step forward and defend their role and agency. Women became major spokespersons for American Islam. Many mosques have become community centers where young women have an expanded role (Haddad, Smith and Moore 2006). There are several women chaplains at private American universities, and several board directors of mosques are women. Youth organizations also began to proliferate, ranging from groups connected to the main organizations to new ones such as the SuShi (Sunni/Shia) group in Washington, DC, interested in exploring intra-faith dialogue and inter-faith activities. Young Muslims continue to seek to create a "true Islam," as they see themselves as "true Americans."

There has also been a rise in the number of organizations catering to the needs of young Muslim Americans, inevitably making space for the creation of unique American Muslim cultural traditions. A good example is the effort of the Muslim American Society, which initiated the Muslim Boys and Girls Scouts (Masood 2005). While they follow the same basic model as the traditional scouting organizations, substitutions have been made. In order to earn badges, for example, Muslim scouts may memorize the Quran or participate in other Islamic activities. While the values imparted teach the importance of brotherhood and sisterhood, they are grounded in Islamic values. The Muslim Student Association has also long played a pivotal role in cultural production by leading activities on American college and university campuses and are now expanding their activities into high schools. Other changes are taking place among Muslim Millennials. Some American Muslims are beginning to defy their parents' wishes and intermarry across ethnic lines. Young women are holding *hijab* parties and Muslim proms. Increasingly, unlike their parents' generation, which adopted Arabic phrases as a sign of distinction, they refer to Allah as God. College students have taken to holding fastathon fundraisers during Ramadan, inviting non-Muslims to join them in fasting for a day and donate the receipts to feed the hungry. They have also become very involved in interfaith activities on campuses and do volunteer work, participating, for example, in Habitat for Humanity projects building and refurbishing homes for the needy.

While Islamic exceptionalism sought to ground the American Muslim experience in reconstituted cultures of the Muslim world, and insisted that it should be adopted as a way of life, young Muslims are seeking to take charge of their own identity and are creating a comfort zone on their own terms within the American context. This manifests itself in an effort to form a distinct American Muslim culture in the arts, music, film, and novels. Young Muslims are doing this by appropriating already existing American cultural practices and "Islamicizing" them. All these processes contribute to the production of an American Muslim youth culture.

Muslim youth write to validate their experience as truly American, exposing the tensions they feel living on the cusp of contending, competing, and contesting cultures. At the same time, they have to confront racism and "othering" on both sides of the divide. Their narratives expose their experience of oppression and intolerance in the dominant society as they attempt to contest their marginalization. They also critique some of the patterns, norms, and values espoused by their parents, feeling that they can serve as barriers to their own aspirations. The youth want to reclaim the right to be different as guaranteed by the Constitution, "insisting on the power that stories have to generate hope and engagement, personal dignity and active citizenship, the pride of identity, and the humility of human connectedness" (Solinger, Fox and Irani 2008: 1).

As part of this enhanced engagement with the American mainstream, young, often second-generation Muslim authors attempt to move beyond the immigrant tendency to address a niche clientele. They are increasingly writing for a general American audience, recording the American Muslim experience in the United States in novels, biographies and memoirs, poetry, and plays. They see themselves as voices of reason resisting the onslaught of negative portrayals of Islamophobic texts. Others have written progressive interpretations of Islam countering the tendency of the media to relegate Islam to an expression of terrorist ideology (Aslan 2007; Safi 2003), while some have produced books advising young people on how to maneuver in the toxic atmosphere in which they live (Malek 2011: 15). New magazines and blogs also cater to issues facing young Muslims.

At the same time, there are some in the Muslim community who oppose writing about problems and equate it with airing "dirty laundry." Immigrants from cultures that value privacy may look askance at those who want to write about what it means to be a Muslim. They fear that if they open themselves up, they will be vulnerable to the general American public who may ridicule their authentic experiences (Solinger, Fox and Irani 2008). Still, more and more young Muslims have ventured into participating in the media. They are experimenting with fashioning an Islamic media as a means of explaining how they see their Islamic identity. They are eager to discuss new ideas and interpretations of what it means to be Muslim American. These new forms of communication attempt to counter the dominant media which bombards Muslims with accusations that undermine their self-assurance and their faith. Muslim media provide an Islamic response, constructing a comfort zone where they are able to counter negative images. Armed with these interpretations, they can confront the dominant hostile environment and operate within it (Curran and Couldry 2003: 7). Participation in new forms of media helps to empower the youth to define themselves apart from the subjugation of their detractors. While defending the faith, they find new and creative means of expression of that faith.

Young American Muslim women have taken the lead in defining appropriate and appealing styles of dress. While many in the general American public perceive Islamic dress, particularly the headscarf, as oppressive to women, believing that it is imposed on them by men, young Muslim women who choose to don Islamic attire are increasingly engaged in making a fashion statement. They have come up with creative ways to dress within the limits of Islamic modesty without abandoning jeans and brand names. And the fashion industry has taken note. Some designers now accommodate Muslim preferences by selling slightly longer tunics, and shops such as *Urban Outfitters* are incorporating symbolic items like the Palestinian *kefiyya* in their displays.

Young Muslims are not reluctant to engage in every genre of music and make it their own. Kareema Salama sings Islamic country music, while Pakistani Americans from Boston have a punk garage band called the *Kominas*. Hip-hop is one of the most notable ways in which mainstream music interacts with American

Muslim culture and serves as a well-documented avenue through which many trace their religious awakening. Rap music produced by the children of Muslim immigrants, as well as by African-American Muslim converts, has become very popular among both second-generation youth and the African American community. Furthermore, while some American Muslims have excelled in traditional Islamic arts, others have become noted photographers and filmmakers. Still other – among them, the Axis of Evil Comedy Tour, Azhar Usman, Allah Made Me Funny, and Hijabi Monologue – are engaged in ensemble performance and standup comedy.

Conclusion

The terrorist attacks of 9/11 pushed Muslims – particularly American-born or American-raised Muslims – to reassess what it means to be American and Muslim. While many Americans may see the two as incongruent or as mutually exclusive, Muslim Americans, and especially the youth, are increasingly striving to reclaim their faith from the demonizers, the hijackers, and the foreign interpreters.

On arriving at Ellis Island, earlier immigrants were met with the American promise: "Give me your tired, your poor, your huddled masses yearning to breathe free, the wretched refuse of your teaming shore." The new immigrants are for the most part college educated, part of the rising professional middle classes of the Muslim world. They are engaged daily in contributing to America's economic and political power. They definitely do not see themselves as "huddled masses" or "wretched refuse." Yet they often feel that they are treated as such.

While the immigrant generation has attempted to maintain its culture by remembering and attempting to reinvent it in the Western context, the responses of the American-born generation have varied according to their acceptance by the host culture and their ability to fully participate in American political, social, and economic life. Raised in schools where the values of multiculturalism and pluralism are venerated as the founding principles of the nation, they often experience discrimination both as racism and increasingly as a vocal devaluation of their religion, keeping them on the margins of society.

These youths are in the process of fashioning a new Muslim-American way of being and attempting to open up American society to Muslim participation and sense of belonging while holding on to the faith. Unlike their parents' generation, they are engaged in American social and political institutions. Many are not seeking to be doctors and engineers, the professions most valued by their parents, but are exploring new professions and embarking on careers as lawyers, novelists, comics, musicians, journalists, public intellectuals, scholars, and government officials. They have assumed agency by participating in public forums. They are comfortable in their newly-fashioned identity of Muslim Americans, fully aware that there are many in the United States who continue to see them as alien based not only on race or politics but, more importantly, on religion. Many devote time to the struggle for religious, political, and human rights as they attempt to fulfill their obligations within society. They are not hiding behind walls of silence but, instead, are articulating their rights as citizens through mastery of the dominant discourse, citing not only their birthright but also their allegiance to the national values of tolerance and acceptance. In this, they are rising above racial, political, and religious profiling by engaging America through discourse, storytelling, humor, ironic self-deprecation, performance, interfaith activities and political dialogue, film, and peacemaking.

Defenders of the "old" Judeo-Christian covenant continue to promote America as a pluralistic, multicultural, multi-faith society open to incorporating all citizens, regardless of their faith. Adherents to this vision of America were among the first to reach out after 9/11 to the beleaguered Muslim community, which saw an outpouring of support from concerned neighbors, rabbis, and ministers. Lined up against them are the defenders of the "new" Judeo-Christian exclusivism forged between the neoconservatives and evangelicals preaching a God of vengeance and war who does not tolerate other faiths, especially Islam.

The events of 9/11 appear to have brought tremendous pressure to bear on Muslims to become "Americans." The question is whose standard of what it means to be American is to be implemented? Anti-Muslim activists have continued the drum beat to incite fear of the presence of Muslims in the West as an imminent threat not only to the "unique" Western culture of liberalism, democracy, tolerance, pluralism, and multiculturalism, but also to the age-old Judeo-Christian West itself. The question persists: Do the democratic principles espoused by the West and spelled out in the American Constitution allow for religions with a distinctive culture and alternate values to flourish in their midst? Put simply, will Muslims be allowed to propagate and maintain a culture and a religion of their choice in a political climate that increasingly demonizes Sharia law, which critics simplistically equate solely with punishments? Many Muslims increasingly feel that they have been stripped of the right to define their own faith since the Sharia text, in fact, articulates the core of the faith and practice of Islam. They continue to wonder what kind of Islam America will tolerate and who determines the parameters of the faith. The situation remains in flux. They are American citizens but are considered suspect by many Americans. They believe that such demonization is essentially un-American, since it tarnishes them not because of anything they have done, but because they share a faith that has been associated with extremists overseas. They wonder whether Muslims in the United States will have the liberty to define what it means to be a Muslim without being hampered by the Islamophobes and the security agencies of the state. More importantly, will Muslims be allowed to have a say in what it means to be an American?

For the second generation, the Islamic exceptionalism that was promoted by their immigrant parents has become unworkable, as it suggests disloyalty to the nation. Muslim engagement with the American public affirms that they have not been silenced by their demonizers. By daring to voice their experience and contest those who seek to harm them, they are hoping for empathy as well as justice. They believe that they are engaged in an effort to re-appropriate the right to define themselves, rather than be defined and quarantined by their adversaries and detractors. In the final analysis, engagement is an act of peaceful defiance and an affirmation of the right to break out from the isolation imposed by the security agencies. It is the affirmation of their belief in the American promise, the American dream, and the American justice system. Rather than victims of history, they see themselves as agents of change, eager to help restore America to its promise of liberty and justice.

References

Alba, Richard. 2012. *Blurring the Color Line: The Chance for a More Integrated America.* Cambridge, MA: Harvard University Press.

Aslan, Reza. 2009. *How to Win a Cosmic War: God, Globalization, and the End of the War on Terror.* New York: Random House.

Bakalian, Anny, and Mehdi Bozorgmehr. 2009. *Backlash 9/11: Middle Eastern and Muslim Americans Respond.* Berkeley, CA: University of California Press.

Cerulo, Karen. 1997. "Identity Construction: New Issues, New Directions." *Annual Review of Sociology* 23(1): 385–409.

Cole, David, and Jack Dempsy. 2006. *Terrorism and the Constitution: Sacrificing Civil Liberties in the Name of National Security.* New York: The New Press.

Curran, James, and Nick Couldry (eds.). 2003. *Contesting Media Power: Alternative Media in a Networked World.* Oxford: Rowman & Littlefield Publishers.

Fukuyama, Francis. 1992. *The End of History and the Last Man.* New York: Free Press.

Haddad, Yvonne. 2004. *Not Quite American? The Shaping of Arab and Muslim Identity in the United States, An Edmondson Historical Lecture.* Waco, TX: Baylor University Press.

Haddad, Yvonne. 2011. *Becoming American? The Forging of Arab and Muslim Identity Pluralist America.* Waco, TX: Baylor University Press.

Haddad, Yvonne, Jane Smith, and Kathleen Moore. 2006. *Muslim Women in America: Gender, Islam, and Society.* New York: Oxford University Press.

Hagopian, Elaine C. (ed.). 2004. *Civil Rights in Peril: The Targeting of Arabs and Muslims.* Chicago: Haymarket Books.

Herberg, Will. 1955. *Protestant, Catholic, Jew: An Essay in American Religious Sociology.* Garden City, New York: Doubleday.

Huntington, Samuel. 1996. *The Clash of Civilizations and the Remaking of the World Order.* New York: Simon & Schuster.

Iftikhar, Arsalan. 2012. "Muslims 2012: The Most Radioactive Voting Bloc in America." *The Islamic Monthly* (Winter/Spring): 38–39.

Krammer, Arnold. 1997. *Undue Process: The Untold Story of America's German Alien Internees.* Lanham, MD: Rowman & Littlefield.

Malek, Alia. 2011. *Patriot Acts: Narratives of Post-9/11 Injustice.* San Francisco: McSweeney's Books.

Mamdani, Mahmood. 2004. *Good Muslim, Bad Muslim: America, the Cold War, and the Roots of Terror.* New York: Pantheon Books.

Masood, Maliha. 2005. "Caught between Worlds: A Pakistani-Muslim Adolescence in America." In *Waking Up American, Coming of Age Biculturally: First Generation Women Reflect on Identity*, edited by Angela Jane Fountas, pp. 53–62. Emeryville, CA: Seal Press.

Safi, Omid. 2003. *Progressive Muslims: On Justice, Gender, and Pluralism.* Oxford: Oneworld Publications.

Samhan, Helen Hatab. 1987. "Politics and Exclusion: The Arab American Experience." *Journal of Palestine Studies* 16(2): 11–28.

Siddique, Kaukab. 2012 "Muslim Elites Learning the Hard Way." *New Trend Magazine*, April 1.

Solinger, Rickie, Madeline Fox, and Kayhan Irani. 2008. "Introduction." In *Telling Stories to Change the World*. New York: Routledge.

Suleiman, Michael. 1999. "Islam, Muslims and Arabs in America: the Other of the Other of the Other . . ." *Journal of Muslim Minority Affairs* 19(1): 33–47.

Winthrop, John. 1867 [1630]. "City Upon a Hill." In *Life and Letters of John Winthrop*, edited by Robert C. Winthrop.

Wuthnow, Robert. 2007. *America and the Challenges of Religious Diversity*. Princeton: Princeton University Press.

6 The politics of belonging

Religiosity and identification among second-generation Moroccan Dutch

Marieke Slootman and Jan Willem Duyvendak

In the last two decades, in many Western countries, Islam has been increasingly articulated as a major source of boundaries and cleavages. This is also the case in Dutch society. Islam is increasingly regarded as incompatible with "Western" and "Dutch" values, and Muslims are perceived as a threat to what is regarded as Dutch culture. Dutch citizens with Moroccan and Turkish immigrant parents are portrayed as foreigners because they are Muslims and are therefore assumed to have a "traditional" – and hence incompatible – culture. Being Dutch has become increasingly defined by being modern (and individualistic), progressive (including tolerance of homosexuality), and secular. The centrality of religion in the Dutch framing of who belongs and who does not is in contrast with the situation in other countries where religion as such has been far less embattled, such as the United States, and impacts the meaning of being Muslim in particular ways.

What does it mean to be a Muslim in this political climate? How can we understand the religiosity and religious identities of second-generation Moroccan Dutch in the Netherlands? Does the exclusionary citizenship discourse discourage people from identifying as Muslim, or do people over-emphasize their identification as Muslim and strengthen their traditions because of this politicization of Islam, which then leads to a "reactive" Muslim identity? Or is identification as Muslim largely unaffected by the political discourse, and can we therefore conclude that being Muslim is the same across many countries, irrespective of political climate?

In this chapter, we explore what being Muslim means for second-generation Moroccans in the Netherlands and how this is affected by the political landscape. We contribute to the debate as to whether Muslim religiosity in Europe is "reactive." Originally, the idea of reactive identity is used in relation to ethnicity, which often solidifies in reaction to exclusion (Portes and Rumbaut 2001; Rumbaut 2008). This can also happen to religious identification; it may strengthen in the face of exclusion. In support of the idea that Muslim religiosity is partially reactive, Connor (2010: 376) concludes, based on data from the European Social Survey, that "less welcoming immigrant contexts are associated with higher religious outcomes among Muslim immigrants in comparison to the host region's religiosity." Torrekens and Jacobs dispute this conclusion that being Muslim is reactive. Based on analyses of survey data from the EURISLAM project, they argue there is no relation between Muslims' religiosity and the national political opportunity structure, nor between Muslims' religiosity and the national discursive climate.[1] Both articles share, however, an understanding of reactive religiosity as "retention," a reflection and reinforcement of ethnic heritage (Connor 2010: 394; Torrekens and Jacobs 2016: 326). Without going into the methodological characteristics of these two studies, in this chapter we evaluate their two claims as to whether Muslim religiosity is or is not reactive (understood as retention), a topic extremely pertinent in the anti-Islam Dutch context.

This chapter presents our argument in two parts. In the first part, we sketch the political landscape. We describe the Dutch politics of belonging and the immigration background of the second generation, and thereby provide the context needed to understand individual experiences. In the second part, we present the experiences of Moroccan-Dutch individuals based on data from our own mixed-methods study and from other empirical studies. We describe what being Muslim means for (some) second-generation Moroccan Dutch, based on quantitative and qualitative data.

Dutch politics of belonging

"Identification" and "culture" have become central tenets of the Dutch politics of belonging. In the words of a Dutch MP, directed at non-Western immigrants and their descendants living in the Netherlands: "Migrants should make explicitly clear their inner commitment to their new 'home' country" (Huizinga-Heringa in the Dutch Parliament in 2004; see Duyvendak 2011: 100). Not only are immigrants and their offspring required to feel at home and identify with their nation of residence, but they are also expected to internalize what is projected as "the" national culture.

The alleged failure of "multiculturalism"

This discourse, which demands inner commitment, is a reaction to the idea that the "integration" of immigrants has failed, for which the political strategy of liberal multiculturalism is blamed (Koopmans et al. 2005; Sniderman and Hagendoorn 2006).

Until the second half of the 1980s, immigrants arriving from Mediterranean countries to work in lower-skilled jobs were not required (nor impelled) to adapt to the Dutch culture and identity. This gave the Netherlands its tolerant image. Politicians from almost all political parties erroneously claim today that it was due to a multiculturalist ideal that immigrants were not asked to assimilate, and instead were encouraged to maintain their own identity, language and culture. However, this approach of "maintenance" of immigrants' culture had little to do with the political ideal of multiculturalism (Bertossi, Duyvendak, and Schain 2012). Rather, it was initially built on the assumption, both of the original immigrants themselves and the broader society, that the migrants would eventually return to Morocco and Turkey.

Nevertheless, many stayed in the Netherlands. The Dutch government continued the maintenance policy of Moroccan and Turkish identities and languages until the late 1980s, although the goal shifted from facilitation of return to support of socioeconomic integration. In other words, socio cultural differences were not valued for their own sake in Dutch policies, as in "true multiculturalism;" a misunderstanding made by many politicians and scholars alike (see Koopmans et al. 2005; Sniderman and Hagendoorn 2007).[2]

Instead, as one of us has contended elsewhere, there has been increasing unease with cultural differences in recent decades (Hurenkamp, Tonkens, and Duyvendak 2013), which can be better explained by progressive monoculturalism than multiculturalism. We elaborate on this argument below.

A culturalization of citizenship

Not only immigrants and their offspring, but many native Dutch as well, struggle to feel at home in the Netherlands (Duyvendak 2011). More social cohesion and more "shared Dutch citizenship" are billed by politicians as the solution. This has led to a public and political debate about what different ethnic and religious groups within the nation, in cities, and in neighborhoods have – or should have – in common. How can they together shape the public domain and its democratic values? The Dutch answer, partly in reaction to the essay "The Multicultural Drama," which blames the elites for being too relativist and proposes the creation of a strong national identity (Scheffer 2000), has been to foreground citizenship on the national level. This national citizenship does not rest on the traditional elements of citizenship: formal duties and juridical rights of members of a political community. Instead, it focuses on cultural elements with the aim of shaping a more homogeneous cultural community. "Good citizenship" then has come to depend not so much on working, paying taxes, or voting, but on criteria such as "proper" cultural practices, "acceptable" women's clothing, feelings of belonging and loyalty, secularism and the display of "appropriate" emotions at the right moments (Hurenkamp, Tonkens and Duyvendak 2012). This need to adapt to the Dutch national culture (not just to the nation's laws, but also to unwritten cultural expectations) has been explicitly formulated, as a 2011 policy letter by the Minister of Integration shows:

> The fundamentals that shape social life in the Netherlands are historically formed and are points of reference, which many Dutch share and which are not to be lost. This is not only about the attainments and the principal values that form the foundation of the Dutch nation state, but also about points of reference that have evolved historically and culturally, like the Dutch language, certain monuments or architectural characteristics or the unwritten ways and codes of behavior that have developed during the course of history.
>
> (Dutch Parliament, 2011, pp. 7–8, translated by the authors)

This culturalized citizenship discourse has not only pervaded the political realm but has also left its mark on actual policies. For example, compulsory "civic integration" programs, which address presumably uniform and undisputed Dutch cultural habits and Dutch history, have been implemented for permanent immigrants from outside the European Union (including those who have lived in the Netherlands for decades).

In short, in order to be accepted as a full-fledged citizen, one needs to feel at home in the Netherlands, demonstrate knowledge of "Dutch" traditions, practice "Dutch" customs and internalize "Dutch" morality. We call this trend a culturalization of citizenship (Duyvendak, Geschiere, and Tonkens 2016) requiring an affective relation of the migrants to their new nation. This Dutch culturalized and emotive discourse about national belonging appears to be very demanding and rather exclusionary, as we will explain now.

Defining the progressive Dutch identity

How is this national identity – this Dutchness – defined? Is this a rather open and inclusive definition, potentially including immigrants as well? Or are immigrants, perhaps paradoxically, asked to integrate into something they will never be considered part of? As we will show, it tends to be the latter: conceptions of Dutch identity and the Dutch nation are strengthened by ahistorical, essentialist definition of who is not Dutch. Hence, Dutchness is defined in contrast to the cultural "Other," in particular the Muslim immigrant (Van Reekum and Duyvendak 2012).

Nearly all political parties, including the right-wing populists, define "modern" progressive values – particularly in the fields of religion, gender and sexuality – as core Dutch characteristics. Secularism, gender equality, and the acceptance of homosexuality serve as ideological benchmarks to test whether immigrants have entered "modernity," the singular condition that allows for their belonging in Dutch society (Mepschen, Duyvendak, and Tonkens 2010). Recent analyses of new political cleavages in Western Europe have often overlooked the pivotal role played by the rhetoric of sexual and gender progress (Uitermark, Mepschen, and Duyvendak 2014). The rise of populism in Western Europe is then mistakenly analyzed as a linear shift toward conservatism. This misunderstanding is due to the conflation of progressiveness and pro-immigration viewpoints. Our research, however, shows that populists combine the framing of Dutch national culture as morally progressive with a virulent anti-immigration agenda. Therefore, when political scientists Kriesi et al. (2012: 171) conclude that the "cultural liberalism of the most educated has declined quite considerably [which] probably reflects . . . the general hardening of the Dutch attitude to immigration," they miss the cardinal point that Dutch anti-immigration discourse goes hand-in-hand with a rhetoric of gender equality and sexual emancipation. Tolerance toward one group, such as the LGBT community, does not imply tolerance toward other dimensions of difference, such as ethnicity or religion.

The Moroccan and Turkish Dutch as the immigrant and Muslim "Other"

In this discourse, in which Dutch identity is defined in progressive and secular terms, immigrants from Morocco in particular and, to a somewhat lesser extent, immigrants from Turkey are presented as ethnic "Others" who demarcate the contours of Dutch identity. This focus on Moroccan Dutch originates in a combination of both their relatively low socioeconomic position and their relatively traditional and religious sociocultural position. Based on their overrepresentation in crime and school dropout rates, for example, Moroccan Dutch have come to be associated with a variety of social problems. However, instead of attributing this overrepresentation to class position or societal mechanisms such as discrimination and stigmatization, the prevailing view has linked these issues with "Moroccan culture" itself, which is therefore seen as backward and a disturbing factor in Dutch society. Recently, Moroccan culture has often been replaced by Islam as a reason for Moroccans in the Netherlands supposedly not being integrated.

The largest Muslim groups in the Netherlands are the Moroccan and Turkish Dutch, who also form the largest ethnic minority groups. The most recent estimations of religious affiliations stem from 2008, when 296,000 of the estimated 825,000 Muslims in the Netherlands were of Moroccan descent and 285,000 were of Turkish descent (Statistics Netherlands 2012b: 44). Nowadays, first- and second-generation Moroccan and Turkish Dutch comprise 2.2 respectively 2.4 percent of the Dutch population (375,000 and 396,000 of a total of 16 million) (Statistics Netherlands 2014: 26). In large cities, the share of Moroccan and Turkish Dutch is much higher. For example, among the ten-year-olds in Amsterdam, this share is nearly 28 percent (Research and Statistics Amsterdam 2014: 67). In some Amsterdam and Rotterdam neighborhoods, Moroccan and Turkish Dutch together comprise between 40 and 50 percent of the population. In these neighborhoods, they are the largest and often most established ethnic groups (including the ethnic Dutch), particularly among the younger cohorts (Crul and Schneider 2010).

The first generation of Moroccan immigrants arrived in the Netherlands in the late 1960s and 1970s, when young men came to work as "guest workers" in lower-skilled jobs. Many of them came from rural areas and had extremely low formal education levels. Most of them were Muslim. Later, when it became clear that they would stay, their families came to the Netherlands as well. Many families had relatively traditional norms and practices. As we will show later, large shares of the second generation are also religious and/or call themselves "Muslim," in contrast to the secular, or rather atheist, Dutch.

While most of the early Moroccan immigrants had low levels of formal education and remained in the lower socioeconomic strata, much of the second generation shows enormous advancement. Since the 1990s, the share of second-generation youth with a Turkish or Moroccan background starting in higher education has increased from 20 to over 40 percent (Statistics Netherlands 2012a: 85). Nevertheless, this contrasts with another large share that lags behind (Crul and Doomernik 2003). Despite the steady increase, the average education level among the second generation is still lower than among ethnic Dutch (Statistics Netherlands 2012a).

Increasingly, and not only in the Netherlands, Islam has been framed as inherently irreconcilable with progressive Western values (Uitermark, Mepschen and

Duyvendak 2014). In this sense, Islam as a religion has replaced Moroccan ethnicity as the "Other" which denotes the Dutch identity as an entity that is culturally distinct. The argument is the same: ethnicity or religion is used to emphasize
the irreconcilability with what is seen as the Dutch culture. Actually, the framing
of cultural boundaries in terms of religion is even more exclusionary than the
framing in ethnic terms, as the religious framing resonates with the global, essen-
tializing "clash of civilizations" discourse.

The immigration of Muslims is seen as a threat to the stability of the Dutch
secular and liberal moral order, and cultural protectionists have set out to guard
Dutch cultural and sexual liberties against the alleged dangers posed by Muslim immigrants. Although political actors vary in the level of exclusion that they
advocate, the populist anti-Islam politician Geert Wilders has managed to draw a
lot of media attention and significant electoral support with his extremely exclusionary anti-immigrant and anti-Muslim statements.

The nativist dimension of Dutch identity

So, then, is cultural adaptation indeed the key to acceptance? And do Dutch politicians believe in the end that Muslim migrants can and will assimilate? To answer
these questions, we have to take into account another exclusionary layer added to
the Dutch dominant citizenship discourse: nativism. Nativism is anchored in the
idea that those whose families have been on Dutch territory for centuries should
have a bigger say about "our" culture and identity, have more rights, and eventually belong "more" (Duyvendak 2011). The profoundness of this Dutch nativism
is reflected in the widespread and consistent use of the term *allochtonen* (literally meaning not from this soil, see Geschiere 2009) to denote "non-western"
immigrants and their children, and sometimes their grandchildren, in opposition
to *autochtonen* (from this soil). Labeling Dutch-born children, of whom the large
majority have Dutch nationality, as *allochtonen*, places them in an outsider position. It is exactly for this reason that, very recently, these labels have been aban-
doned from formal governmental vocabulary.

This nativist layer makes national belonging even more exclusionary. Whereas
the emotive and culturalist demands imply that adaptation of first- and second-
generation immigrants, and thereby acceptance as full-fledged citizens, is eventually possible, the nativist layer implies that immigrants and their direct offspring
will never fully belong; at least not as much as "natives," who are Dutch in the full-
est sense, and are the supposed true citizens of the country. This results in minority individuals, particularly Muslims, being treated with suspicion regardless of
their actual cultural practices and identifications. The nativist position present in
populist discourses not only frames Muslim migrants as foreign (non-native) to
the Dutch culture, but often as unassimilable. It presents the gap between migrants
and natives as by definition unbridgeable, in the sense that over time migrants can
perhaps become slightly more native, but they can never become "real" natives.
In addition, the nativist layer of the Dutch discourse fully legitimizes the othering of those with immigrant backgrounds, placing exclusionary practices beyond

dispute. Therefore, politicians of many strands have been sending a paradoxical message to these migrants, i.e., to totally assimilate into a culture in which they are regarded unassimilable.

Such culturalized citizenship discourse, in which Islam has come to be portrayed as inherently different from "the" national culture, can be found in many other countries. However, the extent to which Islam is perceived as being in deep opposition to a progressive, secular national culture seems to be unparalleled (perhaps with the exception of Denmark). How, in this context, can we understand being Muslim?

Being Muslim in the Netherlands

We present our exploration of individual experiences in three steps. First, we rely on quantitative data to describe the self-identifications of Dutch-born individuals of Moroccan descent. We show that they identify relatively strongly with the label "Muslim" and that this religious identification is intertwined with identification as "Moroccan." Second, we quantitatively explore religiosity among these second-generation Moroccan Dutch and how this religiosity is related to their self-identifications. Third, we use qualitative data to interpret the quantitative findings and to further explore the themes of religious identification, religiosity, and the impact of the political context. Before we turn to our analysis of the data, we first describe the data sources used.

Data

Central to our chapter is the survey data derived from the international TIES project (The Integration of the European Second Generation), which focuses on children of immigrants born and educated in their countries of residence. The Dutch part of the TIES dataset is based on structured surveys among 1,505 respondents aged between 18 and 35 years in the cities of Amsterdam and Rotterdam in 2006–2007, who come from three ethnic groups: second-generation Moroccan Dutch, second-generation Turkish Dutch (with at least one parent born in Morocco or Turkey), and an ethnic Dutch control group of Dutch descent (with both parents born in the Netherlands).

In order to help interpret the quantitative findings, we use the findings of various qualitative studies conducted among second-generation Moroccan Dutch in the Netherlands. Some of the findings used stem from eleven semi-structured interviews that we conducted with university-educated second-generation Moroccan-Dutch adults. At the time of the interviews, they had jobs matching their education level (so, these were individuals who exceed the socioeconomic criterion for integration). Respondents were over thirty years old and had at least one parent who migrated from Morocco. They were born in the Netherlands or arrived at a very young age, before they entered the educational system. The quotes are translated from Dutch, and pseudonyms are used here. (For additional information about the interviews, see Slootman 2014.)

Religious identification as "Muslim"

Central to our analysis is the distinction between two dimensions of being Muslim: the use of the label "Muslim" versus religiosity in terms of practices. The distinction between "identification with a label" and "content" follows from the view, inspired by Barth (1969), that ethnic boundaries are constructions between groups that perceive themselves as different, and do not necessarily reflect preexisting cultural differences. This means that ethnic labels do not necessarily reflect homogeneous and distinctive cultures; they do not reflect some sort of definite sociocultural "content." This separation of label and content can also be applied to other social boundaries, such as those defined in religious terms.

All second-generation Moroccan-Dutch respondents were asked to identify with each of the following three labels: "Muslim," "Moroccan," and "Dutch." We also looked at pairwise comparisons, using the gamma (γ) test of significance. Among second-generation Moroccan Dutch, identification with the label "Muslim" is strong (see also Slootman 2016; Statistics Netherlands 2012b). When asked to what extent one feels Muslim, 83 percent of the Moroccan Dutch TIES respondents answered "strong" or "very strong," and only six percent did not identify as Muslim at all or did so only weakly (see Table 6.1). Although these data seem important, they do not reveal what it means for a person to give a certain answer. As we explained, we do not assume that answers to this question have any other meaning than that people express a certain affiliation with the label Moroccan, or Muslim, or Dutch at a certain moment in time. Men and women do not differ in their identification as Muslim (γ = .025; p = .764). Also, educational level does not appear to have a large effect on religious identification among Moroccan Dutch. The majority (85 percent) of respondents with lower levels of education identify as Muslim (very) strongly, versus 77 percent of those who are more highly educated (HBO and university level) (γ = −.161; p = .074).

Identification as Moroccan appears to be nearly as strong as identification as Muslim: 78 percent of the Moroccan Dutch respondents feel Moroccan strongly and very strongly. It appears that feeling Muslim and feeling Moroccan are closely associated (γ = .660; p < .005). Those who identify relatively strongly as Muslim are also very likely to identify relatively strongly as Moroccan. The

Table 6.1 Identification with three labels of Moroccan-Dutch respondents

Label	Not at all/ very weak %	Weak %	Not strong/ weak %	Strong %	Very strong %	Total %
Muslim	4	2	11	30	53	100
Moroccan	3	3	16	40	38	100
Dutch	9	10	38	30	13	100

Note: This table reflects the answers to the three questions: "To what extent do you feel Muslim/Moroccan/Dutch?" About 400 Moroccan-Dutch respondents answered all of these questions in 2006–2007.

Source: The Integration of the European Second Generation (TIES)

vast majority (86%) of the respondents who strongly or very strongly identify as "Muslim" also strongly or very strongly identify as "Moroccan."

Identification as Dutch is clearly weaker, although this does not mean that the Moroccan Dutch respondents do not identify as Dutch at all. Although one-fifth of the respondents indicate that they do not feel Dutch or feel Dutch only weakly, this still means that eighty percent feels Dutch more than weakly. Nearly half feels Dutch strongly or very strongly. Feeling Dutch is negatively associated with feeling Muslim. This association is significant but only weak ($\gamma = -.146$; $p = .025$). Feeling Dutch is not significantly associated with feeling Moroccan ($\gamma = -.086$; $p = .201$).

In short, both religious and ethnic identifications are relatively strong among the Moroccan Dutch TIES respondents, and these two dimensions are closely associated (see also the findings of Van Heelsum and Koomen 2016). Clearly, the negative image of Islam does not prevent second-generation Moroccan Dutch from identifying as Muslim. The negative association between identification as Dutch and as Muslim could imply that some respondents perceive being Dutch and being Muslim as oppositional, although the correlation is surprisingly weak in the light of the exclusionary Dutch discourse.

Apparently, the exclusionary discourse about Muslims does not make the second-generation refrain from identifying as Muslim. However, does this also mean that they feel and behave religious? Or is this identification with the label Muslim separated from any religious practices? Is it perhaps solely a reaction to the discourse, without any other (more intrinsic) reasons?

Rumbaut's notion of a reactive ethnicity primarily refers to the label-dimension, as he speaks of a heightening of group consciousness and a hardening of identity boundaries in the face of a hostile context (2008: 3). He does not speak about becoming more religious or more traditional; about the content. Neither the analysis of Connor (2010) nor the one by Torrekens and Jacobs (2016) explicitly distinguish between label and content; both Connor and Torrekens and Jacobs use these two dimensions of identification and behavioral practices together within one variable.

To begin to answer the question of to what extent being Muslim is reactive, i.e., how it is influenced by the political context, we explore whether a strong identification as Muslim is accompanied by religiosity. Does identification as Muslim reflect any religious content? Or is it instead a label that only functions to articulate a reactive social identity in the face of the politicized discourse? And if it reflects religious content, how does this relate to the political context?

The relation between label and content

With regard to religiosity, second-generation Moroccan Dutch youth differ from ethnic Dutch. Among the TIES respondents, 90 percent of the Moroccan respondents answered the question, "Do you currently have a religion?" with "yes," whereas only 20 percent of the ethnic Dutch respondents answered this question affirmatively. Not only do the Moroccan Dutch indicate that they are religious far more often than ethnic Dutch respondents, they also adhere to a different religion.

Whereas 83 percent of the ethnic Dutch believers in the TIES data adhere to Christianity, 98 percent of the Moroccan Dutch believers adhere to Islam. The 2012 report of Statistics Netherlands also shows that religiosity continues to be high over the years (Statistics Netherlands 2012b).

The correlation of the answers to the question "To what extent do you feel Muslim?" (the label) with various religious practices and views (the content), shows that these religious content-variables all significantly correlate with identification as Muslim. Several variables were included in this analysis, such as the role that religion plays for someone as a person (personal importance of religion, thinking about religion, and seeing oneself as a "real" Muslim); religious behavior (fasting, eating halal, visiting the mosque); wearing a headscarf; and political religious norms (the ideas that religion should be represented in politics and society, and that religion should be the ultimate political authority).

The results indicate that religious identification often, at least partly, goes hand in hand with greater adherence to religious practices, stronger religious views, and stronger emotions with regard to religion and fellow believers. This finding challenges the idea that religious identification only functions as a way to demarcate a social identity – and has solely external reasons – and does not reflect some sort of religious content. At the same time, the fact that most of the correlations are not strong but are moderate at most (with correlation coefficients below 0.300) shows that religious identification is not simply a reflection of religiosity, and that religious content therefore cannot be regarded the sole explanation for religious identification. Other, more external, reasons must exist. Are we looking at an at least partially reactive identity? Qualitative studies, including our own, help us further understand the reasons and meanings of identification as Muslim.

A (partially) non-reactive identity

First of all, in support of the quantitative findings, the qualitative studies show the presence and salience of religious identity for second-generation Moroccan Dutch individuals (Buitelaar 2009; De Jong 2012; Ketner 2010; Stock 2014). In all but one of our interviews, which at first instance did not focus on religion, respondents introduced the label Muslim when they reflected on the use of the labels Moroccan and Dutch. They all labeled themselves (among others) as "Muslim." In some instances, Moroccan and Muslim were mentioned in one breath, as being two sides of the same coin. In other moments, particularly in the interviews with strongly religious people, these identities were explicitly separated. In response to the question how they identified in ethnic and national terms, most respondents said they felt both Dutch and Moroccan, and added that they also felt Muslim, and many proceeded by saying that they felt "more Muslim than Moroccan," or that "Muslim" felt as their most salient identity. See, for example, Hind's words:

> I think . . . when I am being honest with myself – I don't feel really connected with the Moroccan culture or so . . . I DO feel connected with being Muslim. Much more than with being Moroccan.

In the interviews, various reasons for their religious identification emerged. First of all, for these respondents their religious identification originated in their upbringing. As is the case for nearly all second-generation Moroccan Dutch, Islam had been a self-evident ingredient of their upbringing. Islam was a natural aspect of their parents' lives and worlds; for their parents, being Moroccan and being Muslim were strongly intertwined. In our study, all but one of the respondents (the one that did not call herself "Muslim") were raised as Muslim, although the level of religiosity and the intensity of the practices varied. For most respondents, this religious upbringing merely consisted of non-reflective adherence to certain norms and practices. Some respondents went to Quran school when they were young.

Furthermore, as a result of this upbringing, being Muslim constitutes part of the second generation's relationship with their parents. Respondents saw their identification as Muslim partly as a mechanism to preserve the social bonds with their parents; as a way to show respect. Even those for whom Islam was not more than a source of inspiration, or an identity, said they visited their parents on religious holidays, and as a token of love and respect they would not confront their parents with their changed religious views. One respondent, Said, even saw religion as "a ticket to entry" with his parents; a basic condition for maintaining a good relationship. The consideration of their parents is not unique to the adult second generation, also for the younger cohorts it is important to pay respect to their parents (Ketner 2010).

This does not mean that Islam has no meaning for the second generation themselves. Although a few respondents explained that they "did not believe" at all, for many, their religion indeed has intrinsic value, although the meaning, scope, and salience varies. This intrinsic value is further explained by Buitelaar (2009), who shows that for the higher educated daughters of Moroccan immigrants she studied, Islam is a source of strength, inspiration, and consolation. For them, Islam provides a sense of security, guidance, and a moral compass. Some value the sense of connection and belonging with a worldwide *umma* (community of believers). Similarly, most of our interview respondents describe Islam as a source of inspiration that provides a specific worldview. For some, Islam is more consequential in how they live their lives; they abide by an encompassing set of guidelines for living. And even many of the respondents who are not very religious comply with some behavioral guidelines (such as alcohol abstinence).

The guidance that religion can provide, by offering a moral compass and behavioral guidelines, is particularly important for adolescent children of immigrants whose parents remain oriented toward the country of origin, whereas their own futures lie in the country of residence (Slootman and Tillie 2006; De Koning 2008). In the development of a personal identity in a "new" country, where their parents are foreign, religion can provide a helpful anchor, particularly when it provides answers to existential questions and behavioral guidelines in the form of clear prescriptions about what is *halal* (admissible) and *haram* (forbidden) (De Koning 2008; Ketner 2010).

A (partially) reactive identity

Clearly, the analysis above shows that religious identification and religiosity is not reactive – or, more precisely, being Muslim is at least not only reactive. It is not (only) shaped by the political discourse: it has historical roots, intrinsic meaning, and social functions. Does this mean that Torrekens and Jacobs (2016) are right in their conclusion that Muslim identification and religiosity is not affected by the discursive context at all? No, it does not. We found evidence that the political context does affect the religious identification and religious content of second-generation Moroccan Dutch.

All our interview respondents mentioned that the dominant Dutch integration discourse was stigmatizing and exclusionary. This result corroborates one of the main conclusions of a large recent study of the Dutch Institute for Social Research (SCP 2015). Our respondents perceived an omnipresence of stereotypical images in which "the Moroccan culture" and "Islam" are presented as backward and inherently incongruent with being Dutch. Although they felt they did not fit the negative stereotypes presented, respondents nevertheless felt that the characterizations of Moroccan-Dutch citizens and Muslims by politicians and others in the media were directed at themselves, which they found extremely frustrating.

The political context and "the Dutch discourse" affect how Moroccan-Dutch individuals are treated in everyday social contexts. The interview respondents in our study recalled many instances in which they felt addressed as Moroccan or Muslim (often, these two labels were mentioned within one breath). Although the respondents did not interpret these instances necessarily as examples of discrimination – as "there were no negative intentions" – these were recalled with annoyance. This is not surprising, as being labeled by ethnic Dutch as "Moroccan" or "Muslim" is an experience of exclusion. After all, regardless of one's own self-identification, such external labeling by others – of ethnic-Dutch descent – denies one's agency and one's belonging, particularly when "Moroccan" and "Muslim" are widely presented as identities that preclude being Dutch.

In a broader sense, the increasing emphasis on religion makes the religious identity "inescapable;" see the words of Bouchra below. Many respondents felt that the fact that they were seen as Muslim had come to determine who they are in Dutch society. Such change is also experienced by respondents in the other Dutch studies (see for example Buitelaar 2009: 144; De Koning 2008; and SCP 2015).

> I think that previously I was more often addressed in terms of my ethnicity. In my perception, after September 11, the focus has shifted to the religious identity. . . . Yes, this religious identity, it's simply inescapable. It seems as if the entire debate about identities has been reduced to the religious identity.

In addition, feelings of exclusion push the orientation toward the *umma*. Hicham and Bouchra described how this worked for them:

> As a practicing Muslim, you become more outspoken about: I am Muslim, and I pray five times a day, take it or leave it. Whereas before, when the theme of religion was discussed, this much less felt as some essential aspect of

yourself. It just was one of your characteristics. But now, it has become some sort of make-or-break point: take it or leave it, it is important to me. Things you were less conscious about before, have gained in importance. . . . I think fear and insecurity makes you search for some guidance. . . . It makes you think about your identity, and make choices more deliberate, and makes you articulate them more. . . . I think over time, the balance has shifted to more-Muslim, more-Moroccan, and more-Arabic, because of everything that happens here.

Living in the diaspora in the Netherlands only strengthens my identification with the *umma*. But also – just like you just said – the current societal climate, in which an identity . . . in this case an Islamic identity . . . this practically forces you to unite. [MS: Unite with whom?] With fellow believers.

As the widespread emphasis on religion made them identify more with the Muslim label, raised their interest in Islam, and for some even strengthened their religiosity, we can speak of an (at least partially) reactive identification. This conclusion supports Connor's argument, challenging that of Torrekens and Jacobs. The findings of Van Heelsum and Koomen (2016) indicate that the tone of the attention does not matter that much, as they show that even "positive" media attention increases the affirmation of religious identity.

Acts of retention?

Just like Connor, Torrekens and Jacobs refer to a frame in which reactive religiosity is presented as a reflection and reinforcement of ethnic heritage, as a hostile environment supposedly brings about a traditional turn (Alba 2005; Reitz et al. 2009). We agree with Torrekens and Jacobs that such a traditional turn is hard to find. The Dutch qualitative studies support the claim that Muslim religiosity among second-generation Moroccan Dutch is not an act of ethnic or religious retention. That does not mean, however, as Torrekens and Jacobs conclude, that there is no reactive response. Instead, it works in other ways, not necessarily "retentionary" or "traditional." A closer look at the relation between ethnicity and religion (a topic not studied by Torrekens and Jacobs) shows that being Muslim for second-generation Muslims is not an act of retention, that it is not merely a re-activation of their parents' heritage.

In several of the interviews, the participant mentioned being Muslim and being Moroccan in one breath whereas several moments later the same person explicitly distinguished between the religious and the ethnic dimension. Ahmed's comments illustrate this paradox:

I am Muslim by birth, and I am raised as a Muslim. So, within the context of our home and my family, we have been raised as Moroccans, according to Moroccan norms and values, and Moroccan child rearing practices.

I do not feel really confident about me being Moroccan . . . but I know about one thing: I am a Muslim. This is the most prominent dimension of my identity. That, I have in common with others.

Often, these two dimensions, ethnic and religious identity, are seen by the interviewees as strongly related, while at other moments the dimensions are explicitly separated, sometimes even within the same interview. How can we understand this? These contrasting perspectives point to a paradoxical relation between ethnicity and religion that is important to understand, as it sheds light on the position of the second generation with their parents on the one hand, and the Dutch political context on the other.

First of all, the interviews clearly support the picture sketched by the quantitative data, that being Moroccan and being Muslim are strongly intertwined. This equation of being Moroccan and being Muslim mirrors the dominant Dutch discourse about the Other, in which Moroccan and Muslim are highly conflated, as we have seen. Although the definition of the Other shifted from the ethnic to the religious dimension, the definition still applies to the same category of people (particularly those with a specific ethnic background: Moroccan), with the same stereotypes (traditional and therefore "backward" and incongruent with being Dutch). Additionally, and not linked to the Dutch political climate, the entwinement of the ethnic and religious labels can be understood by the fact that the second generation was raised by Moroccan parents, for whom Islam was a natural part of their culture. In this upbringing, being a "good Moroccan" meant being a "good Muslim," and the other way around. Apparently, this equation of religiosity and ethnicity reflects omnipresent dominant discourses.

At the same time, many of the respondents, particularly those who are more religious, explicitly distinguish the ethnic and religious dimension, when they for example explain that they feel "more Muslim" than "Moroccan." This separation points to acts of reinvention, to new spaces being created, to their interpretation of Islam becoming more "modern," in ways not visible in (many) quantitative studies. The second generation does not simply copy the hearsay religiosity of their parents. Instead, they feel an obligation to educate themselves in Islam and to make up their minds about their religion as individuals.

Among Muslim youths, De Koning (2008) observes an urgent quest for what he calls a "pure" Islam: religious interpretations that are stripped of "cultural" (Moroccan) elements. With this endeavor, the second generation distances themselves from their parents and actively construct their own stances, connected with the challenges of their own lives as young Muslims in the Netherlands (see also Ketner 2010). Their use of Islamic discourse enables them to negotiate expansion of their freedom, without alienating themselves from their parents (De Koning 2008; Buitelaar 2009: 179). In other words, for the second generation being Muslim is a way to create their own positions and new spaces. It enables them to distance themselves from the traditions of the first generation and adapt to a more modern and individualized lifestyle oriented to participation in Dutch society, while at the same time doing justice to their background and nurturing the bonds with their parents. From this perspective, the conclusion drawn by Statistics Netherlands (2012b) that (Muslim) religiosity and integration into Dutch society can be very well combined (2012b, 21) is only logical; just like its expectation that Islam in the Netherlands will become increasingly separated from countries of (parental) origin strengthen this picture (2012b, 19).

Paradoxically, although the Muslim youth have partially internalized the idea that being Muslim is defined in opposition to being Dutch, their identification as Muslim helps to transcend another (perceived) opposition, that between "Moroccan" and "Dutch." Stressing their Muslim identity instead of their Moroccan identity helps them to position themselves within Dutch society (De Koning 2008: 298); to claim their belonging in Dutch society. This is not an easy matter at all, because how they see Islam (as individualized and emancipative) greatly differs from how Islam is portrayed in the Dutch debate (De Koning 2008: 298; see also Ketner 2010: 50).

Although these descriptions are focused on being Muslim and seem to suggest that religiosity and religious identity is all pervasive, the interviews were certainly not dominated by quotes about Islam and being Muslim, and the role religion played for the various respondents varied greatly. As we have seen, for some, religious rules and practices (such as praying, fasting, visiting the mosque, wearing a headscarf, and having certain drinking and eating prescriptions) were consequential guiding principles. For others, Islam provided merely a "source of inspiration," while some who identified as Muslim did not believe at all. Considering the variations, it is important not to overestimate the role of religion for all Muslim individuals. Stock (2014) urges us in similar words to see the religious dimension in the right proportion. In the narratives of second-generation Moroccan (and Turkish) Dutch that she studied, religion is presented as an important aspect of people's personal lives, but at the same time has a rather marginal position in their life stories. This means that the importance of religion for them as individuals should not make us interpret all of their experiences and identities in religious terms (Stock 2014: 425). When we only focus on "Muslim" aspects of their lives, we might unintentionally exaggerate the importance of these aspects.

Conclusion

How does the culturalized citizenship discourse in the Netherlands, which has increasingly focused on a supposed cultural and religious Otherness of Muslims, impact being Muslim for the second-generation Moroccan Dutch? And what can we say about the Dutch discourse based on our empirical findings?

Based on quantitative and qualitative data, we have concluded that identification as Muslim is relatively high among this second generation. For some, this partially reflects the intrinsic value of religion and personal religiosity, in line with the conclusions by Torrekens and Jacobs. Being Muslim provides a source of inspiration and practical guidance, and a sense of belonging with a worldwide community. In addition, for second-generation Moroccan Dutch, being Muslim is also a continuation of their upbringing and a way to preserve bonds with their parents. However, their being Muslim cannot be totally separated from the exclusionary political context. The societal salience of religion as a social boundary enhances the salience of the Muslim identity for Moroccan-Dutch individuals and increases their orientation toward Islam. In that sense, we can clearly say that being Muslim is at least partially reactive.

But what is the character of this "reaction?" Is it necessarily traditional, or perhaps more modern? Second-generation Moroccan Muslims do not copy the religious experience of their parents. What it means to be Muslim changes over time. The meaning of Islam for these young Muslims is by no means self-evident. They craft their own, de-culturalized, version of their religion, in which they nurture the bonds with their parents, while at the same time they negotiate space to participate in their own ways in Dutch society. They use Islam to transcend the opposition between Moroccan and Dutch and to create their own space and identity, oriented toward Dutch society, rooted in a Moroccan Muslim background.[3] For them, Islam is not necessarily in opposition with being part of a "modern" society such as the Netherlands; a perspective that conflicts with the Dutch culturalized discourse.

We conclude that the public debate does influence being Muslim in the Netherlands, as do many other factors. The continuous emphasis placed in broader society on "Islam" and the "Muslim identity," in which all Muslim individuals are reduced to a singular Muslim identity, makes this religious part of their identity extra salient and triggers a conscious search for the personal meaning of Islam for young individuals who suffer from the oppositional definition in the dominant political discourse.

Still, for many Muslims in the Netherlands, where being Dutch is so deeply defined as "secular" and "progressive," this oppositional definition remains problematic. Even the adoption of a "de-ethnicized" Islam (an Islam that detaches being Muslim from being Moroccan, which is an Islam that is increasingly more modern in many respects) impedes the group's acceptance as part of the Dutch nation. As long as this evolving religiosity is not recognized and continues to be understood as traditional and as a turning away from Dutch society – and as long as the excessive emphasis on the supposed crucial role of religion and the presentation of Islam as inherently "backward" and incongruous with being "native" Dutch will not change – this will complicate the efforts of Muslim youths to become (and be seen as) fully-fledged citizens. In other words, the future will tell if Islam will keep functioning as a central social marker or if it will fade as a social boundary.

Notes

1 Strikingly, in Torrekens and Jacobs's article, contrary to our assessment of the Dutch discourse, the discursive climate in the Netherlands is considered relatively open (in comparison to Belgium, Switzerland and Germany). Although in our chapter we do not make an international comparison, we want to remark that the analysis leading to this assessment of the Dutch discourse might be too positive, as it ignores the tone of voice and prominence of the spokesperson. They operationalized the national discursive climate as the number of claims made in a selection of national newspapers; "positive" and "negative" claims were scored +1 and –1, respectively. This fails to do justice (a) to the sometimes extremely insulting tone of voice in the Netherlands (such as "Do you want less Moroccans? We take care of it!"), and (b) the varying resonance of statements, depending on the spokesperson (such as leaders of political parties).

2 For a critique of this multiculturalist interpretation of Dutch policies, see Duyvendak, Pels, and Rijkschroeff 2009; Duyvendak and Scholten 2012; Duyvendak et al. 2013.
3 Of course, the results of this chapter do not apply to all second-generation Moroccan Dutch, nor to all Muslims. For example, another (smaller) part consists of individuals who distance themselves from Dutch society and strengthen the discourse in which Islam and Western values are presented as entirely oppositional and incongruent.

References

Alba, Richard. 2005. "Bright vs. Blurred Boundaries: Second-Generation Assimilation and Exclusion in France, Germany and the United States." *Ethnic and Racial Studies* 28(1): 20–49.

Barth, Fredrik. 1969. "Introduction." In *Ethnic Groups and Boundaries: The Social Organization of Culture Difference,* edited by Fredrik Barth, pp. 9–38. London: Allen and Unwin.

Bertossi, Christophe, Jan Willem Duyvendak, and Martin Schain (eds.). 2012. "The Problems with National Models of Integration: A Franco-Dutch comparison." Special Issue of *Comparative European Politics* 10(3).

Buitelaar, Marjo. 2009. *Van Huis uit Marokkaans. Levensverhalen van Hoogopgeleide Migrantendochters.* Amsterdam: Bulaaq.

Connor, Phillip. 2010. "Contexts of Immigrant Receptivity and Immigrant Religious Outcomes: The Case of Muslims in Western Europe." *Ethnic and Racial Studies* 33(3): 376–403.

Crul, Maurice, and Jeroen Doomernik. 2003. "The Turkish and Moroccan Second Generation in the Netherlands: Divergent Trends between and Polarization within the Two Groups." *International Migration Review* 37(4): 1039–1064.

Crul, Maurice, and Jens Schneider. 2010. "Comparative integration context theory: participation and belonging in new diverse European cities." *Ethnic and Racial Studies* 33(7): 1249–1268.

De Jong, Machteld. 2012. *Ik ben die Marokkaan niet! Onderzoek naar identiteitsvorming van Marokkaans-Nederlandse hbo-studenten.* Amsterdam: VU Uitgeverij.

De Koning, Martijn. 2008. *Zoeken naar een "Zuivere" Islam. Geloofsbeleving en Identiteitsvorming van Jonge Marokkaans-Nederlandse Moslims.* Amsterdam: Bert Bakker.

Dutch Parliament [Tweede Kamer]. 2011. *Integratiebeleid. Visie op Integratie, Binding en Burgerschap.* TK. 32824, nr. 1. June 16, 2011.

Duyvendak, Jan Willem. 2011. *The Politics of Home. Belonging and Nostalgia in Western Europe and the United States.* New York: Palgrave Macmillan.

Duyvendak, Jan Willem, and Peter Scholten. 2012. "Deconstructing the Dutch Multicultural Model: A Frame Perspective on Dutch Immigrant Integration Policymaking." *Comparative European Politics* 10(3): 266–282.

Duyvendak, Jan Willem, Peter Geschiere, and Evelien Tonkens. eds. 2016. *The Culturalization of Citizenship: Belonging and Polarization in a Globalizing World.* Basingstoke, UK: Palgrave.

Duyvendak, Jan Willem, Trees Pels, and Rally Rijkschroeff. 2009. "A Multicultural Paradise? The Cultural Factor in Dutch Integration Policy." In *Bringing Outsiders In: Transatlantic Perspectives on Immigrant Political Incorporation,* edited by Jennifer Hochschild and John Mollenkopf, pp. 129–139. Ithaca, NY: Cornell University Press.

Duyvendak, Jan Willem, Rogier van Reekum, Fatiha El-Hajjari, and Christophe Bertossi. 2013. "Mysterious Multiculturalism. The Risks of Using Model-Based Indices for Making Meaningful Comparisons." *Comparative European Politics* 11(5): 599–620.

Geschiere, Peter 2009. *The Perils of Belonging: Autochthony, Citizenship, and Exclusion in Africa and Europe*. Chicago: University of Chicago Press.

Hurenkamp, Menno, Evelien Tonkens, and Jan Willem Duyvendak. 2012. *Crafting Citizenship. Negotiating Tensions in Modern Society*. Basingstoke, UK: Palgrave Macmillan.

Ketner, Susan. 2010. *Marokkaanse wortels, Nederlandse grond. Jonge moslims over opgroeien in Nederland* [*Moroccan roots, Dutch soil. Young Muslims about growing up in the Netherlands*]. Utrecht: Verwey-Jonker Instituut.

Koopmans, Ruud, Paul Statham, Marco Giugni, and Florence Passy. 2005. *Contested Citizenship: Immigration and Cultural Diversity in Europe*. Minneapolis, MN: University of Minnesota Press.

Kriesi, Hanspeter, Edgar Grande, Martin Dolezal, Marc Helbling, Dominic Höglinger, Swen Hutter, and Bruno Wueest. 2012. *Political Conflict in Western Europe*. Cambridge: Cambridge University Press.

Mepschen, Paul, Jan Willem Duyvendak, and Evelien Tonkens. 2010. "Sexual Politics, Orientalism, and the Multicultural of Citizenship in the Netherlands." *Sociology* 44(5): 962–979.

Portes, Alejandro, and Rubén Rumbaut. 2001. *Legacies: The Story of the Immigrant Second Generation*. Berkeley, CA: University of California Press.

Reitz, Jeffrey, Rupa Banerjee, Mai Phan, and Jordan Thompson. 2009. "Race, Religion and the Social Integration of New Immigrant Minorities in Canada." *International Migration Review* 43(4): 695–726.

Research and Statistics Amsterdam 2014. *Amsterdam in Cijfers, Jaarboek 2014*. Amsterdam: O+S Amsterdam.

Rumbaut, Rubén. 2008. "Reaping What You Sew: Immigration, Youth, and Reactive Ethnicity." *Applied Developmental Science* 22(2): 1–4.

Scheffer, Paul. 2000. "Het multiculturele drama." *NRC Handelsblad*, 29 January.

SCP. 2015. *Werelden van Verschil. Over de Sociaal-Culturele Afstand en Positie van Migrantengroepen in Nederland*. Den Haag: Sociaal en Cultureel Planbureau [Netherlands Institute for Social Research].

Slootman, Marieke. 2014. "Reinvention of Ethnic Identification among Second-generation Moroccan and Turkish Dutch Social Climbers." *New Diversities* 16(1): 57–70.

Slootman, Marieke. 2016. "Substantive Signifiers? Ethnic and Religious Identifications among Second-generation Immigrants in the Netherlands." *Identities* 23(5): 572–590.

Slootman, Marieke, and Jean Tillie. 2006. *Processen van Radicalisering. Waarom Sommige Amsterdamse Moslims Radicaal Worden*. Amsterdam: IMES.

Sniderman, Paul, and Louk Hagendoorn. 2006. *When Ways of Life Collide: Multiculturalism and Its Discontents in the Netherlands*. Princeton, NJ: Princeton University Press.

Statistics Netherlands. 2012a. *Jaarrapport Integratie 2012*. Den Haag: CBS.

Statistics Netherlands, 2012b. *Moslim in Nederland*. Den Haag: CBS.

Statistics Netherlands. 2014. *Jaarrapport Integratie 2014*. Den Haag: CBS.

Stock, F. 2014. *Speaking of Home: Home and Identity in the Multivoiced Narratives of Descendants of Moroccan and Turkish Migrants in the Netherlands*. University of Groningen (Doctoral dissertation).

Suárez-Orozco, Carola, and Marcelo Suárez-Orozco. 2001. *Children of Immigration*. Cambridge, MA: Harvard University Press.

Torrekens, Corinne, and Dirk Jacobs. 2016. "'Muslims' Religiosity and Views on Religion in Six Western European Countries: Does National Context Matter?" *Journal of Ethnic and Migration Studies* 42(2): 325–340.

Uitermark, Justus, Paul Mepschen, and Jan Willem Duyvendak. 2014. "Populism, Sexual Politics, and the Exclusion of Muslims in the Netherlands." In *European States and their Muslim Citizens*, edited by John Bowen, Chistophe Bertossi, Jan Willem Duyvendak, and Mona Krook, pp. 235–255. Cambridge: Cambridge University Press.

Van Heelsum, Anja, and Maarten Koomen. 2016. "Ascription and Identity. Differences between First- and Second-generation Moroccans in the Way Ascription Influences Religious, National and Ethnic Group Identification." *Journal of Ethnic and Migration Studies* 42(2): 277–291.

Van Reekum, Rogier, and Jan Willem Duyvendak. 2012. "Running from Our Shadows: The Performative Impact of Policy Diagnoses in Dutch Debates on Immigrant Integration." *Patterns of Prejudice* 46(5): 445–466.

Part III
Education and integration

7 Muslim integration in the United States and England

The role of Islamic schools

Jen'nan Ghazal Read and Serena Hussain

The role of religion in schools is one of the most controversial issues in educational arenas in the West today (Halstead and Pike 2006; King 2010; Dronkers 2016). Historically, debates over faith-based education focused on Catholic and Jewish schools because they occupied the largest portion of the religious school market (Jones 2008; Uecker 2009). More recently, Islamic schools have entered into the debate due to concerns over their role in isolating Muslims from mainstream society (Merry and Driessen 2016). This is particularly true in the U.S. and England, countries that have been targeted by Islamic extremists while witnessing an exponential rise in the number of Muslim immigrants and Islamic institutions in major metropolitan areas over the past decade (Abrams 2011; Miah 2016).

As stated above, arguments over faith-based schools are not new nor are they limited to Islamic schools. Some contend that faith-based schools provide social and academic advantages that can be absent in public school settings (King 2010). Others criticize private schools for their exclusivity, while others focus the erosion of social cohesion that can be produced by isolating children and their families from mainstream institutions (Burtonwood 2003; Short 2003). These debates have become especially pronounced in recent years with respect to Islamic schools in the West. In 2001, a series of riots in northern England followed by the terrorist attacks in New York City and Washington, DC led to increasing concerns regarding the detrimental impact of the physical separation of Muslim communities and institutions from broader society (Hussain 2008a; Read 2008; Briskman and Latham, 2017). In England, new policies promoting social cohesion placed the segregation of young South Asian Muslims at the core of the 2001 riots (Kundnani 2001; Miah 2013).

Despite the prominence of the topic, much of the debate had been conducted at the level of what Grace (2003: 150) describes as "assertion and counter-assertion" with less academic attention to the role of Islamic schools in promoting or discouraging social cohesion (Miah 2013; 2015).

Social cohesion refers to the interconnectedness of people from different groups that influences and is influenced by their degree of participation in civic and public life (Tolsma, Van der Meer, and Gesthuizen 2009). This study sets out to address this gap. The analysis draws on extensive qualitative data gathered at three Islamic schools (with students aged 7 to 15) to explore: 1) what motivates parents to send their children to private Islamic schools rather than public ones? 2) How do students feel about their experiences in the schools and communities? 3) To what extent does belonging to an Islamic school community inhibit or promote the engagement and interaction of Muslims with non-Muslim communities and institutions?

Before addressing these questions, we first provide a brief history of Islamic schools in the U.S. and England. We then situate these two cases in the larger literature on faith-based schools and social cohesion. We identify several research questions from the literatures and explore them empirically with rich qualitative data, which we describe in detail in the data and methods section. The findings are organized around the three questions listed above, and the conclusion discusses the implications of our findings for future research on Muslim communities in the West.

Islamic schools in the United States and England

An increase in the size and number of non-Jewish and non-Christian populations in the U.S. and England over the past few decades has fuelled demand for educational establishments to reflect the teachings of other faith groups (Merry and Driessen 2005). The earliest U.S. Islamic schools emerged in the 1970s and grew significantly in the 1980s and 1990s (Haddad, Senzai and Smith 2009), with an estimated 300 schools across the country today (Islamic School League of America 2014). In England, the first Islamic independent schools came about in the late 1970's and today number close to 200, with the majority having been established in the last decade (Abrams 2011). In both countries, the establishment of Islamic schools filled a void that was missing in state schools (known as public in the U.S.), which observed Christian religious holidays (and Jewish ones in the U.S.) but made little accommodation for Muslims when it came to religious practices such as the five daily prayers, Ramadan, or Eid festivals. Islamic schools aimed to provide an environment in which the practices and teachings of Islam could be incorporated into an ordinary day's learning. In this respect, Islamic schools do not differ from other faith-based schools in their aim to provide a space in which children can learn mainstream subjects in the context of their faith (Merry and Driessen 2009; Thohbani 2010; Tarc 2016).

A key difference between the U.S. and British contexts is that U.S. Islamic schools receive no direct federal aid and have only minimal accountability to the state. In contrast, many Islamic schools in England receive state funds, and even those that do not must still undergo inspections from the Office for Standards in Education, Children's Services and Skills (OFSED) to determine whether they fulfil government requirements as independent schools. While U.S. Islamic schools have fewer federal and state restrictions, most strictly monitor testing and strive for high educational standards in order to publicize their attainment rates and attract more students.

Faith-based schools and social cohesion

Strong claims are often made in relation to the impact faith schools have on the personal and intellectual autonomy of students (Jones 2008). It is argued that young people who attend faith schools are limited to a single ideological approach for viewing the world. They are further restricted in their ability to challenge the legitimacy of such perspectives, due to limited interaction with those beyond their own faith group (Halstead and McLaughlin 2005). Furthermore, faith schools are often sites for intensive development of religious identities which can coincide or conflict with ethnic identities and in turn create and maintain notions of distinctive group boundaries (Alleyne 2011; Tarc 2016).

Others debate the wider consequences faith schools might have on societal cohesion (De Jong and Snik 2002). Opponents argue that faith schools damage integration by encouraging the physical separation of groups and claim that the educational segregation of children results in parallel communities rather than integrated ones (Halstead and McLaughlin 2005; Miah 2015). Critics further contend that childhood socialization in restricted settings results in children being ill-equipped to deal with social diversity, particularly when ideological approaches in the schools are in conflict with mainstream ones (King 2010). Thus, faith schools could hinder the ability and willingness of young people to integrate into wider society, even after they have left the school system.

These debates have historically centered on Christian and Jewish schools but have more recently shifted to Islamic ones. Professor Richard Dawkins, perhaps Britain's most well-known opponent to faith schools appeared on "The Big Debate" (aired by the BBC on January 29, 2008) and argued that, compared to attending Christian schools, attending Islamic schools was far more damaging to children's right to choose their own religious persuasion because of the Sharia's position on apostasy. More recently, BBC Radio Four's "Moral Maze" (broadcast on July 19, 2017) discussed how the "apartheid" of segregating the sexes in Islamic schools was in conflict with British values and gender equality, even though single sex schools are overwhelming regarded as positive for educational outcomes. Although these arguments focus on the rights of the child, a core oppositional position to Islamic schools in recent times is propelled by fear associated with the perceived level of integration of Muslims, more broadly, compared to other minority religious and ethnic groups.

The aftermath of the 9/11 and 7/7 bombings resulted in waves of heightened moral panic regarding Muslims on the shores of Western nations (Piševm and Milenkovic 2016). Amidst fears regarding a dangerous enemy potentially already thriving within national borders were concerns regarding the role of Islamic schools in radicalizing young Britons and Americans. In 2002, Peter Smith, the General Secretary of the Association of Teachers and Lectures in the UK, publicly expressed concerns about a fictional "Osama bin Laden Academy" during his address at the National Union of Teachers conference. Understandably, public comments like these did little for the credibility of established Islamic schools, which had already been catapulted into the limelight after the events of the prior year. This discourse has continued in the British press with reports of Islamic schools acting as "Trojan Horses" in our midst by enforcing anti-Western teachings (Miah 2017).

Islamic schools have also faced levels of criticism for their lack of "tolerance" teaching within schools, a measure evaluated during compulsory school assessments. The singling out of Islamic schools within debates on faith schools and tolerance is shown to be unfair and disproportionate when scores for tolerance teaching for other faith schools are also studied. For example, 32% of Islamic schools compared with 42.5% of Evangelical Christian schools were marked poorly on this measure during OFSTED assessments in 2004, yet the issue has been highlighted more intensely in relation to Islamic schools (Meer 2007). A decade on, such examples continue as illustrated by the OFSTED report on the Al Hijra school in Birmingham, which received damming criticism for being unsafe, inconsistent, and requiring "special measures," even though the school produced an 88% GCSE A–C pass rate (BBC 2017).

The spatial separation of communities more generally, particularly Muslim communities, was raised as a concern to be addressed by public policy (Cantle 2004; Taylor-Gooby and Waite 2014). Residential and educational isolation is argued to remove opportunity for inter-group contact, which results in divided societies (Kundnani 2001; Meer 2007). Islamic schools are seen as instrumental in contributing to this precisely because they provide separate spaces for Muslims. But a comprehensive review of empirical studies on the relationship between diversity and social cohesion found that the evidence has been "mixed at best" as to whether inter-group mixing produces positive outcomes for inter-group relationships and social cohesion (Tolsma, Van der Meer, and Gesthuizen 2009).

Furthermore, there is a growing body of evidence that illustrates the benefits of providing separate space for faith education, not only for the students but also for society as a whole. This line of reasoning argues that faith schools provide "safer" environments by protecting against religious prejudice, thereby allowing students to claim a legitimate "minority" identity within society (Ghuman 1996; Zine 2001; Miah 2013). Khan (2010) argues that this is particularly important for young people who are at greater risk of alienation from mainstream society. He discusses how the absence of safe spaces can lead to the individual's rejection of authority, which results in disenfranchisement. When provided with safe spaces, children can develop self-esteem, allowing them to have more confidence and self-awareness when contact with others eventually takes place (Short 2003; Valins 2003; Miah 2015).

Several studies have lent some support to the need for safe spaces, finding that state schools have generally failed Muslim students both academically and socially (Meer 2007). For example, the 2001 and 2011 Censuses for England and Wales demonstrated that Muslims were among the lowest performing students, being the group least likely to leave school at sixteen with satisfactory qualifications, when compared with all other faith groups (Hussain 2008a; Hussain 2017). Hussain's study discusses a number of arguments for the disproportionately low achievement on the part of Muslim students in mainstream education. One such argument points to the increase of Muslim-specific discrimination described as Islamophobia.

In North America, Muslim students also face similar issues surrounding religious intolerance. Abu El-Haj and colleagues (2017) show how educators in liberal democracies, such as the U.S., use narratives of nationalism to position Muslims as racialized others and restrict the freedoms of Muslim youth. Merchant (2016) reports how Muslim students in mainstream schools felt pressure to defend their religion and faced stereotypes about Islam. Zine's (2001) study demonstrated how many students and parents felt that Islamic schools in contrast were "safe havens," providing a space free from the racism and religious discrimination encountered by some in mainstream schools. Merry and Driessen (2009: 102) describe Islamic schools in the U.S. as catering to students "whose cultural identities are hybrid and fluid, whose religious identities are routinely shunned and derided in Western societies and whose psychological and physical safety are important for flourishing." Therefore, debates surrounding the accommodation of Muslims students' religious beliefs and practices, rather than underachievement, have been significant in the North American context.

The studies described above provide important insight into debates surrounding faith-based schools and social cohesion. While some have focused on the experiences of students and their families at faith-based schools, very few have done so for Muslims. Understanding why Muslim families choose Islamic schools over public ones can shed light on the processes that promote or inhibit their interaction with non-Muslim communities – an important component of social cohesion. Accordingly, this study focuses on the following questions: 1) What motivates parents to send their children to private Islamic schools rather than public ones? 2) How do students feel about their experiences in the schools and communities? 3) To what extent does belonging to an Islamic school community inhibit or promote the engagement and interaction of Muslims with non-Muslim communities and institutions?

Research setting

This article draws on extensive qualitative field work conducted over 20 months at three private Islamic schools in urban settings in North Carolina (U.S.) and Oxfordshire and Lancashire (England) during 2010 and 2011. Because the countries differ on a number of key factors, we carefully selected the schools based on the following common denominators: 1) comprised primarily of immigrants (rather than converts); 2) mono-ethnic community or presence of a dominant ethnic group; 3) similar socioeconomic backgrounds of the parents; 4) similar age range of students (ages 7–15) and 5) fee paying (i.e., rather than state-funded in the case of England). The population sizes of the English schools were smaller than the U.S. school, thus two schools were included to gain a more equal number of student and parent interviews. It is worth noting that the schools included in this study may differ from other Islamic schools in England and the U.S. The most obvious way they differ within the British context is that there are state-funded Islamic schools as well as fee-based ones. The ethnic make-up of other schools can also vary, with some having one or two dominant ethnic groups and others having many.

To gain access to the schools, the co-authors contacted school administrators and arranged face-to-face meetings to explain the research and provide sample consent forms for input and approval. Both authors have extensive research experience working with Arab and Muslim communities and were able to provide examples of past research when requested in order to demonstrate credibility. The second author, who was highly experienced in qualitative interviewing of Muslim adolescents and their families, collected the overwhelming majority of data. The data derive from in-depth interviews, focus groups, and participant observation with five groups of participants in each setting, all of whom provided written consent or guardian consent, in the case of students. The five groups included: 1) students who were attending an Islamic school at the time of the study; 2) teachers and administrators at the schools; 3) parents of students who had attended or were attending an Islamic school; 4) Muslim university students who studied at an Islamic school for some of their school career; and 5) Muslim university students who had not been part of an Islamic school system.

The authors conducted in-depth interviews with 15 mothers and multiple school administrators and teachers in both countries. Focus groups with students were also carried out by their grade level, with an average of eight students per session. Focus groups are a particularly useful method for this age group since individual interviews can be intimidating for adolescents. In contrast, group settings can elicit multiple views and experiences and allow youth to speak in a language they would normally employ (Gibson 2012: 148). Finally, in-depth interviews were conducted with 20 Muslim students who were attending universities, half of whom were alumni of Islamic schools and half who had never attended an Islamic school. These latter groups were included to compare the integration experiences of Muslim students once they entered non-Muslim universities.

The interviews and focus groups were all tape-recorded and transcribed verbatim. Each of the co-authors coded the transcripts separately to identify themes and then compared and cross-checked the coding to organize the findings around similarities and differences between countries and within each country. Due to the large number of participants in the study and similarities in their individual-level characteristics (e.g., age, ethnicity), we use the terms student, parent, teacher, and university student throughout the analysis rather than give pseudonyms to each respondent.

Good intentions: parental motivations and student experiences

There were a number of common factors that motivated parents in the U.S. and England to send their children to Islamic schools. A primary one was the belief that mainstream schools in the U.S. and England were unable or unwilling to adapt to the fact that Islam is a lived religion that requires daily practice. Many of the parents described how their children had been bullied in public schools for expressing their Muslim identity. This prompted some to transfer to an Islamic school, which in some cases required the entire family to move. For example, one North African family had relocated from Norway to England to access what they believed were safer school environments. Another British family removed their daughter from a state school due to frustrations over continuous peer harassment and a lack of intervention from school administrators. Parents in the U.S. and England described how Islamic schools provided an environment for their children to practice Islam openly and freely without retribution. In England, this was discussed in terms of "not standing out" due to religious symbols (e.g., *hijab*) or religious practice (e.g., praying). Similarly, discussions among U.S. parents were about protecting their children from feeling self-conscious and ashamed of their heritage. One American parent explained how this shaped her decision to transfer her youngest son from a public school to an Islamic one, even though her other children had all graduated from public schools:

> There seemed to have been an identity crisis with him. I don't know why, my older kids didn't suffer this way. He would come to me and say "Why can't we be like normal people? Why can't I have a tree with lights? Why do I have to fast during this stupid month?" There was an edge to him and I couldn't understand where it came from. Like he truly hated the idea of being a Muslim. But you see he grew up in the era after 9/11 . . . he was a little over a year old when it happened. After 9/11, our older kids were in a haze, they would hear all the comments about Muslims. Our reaction was to ground them in our religion and our heritage. I wasn't even wearing *hijab* then, this happened only in the last decade. I hardly went to mosque, I wasn't that religious but I realized either my kids get grounded in a faith or they are going to grow up feeling lost and ashamed of who they are, their own heritage.
>
> (Parent, U.S.)

Some students shared similar narratives detailing the hostilities they had experienced in public schools. They talked about feeling less anxious and less misunderstood in an Islamic school setting:

> In public school . . . once this person walked up to me and the teacher was right there. And they walked up to me and they were like, "Shut up you Muslim you're going to bomb the school!" And then like she cussed me out . . . and I'm like, "Shut up" and the teacher's like, "Excuse me, what did you say?" And I feel like . . . she hates me because I'm a Muslim.
>
> (8th grade student, U.S.)

Another university student described her experiences of being a Muslim in public school:

> My 6th grade teacher tried to make me come to prayer club. It was in the Bible belt. It was even, like, my friends would be like, "Come to church," and I was like, "No." But those are like extreme areas in the U.S. They're probably not like everywhere, but I think also there's a little bit more pressure, even when I moved to Atlanta, after 9/11 because if they know that you're Muslim, they'll ask you all these questions, and obviously we don't know everything. So, it's a lot of pressure when you can't answer or when you say something and some other kids is like, "What are you talking about? That's not true!"
>
> (University student, U.S.)

In addition to providing a safe environment, another common motivating factor for sending children to an Islamic school was the concern that public schools promoted bad moral behavior. One American parent described how the public school in her area was excellent for accommodating the needs of Muslims, but she decided to send her children to an Islamic school because the environment was more conducive to good moral behavior:

> It's also about the morals and the respect and everything the religion teaches them, which makes them better Muslims and better learners.
>
> (Parent, U.S.)

Concerns over morality were particularly acute with respect to daughters. Parents in both countries demonstrated a greater propensity to sending their female children to an Islamic school in order to protect family honor (Read and Oselin 2008). One female student had been caught talking on the phone with a boy late at night while attending a public school, and her mother met with her teachers to ask that they monitor her more closely. The parents feared she would start having boyfriends like some of the non-Muslim girls at the school. The parents described themselves as not particularly religious but were concerned about their ability to enforce cultural expectations regarding female sexual control. This example highlights a common theme among several parents who distinguished between religious and cultural motivations for sending their children to an Islamic school.

Students were also aware that familial and community expectations for females were quite different from those for males. Two female students in the study explicitly described how their parents had a strong preference for them to remain outside of the labor market. They talked about the need to remain in the home to help ensure family stability and good moral values. During one focus group session in England, a 14-year-old female student was quite vocal about not being allowed to pursue a career. When asked to explain why she felt this was the case, she replied, "Because I'm a girl, and . . . 'cause I'm a girl. That's why. Because I'm a girl."

However, parental intentions did not always translate into reality. Like many adolescents in general, several of the students described navigating around the cultural and religious expectations of their families, presenting one identity at home while crafting another at school and in social circles. This is similar to findings for adolescents, in general, regardless of ethnic or religious background. Given the focus of this study, it was particularly interesting that the Islamic schools, themselves, provided the students with the resources needed to challenge parental expectations, as we describe in the next section.

Intended and unintended consequences

While parents were primarily interested in socializing their children with ethnic and religious values, the schools were primarily focused on academic achievement. This was evident particularly in discussions with administrators and teachers, most of whom worked long hours that extended beyond the norm for their salaried positions. Many of the teachers described their jobs as providing a service to the community by preparing students to excel in mainstream careers while in the safety of a non-discriminatory environment. Likewise, both students and parents generally felt that the Islamic schools provided a better academic environment than surrounding public schools. One university student in England compared his academic achievements with that of his peers who grew up in the same neighborhood and attended the local public school:

> More people where I came from, from my area, went to a certain high school. And most of them were, well let's say if you did well at that school you know it was like in a blue moon. All my friends from my area see it as an achievement that I'm at university, whereas I never saw it as a big deal, 'cause I wasn't around those kind of people. Everyone I was with at Islamic school all aspired to go to uni. Most people I know from my neighborhood aren't at uni or doing very well at all.
>
> (University student, England)

This student was in many ways a "success story" for his community. He was confident, a high academic achiever, actively involved in campus life, had clear professional ambitions, and was very comfortable describing himself as a British Muslim. His case resonates with previous studies that found that UK faith schools (all religious categories) obtained higher examination results than the local public schools and offered an alternative for some families to opt out of underperforming state facilities (e.g., Yeshanew, Shagen, and Evans 2008).

In the U.S., students and parents discussed the school's focus on high academic achievement with mixed feelings. Although they were pleased with the progress of their children, several comments were put forward regarding demanding home-work loads and strict rule enforcement in schools. Although this was believed to enhance children's performance, such "pushy" behavior was described as causing frustration at times. At the same time, students, parents, and teachers in both countries felt that frequent, sustained student-teacher interaction and low student-teacher ratios were the greatest strengths of Islamic schools. This was particularly noted when comparing experiences of mainstream education and Islamic schools in both countries, as illustrated by a UK student:

> this is my least thing that I liked about my [public] school – they used to tell us something, but say if you didn't understand you would ask the teacher and they would say you weren't listening. We would say we were, but we just don't understand it. Then whenever it's a parents' evening and they would tell our parents that your child is like this and they should ask for help. And we would say we do ask for help but they don't give it.
>
> (Year 10 student, England)

An American parent describes how the lack of student-teacher time in public schools was a motivation for choosing an Islamic school for her child:

> My son was not motivated and he is very, very capable. Every single year his teacher recommended that he be evaluated for the academically-gifted program based on his performance in class, and when his dad works with him on math and me on language arts, he's very capable. Yet when they test him he does not test well and they notice he doesn't care. He's not motivated – yet he responds when you give him attention. His class had one teacher and 29 students, 24 of them were boys. I have no idea how she did it. At the Islamic school there are lower ratios so I know that boys who are capable like him are thriving because the attention is focused on them big time. The teacher last year had nine students and a teaching assistant also . . . compare that to 29 at the public school and no assistant!
>
> (Parent, U.S.)

This particular feature of Islamic schools was noted by university students who had been through the Islamic school system. The abundance of peer and teacher support was likened by several students to a family environment, where teachers took on a pseudo-parent role:

> The teachers are like our mothers and all of the people in the school are like our brothers and sisters. So it does feel like a big family.
>
> (Year 8 student, England)

This closeness was also described as a double-edged sword for some parents and students, who felt the boundaries of privacy were sometimes blurred. Students commented on how it was difficult to keep secrets or conceal issues from the rest of the student body and staff.

This family-like environment also came with some unintended consequences, particularly as it related to students pushing the boundaries of familial expectations. The two female students whose families did not want them to pursue careers exemplify this issue. The students' teachers discussed how they were committed to challenging such views and described how they used their authority as religious teachers to persuade parents to reconsider their stance. One teacher at a British school explained,

> I can talk to her father and he will listen. He is far more likely to be receptive to the opinions of a practicing Muslim teacher (me), someone equipped with knowledge about Islam and women's rights, than a teacher at a mainstream school who may be perceived as potentially corrupting her.
>
> (Teacher, England)

In this way, teachers are able to provide a religiously legitimate voice in support of students. Thus rather than reproducing patriarchy, Islamic schools can be an important space in which to challenge and overcome traditionalist views. This is in keeping with previous studies which have described how young Western-born

Muslim women have utilized religious teachings in order to negotiate greater freedom within the public sphere (e.g., Read and Bartkowski 2000). Some have even argued that becoming more religiously observant has been a successful vehicle for daughters to challenge parental restrictions in the private and public realms (Afshar, Aitken and Franks 2005; Hussain 2008b).

Other students relied on school administrators and teachers to help overcome obstacles to achievement presented by a lack of familial human capital. Some parents came from lower socioeconomic backgrounds and lacked educational experiences to pass on to their children. Some parents also felt that academic achievement was less of a priority than good moral behavior. Teachers were attuned to these cases and often spent extra time nurturing such students' skills and encouraging them to reach beyond family expectations. Their adoption of a pseudo-parent role resulted in the transference of human capital from the teacher to the student. In this respect, schools were particularly beneficial in improving the mobility of students from less advantaged backgrounds (e.g., Devereux, Black, and Salvanes, 2005).

Segregation or delayed integration?

A common assumption in public discourse is that Islamic schools segregate and isolate Muslims from non-Muslims, thereby weakening social cohesion. We focused on this issue by asking all the participants in the study whether they felt that being part of an Islamic school community hindered, helped, or perhaps had no effect on their interactions and experiences in non-Muslim arenas. Some of the most telling comments came from university students who had previously attended an Islamic school. Many felt strongly that the Islamic schools gave them the confidence to interact with those from outside of their faith community, and all said that it was important to do so in order to enjoy the full benefits of living in a multi-cultural society. Both the university and middle school students described having a mixture of Muslim and non-Muslim friends, in England and in the U.S. For example, one British engineering student described how he sat with the same two non-Muslim friends in his lectures, played football in a mixed group, and had an active role in Islamic society events. The female students who wore the *hijab* described feeling confident enough to do so at their university and felt that it had not hampered their ability to make non-Muslim friends.

However, the characteristics of such friendships were variable, with many resembling casual friendships rather than close, meaningful ones (Reynolds 2007). Meaningful friendships with non-Muslims were most common among males in the U.S. and least common among females in England.

Parents in the U.S. described how their children were exposed to a great deal of diversity at the Islamic school because the student body originated from an array of countries. When asked about exposing children to religious diversity, many parents described how the residents in their suburbs were predominately non-Muslim and that children often played with the other children in their neighborhoods, met their parents' non-Muslim friends, and took part in extracurricular activities where they had regular contact with non-Muslim children. In England, parents said there were far fewer organized activities with non-Muslims, but also felt their children would not have difficulty engaging with wider society as a result of attending an Islamic day school:

> No, I don't, I don't feel they're missing out. Like I said, I do take my children out, they do communicate with their [non-Muslim] teachers and they do have a chance of seeing the outer world. I don't personally feel that they're missing out. Because in the end they are going to go to a school that is going to have a mixed group, at high school, at university . . . so they will have a chance to mix [with non-Muslims] there.
>
> (Parent, England)

Other parents were less resolute, expressing initial apprehension about whether an Islamic school would be detrimental to their child's social integration:

> I had doubts when my daughter first came here (Islamic school). I brought her for the grammar school exam and she acted out. She did it deliberately because she didn't want to come here. I'm also governor at the primary school, the state school for the younger children. So I'm an all-rounder basically. Not just an Islamic person who carries on with Islamic things. I also go out in the world as well. I encourage the children to do things. You've got to in this country.
>
> (Parent, England)

Another British parent felt that too much emphasis was placed on interacting with non-Muslims. She described how in reality her daughter would finish school, get married, and only need to have regular contact with her family and immediate community. Such sentiments echo those described earlier by a minority of students who claimed their parents did not encourage them to go onto higher education or pursue a career. This finding continues to reflect the reality of many young Muslim women today. For example, Hussain (2017) recently found that in England and Wales, Muslim women of all age cohorts were more likely to report looking after the family and home, compared with other women nationally and of other faith groups. There is also evidence that Muslim women experience greater levels of prejudice and exclusion from the labor market, regardless of qualifications, language skills, and experience (Khattab and Modood, 2017). As a result, there may be a greater hesitancy on the part of families to expose their daughters to negative experiences within the workplace; Muslim women may also have fewer opportunities to leave the home if employment options are not available or financially viable (Hussain 2017).

The overwhelming majority of participants in the study felt strongly that Muslims should not attend Islamic school for the totality of their school career and that doing so could result in difficulties at college or work. Several students spoke about looking forward to attending mainstream schools, in spite of feeling nervous about the challenges larger school grounds and student bodies may bring. The students who had attended an Islamic day school and were now at a mainstream university also described their feelings on this retrospectively. Having a mixture of Islamic and public school experiences was believed to be an optimum combination:

> I'm really glad that I got the kindergarten through 8th grade experience at an Islamic school, but I think as a person living in America you also need to experience the public school system. Because at an Islamic school, you know you only know Muslims and it's good that I went there kindergarten through 8th and you learn your morals and your values, but then you also need to experience what's out there. I know people send their kids to private school and even me if I were a mom and I could afford it I still don't know if I would send my kids . . . because they should experience, they should see what's out there. Even if it's a school filled with like crazy kids. I still think you should experience that.
>
> (University student, U.S.)

Students in our study discussed being able to better navigate mainstream areas as a result of delayed inter-group contact and to have the confidence to openly express their religious identity with their teachers and peers during further and higher education.

These findings support the concept of delayed integration, whereby:

> A minority struggling to maintain its identity often welcomes a limited amount of isolation that might enable it to gain the confidence and security it needs in the early days of its establishment. That confidence, once achieved, might later help in its attempts to assimilate on its own terms.
>
> (Meer 2007: 67)

We also found that the teachers and administrators at Islamic schools often discouraged employment in ethnic enclaves in favor of greater participation within mainstream society (Clark and Drinkwater 2000). They would mentor and advise the students to focus on subjects and areas that would make them competitive for nationally-ranked universities, often talking about career options in the long-term. In this respect our findings are in keeping with the Short's (2003) study on Jewish schools and social cohesion in which he concluded that faith schools may not only be compatible with social cohesion but actually strengthen it. By facilitating greater participation within mainstream arenas, the Islamic schools in our study can be argued, in the same vein, to potentially strengthen integration of Muslim communities by arming young people with qualifications to compete for places in mainstream higher education institutions and the labor force.

Religious schools, religious students?

Another common concern is that Islamic schools are inculcating Muslim youth with religious extremism that will then lead to violence and terrorism. We were acutely aware of this going into the study and paid particular attention to the various ways in which religion can be exhibited – in practice, in dress, in language, in the classroom environment, and so on. We found considerable variability in the degree of religiosity among participants in our study. Some teachers wore the face covering (*niqab*) and observed strict gender segregation, while other teachers at the same school did not affiliate with Islam (either atheist or from other faith backgrounds). Most students and parents described themselves as being somewhere in the "middle" in terms of how religious they were. The American parents described themselves as having moderate Islamic views and several compared themselves to a good Christian, seeing little difference between their religiosity and that of their neighbors.

When asked whether the Islamic school their children attended would be a good fit for all Muslims, two parents commented how it may not suit those with more "extreme" or "stricter" religious views, demonstrating that parents perceived the schools as providing mainstream and moderate versions of Islam (see Saeed 2007). Students also commonly expressed the opinion that parents and communities play a bigger role than the schools in shaping their religious views and behaviors. All agreed that attending an Islamic school made them more aware of their religion but did not necessarily feel that it resulted in them becoming a better Muslim.

We also explored religious identity with Muslim university students who had previously attended an Islamic middle school. Many felt that leaving an Islamic school allowed them to have greater exposure to other Islamic theological perspectives, and several discussed how they welcomed the opportunity to evaluate the religious perspectives they had been taught during Islamic school in relation to other religious teachings. They also described how attending Islamic schools had turned some students away from Islam altogether rather than cementing religious conviction. This was in keeping with the views of parents, students, and teachers in the study who argued that religiosity is not necessarily more pronounced among those who attend Islamic schools.

University students who had not attended an Islamic school likewise agreed that Islamic-school training did not necessarily result in greater piety. Moreover, several of these students described themselves as practicing Muslims who felt no less religious than their counterparts who had attended Islamic middle schools. They also described receiving other types of religious schooling in the form of Islamic Sunday schools in the U.S. or after-school Islamic lessons at mosques in England. However, a key differentiator was that most female students who had attended an Islamic school wore the *hijab* compared to only a handful of those who had not attended an Islamic school. In contrast, there were no obvious physical differences between males who had or had not attended Islamic schools. For example, males who had attended mainstream schools also wore beards, whereas some males who had attended an Islamic school did not.

The results from our interviews with both cohorts were in keeping with the general theme of a growing number of studies on religious identity of young Muslims living in the West. Many students spoke about experiences post 9/11 (and 7/7 in England) and how it had become difficult to be a Muslim living in the West due to media representations and the association of Muslims with terrorism (Zine 2001; Hopkins 2004; Peek 2005; Merchant 2016). At the same time, none of the students felt any contradiction with describing themselves as both "British and Muslim" or "American and Muslim," demonstrating how they interpreted hybrid identities to fit their world view (Jacobson 1997; Saeed, Blain, and Forbes 1999). Therefore, both cohorts of students were able to negotiate their identities in order to promote a sense of belonging in the context of their countries of nationality and their faith, simultaneously.

Conclusion

Debates regarding the compatibility of Islam and Western countries soared after 9/11 and have continued to gain momentum after the July 2005 bombings in London. Since the rise of the Islamic State, there has also been a steady flow of attacks across European cities, including three terrorist attacks in the UK during the Summer of 2017 alone. These events expanded the boundaries of terrorism to include domestic as well as foreign threats, and Muslim youth have come under increasing scrutiny as potential "home-grown" terrorists (Crozier and Davies 2008; Miah 2017). Islamic institutions (mosques and schools) have come under heavy criticism on the grounds that they are either incubating future terrorists or not doing enough to denounce and stop their incubation in other locations (Miah 2013). To date, the vast majority of these debates have played out without the support of rigorous empirical research, thus the degree to which Islamic schools in the West contribute to or detract from civic society is still under-explored. The increase in scrutiny of Islamic schools and university Islamic societies as a result of the 'Trojan Horse' incident described above and the UK government's anti-terrorism strategy, known as PREVENT, has led to greater difficulties around access for researchers.

Accordingly, this study set out to explore whether and how Islamic schools influence social cohesion, using case studies in the U.S. and England. We find that rather than promoting separation, the Islamic schools in our study demonstrated a commitment to facilitating student and family participation in mainstream institutions (e.g., universities, civic organizations, labor force) – outcomes compatible with socially cohesive societies. Moreover, their goal was not to create segregated niches within the mainstream, but rather to blend cultural and religious values in ways that allowed for optimal success in the public and private spheres. In both countries, school administrators and teachers exhibited a clear dedication to achieving the best academic standards possible in order to place students in reputable universities and ultimately successful careers. These findings resonate with Dagovitz's (2004: 165) argument that faith-based schools can contribute positively to society by preparing students to be "good liberal citizens."

Our interviews also revealed that teachers would frequently assume a parental role with students in order to mentor them effectively. This often resulted in an important transference of human capital from the teacher to the student, which was especially crucial for students in homes where academic achievements were less of a priority or where parents lacked formal education themselves. To the extent that religion was critical in student development, it often worked in ways contrary to popular belief, providing a religiously-legitimate voice to parents to encourage their children's academic success when the families had reservations and/or lacked the educational background themselves to support the students. This was particularly important for female students, who often used the assistance of their teachers to challenge patriarchal restraints in the home.

The study did highlight some potential challenges for social cohesion more widely, and integration of individuals who belong to certain cohorts, more specifically. The Islamic schools in the U.S. were more multiethnic, containing linguistic and cultural diversity from Africa, Asia, Europe, and White America (through Muslim convert families), even though students with Middle Eastern heritage made up the largest share. The schools in England were far less diverse and largely reflected the local population in terms of ethnic residential clustering (Hussain 2008a). Thus, the English schools in our study provided less opportunity for contact with children from other cultures during school hours than did those in the U.S. While not all Islamic schools in England are dominated by a single ethnic group, for those that are, a major challenge will be finding ways to facilitate student contact with other groups. In addition, greater residential concentration of Muslim groups in England compared with American Muslims could result in less opportunity for inter-group contact outside of school hours. Unless such students continue their post-Islamic school education in public facilities or become employed outside of their ethnic enclaves, integration is less likely to occur. Our findings also suggest that a lack of inter-group contact could potentially result in more negative outcomes for women than men, given the greater levels of social control imposed on females. Even in the U.S., most students reported that their mothers did not work outside of the home – despite often having a university-level education.

The concerns outlined above are not a feature of Islamic schools per se, but rather of isolated communities. If attending an Islamic school is married with other contextualizing factors such as residential concentration and segregation, the ability of Muslims to engage with those outside of their immediate ethno-religious community will be difficult. Herein lies the biggest challenge in moving forward, especially in England, where communities are more concentrated and generally of lower socioeconomic status than those in the U.S. (Hussain 2008a). Inter-group contact is essential for ameliorating stereotypes and ensuring mutual respect and cooperation among groups with different values and beliefs, whether those differences are based on religion, ethnicity, or some other defining characteristic. At the same time, we found that Islamic schools need not be a source of social fragmentation and can provide a successful vehicle for the promotion of civic engagement and participation for Muslim communities in the West. While these were just three case studies, they demonstrate the need for more in-depth examinations of Islamic institutions in order to more accurately understand their potential role in civic society.

Acknowledgements

This study was funded by a generous grant from the Stuart Family Foundation. The contents of this chapter reflect solely the thoughts of the authors.

References

Abrams, Fran. 2011. "Islamic Schools Flourish to Meet Demand." *The Guardian*, November 28.

Abu El-Haj, Thea Renda, Anne Ríos-Rojas, and Reva Jaffe-Walter. 2017. "Whose race problem? Tracking patterns of racial denial in US and European educational discourses on Muslim youth." *Curriculum Inquiry* 47(3): 310–335.

Afshar, Haleh, Rob Aitken, and Myfanwy Franks. 2005. "Feminisms, Islamophobia and Identities." *Political Studies* 53(2): 262–283.

Alleyne, Richard. 2011. "Richard Dawkins Attacks Muslim Schools for Stuffing Children's Minds with 'Alien Rubbish'." *The Telegraph*, October 8.

BBC Radio Four. 2017. "The Morality of Faith Schools, Moral Maze." Available online at www.bbc.co.uk/programmes/b08y1bzf

Briskman, Linda, and Susie Latham. 2017. "Muslims at the Australian periphery." Australian Studies Centre, Universitat de Barcelona.

Burtonwood, Neil. 2003. "Social Cohesion, Autonomy and the Liberal Defence of Faith Schools." *Journal of Philosophy of Education* 37(3): 415–425.

Cantle, Ted. 2004. "The End of Parallel Lives? Final Report of the Community Cohesion Panel." London: Home Office.

Clark, Ken, and Stephen Drinkwater. 2000. "Pushed Out or Pulled In? Self-Employment among Ethnic Minorities in England and Wales." *Labour Economics* 7(5): 603–628.

Crozier, Gill, and Jane Davies. 2008. "'The Trouble Is They Don't Mix': Self-Segregation or Enforced Exclusion?" *Race, Ethnicity and Education* 11(3): 285–301.

Dagovitz, Alan. 2004. "When Choice Does Not Matter: Political Liberalism, Religion and the Faith School Debate." *Journal of Philosophy of Education* 38(2): 165–180.

De Jong, Johan, and Ger Snik. 2002. "Why Should States Fund Denominational Schools?" *Journal of Philosophy of Education* 36(4): 573–587.

Devereux, Paul, Sandra Black, and Kjell Salvanes. 2005. "Why the Apple Doesn't Fall Far: Understanding Intergenerational Transmission of Human Capital." *American Economic Review* 95(1): 437–449.

Dronkers, Jaap. 2016. "Islamic Primary Schools in the Netherlands." *Journal of School Choice* 10(1): 6–21.

Ghuman, Paul. 1996. "Culture and Cognition: The Intellectual Development of Indian Adolescents." *Scientia Paedagogica Experimentalis* 32(2): 275–290.

Gibson, Jen. 2012. "Interviews and Focus Groups with Children: Methods That Match Children's Developing Competencies." *Journal of Family Theory & Review* 4: 148–159.

Gilbert, David. 2004. "Racial and Religious Discrimination: The Inexorable Relationship between Schools and the Individual." *Intercultural Education* 15: 253–266.

Grace, Gerry. 2003. "Educational Studies and Faith-Based Schooling: Moving from Prejudice to Evidence-Based Argument." *British Journal of Educational Studies* 51: 149–167.

Haddad, Yvonne, Farid Senzai, and Jane Smith. 2009. *Educating the Muslims of America.* New York: Oxford University Press.

Halstead, Mark, and Terence McLaughlin. 2005. "Are Faith Schools Divisive?" In *Faith Schools: Consensus or Conflict?,* edited by Roy Gardner, Jo Cairns, and Denis Lawson, pp. 61–73. London: Routledge.

Halstead, Mark, and Mark Pike. 2006. *Moral and Citizenship Education: Learning Through Action and Reflection.* London: Routledge.

Hopkins, Peter. 2004. "Young Muslim Men in Scotland: Inclusions and Exclusions." *Children's Geographies* 2: 257–272.

Hussain, Serena. 2008a. *Muslims on the Map: A National Survey of Social Trends in Britain.* London: IB Tauris.

Hussain, Serena. 2008b. "Counting Women with Faith: What Quantitative Data can Reveal about Muslim Women in 'Secular' Britain." In *Women and Religion in the West: Challenging Secularization,* edited by Kristin Aune, Sonya Sharma, and Giselle Vincett, pp. 165–182. ALdershot, UK: Ashgate.

Hussain, Serena. 2017. "Muslims in Britain: An Overview." In *Islamophobia: Still a Challenge for Us All,* edited by Farah Elahi and Omer Khan, pp. 16–21. Runnymede Trust: London.

Islamic School League of America. 2014. Available online at http://theisla.org/ (accessed May 30, 2014).

Jacobson, Jessica. 1997. "Religion and Ethnicity: Dual and Alternative Sources of Identity among Young British Pakistanis." *Ethnic and Racial Studies* 20: 238–256.

Jones, Steven. 2008. *Religious Schooling in America: Private Education and Public Life.* Westport, CT: Praeger.

Khan, Saqib. 2010. "The Phenomenon of Dual Nihilism among British Muslim Youth of Bradford, England: Beyond Diasporic and Hegemonic Identity." Presented at *Diasporas: Exploring Critical Issues,* July 7–9, Mansfield College, Oxford. Available online at www.inter-disciplinary.net/at-the-interface/diversity-recognition/diasporas/project-archives/3rd/session-9b-strategic-spaces/ (accessed May 9, 2013).

Khattab, Nabil, and Tariq Modood. 2017. "Accounting for British Muslim's Educational Attainment: Gender Differences and the Impact of Expectations." *British Journal of Sociology of Education* 11: 1–18.

King, Carolyn. 2010. "Faith Schools in Pluralistic Britain: Debate, Discussion, and Considerations." *Journal of Contemporary Religion* 25: 281–299.

Kundnani, Arun. 2001. "From Oldham to Bradford: The Violence of the Violated." *Race and Class* 43: 41–60.

Merchant, Natasha. 2016. "Between a Rock and a Hard Place: Shia Ismaili Muslim Girls Negotiate Islam in the Classroom." *Diaspora, Indigenous, and Minority Education* 10: 98–111.

Meer, Nasar. 2007. "Muslims in Britain: Challenging Mobilisations or Logical Developments?" *Asia Pacific Journal of Education* 27: 55–71.

Merry, Michael, and Geert Driessen. 2005. "Islamic schools in Western Countries: Policy and Procedure." *Comparative Education* 41: 411–432.

Merry, Michael, and Geert Driessen. 2009. "Islamic Schools in the US and Netherlands: Inhibiting or Enhancing Democratic Dispositions?" In *Alternative Education for the 21st Century,* edited by Phillip Woods and Glenys Woods, pp. 101–122. New York: Palgrave Macmillan.

Merry, Michael S., and Geert Driessen. 2016. "On the right track? Islamic schools in the Netherlands after an era of turmoil." *Race, Ethnicity and Education* 19(4): 856–879.

Miah, Shamim. 2013. "Prevent'ing Education: Anti-Muslim Racism and the War on Terror in Schools." In *The State of Race,* edited by Nisha Kapoor and Virinder Kalra, pp. 146–162. Basingstoke, UK: Palgrave Macmillan.

Miah, Shamim. 2015. *Muslims, Schooling and the Question of Self-Segregation.* Basingstoke, UK: Palgrave Macmillan.

Miah, Shamim. 2016. "The Muslim problematic: Muslims, state schools and security." *International Studies in Sociology of Education* 26(2): 138–150.

Miah, Shamim. 2017. *Muslims, Schooling and Security: Trojan Horse, Prevent and Racial Politics.* London: Palgrave MacMillan.

Peek, Lori. 2005. "Becoming Muslim: The Development of a Religious Identity." *Sociology of Religion* 66: 215–242.

Piševm, Marko, and Milos Milenkovi . 2016. "Islam." In *The Anti-Multicultural Rhetoric of Western European Politicians and Anthropologists.* Etnoantropoloski Problemi 8: 965–985.

Read, Jen'nan Ghazal. 2008. "Faith, Fact, and Fiction: What Muslim Americans Really Mean for U.S. Democracy." *Contexts* 7: 39–43.

Read, Jen'nan Ghazal, and John P. Bartkowski. 2000. "To Veil or Not to Veil? A Case Study of Identity Negotiation among Muslim Women Living in Austin, Texas." *Gender & Society* 14: 395–417.

Read, Jen'nan Ghazal, and Sharon Oselin. 2008. "Gender and the Education-employment Paradox in Ethnic and Religious Contexts: The Case of Arab Americans." *American Sociological Review* 73: 296–313.

Reynolds, Tracey. 2007. "Friendship Networks, Social Capital and Ethnic Identity: Researching the Perspectives of Caribbean Young People in Britain." *Journal of Youth Studies* 10: 383–398.

Saeed, Amir. 2007. "Trends in Contemporary Islam: A Preliminary Attempt at a Classification." *The Muslim World* 97: 395–404.

Saeed, Amir, Nigel Blain, and David Forbes. 1999. "New Ethnic and National Questions in Scotland: Post-British Identities among Glasgow Pakistani Teenagers." *Ethnic and Racial Studies* 22: 221–244.

Short, Geoffrey. 2003. "Faith Schools and Social Cohesion: Opening up the Debate." *British Journal of Religious Education* 25: 89–102.

Tarc, Rita. 2016. "Canadian Islamic schools: Unraveling the politics of faith, gender, knowledge, and identity." *International Journal of Qualitative Studies in Education* 29: 130–133.

Taylor-Gooby, Peter, and Edmund Waite. 2013. "Toward a More Pragmatic Multiculturalism? How the U.K. Policy Community Sees the Future of Ethnic Diversity Policies." *Governance: An International Journal of Policy, Administration and Institutions* 27: 267–289.

Thohbani, Shiraz. 2010. *Islam in the School Curriculum: Symbolic Pedagogy and Cultural Claims.* London: Continuum International Publishing Group Ltd.

Tolsma, Jochem, Tom Van der Meer, and Maurice Gesthuizen. 2009. "The Impact of Neighbourhood and Municipality Characteristics on Social Cohesion in the Netherlands." *Acta Politica* 44: 286–313.

Uecker, Jeremy E. 2009. "Catholic Schooling, Protestants, and Religious Commitment in Adulthood." *Journal for the Scientific Study of Religion* 48: 53–367.

Valins, Oliver. 2003. "Stubborn Identities and the Construction of Socio-Spatial Boundaries: Ultra-Orthodox Jews Living in Contemporary Britain." *Transactions of the Institute of British Geographers* 28: 158–175.

Yeshanew, Tilaye, Ian Schagen, and Suzanne Evans. 2008. "Faith Schools and Pupils' Progress through Primary Education." *Educational Studies* 34: 511–526.

Zine, Jasmin. 2001. "Muslim Youth in Canadian Schools: Education and the Politics of Religious Identity." *Anthropology & Education Quarterly* 32: 399–423.

8 Transnational schooling among children of immigrants in Norway

The significance of Islam

Liza Reisel, Anja Bredal and Hilde Lidén

Concerns about the children of non-Western immigrants who are being sent to their parents' home countries, either for schooling or general socialization, repeatedly resurface in the Norwegian integration debate. These concerns center on the real or imagined threats this practice poses for the children's further integration into Norwegian culture and society. In particular, the public discourse tends to focus on children from Muslim families, and questions about forced religious socialization in Quran schools. The Norwegian authorities worry about these children's safety, and also fear that their absence from Norwegian schools will affect their ability to speak Norwegian, follow the curriculum for their age, and reintegrate upon return to Norway. An underlying concern is that such disadvantages may be exacerbated by a strengthened Islamic identity at odds with Norwegian values. A related debate revolves around the possibility of establishing private Islamic schools in Norway. This public debate tends to address many of the same concerns as the debate about schooling abroad, such as language development, religious indoctrination, and potential marginalization.

While these worries about children who spend part of their school-age years abroad are not specific to the Norwegian context (see Hamann, Zúñiga and Sánchez García 2010; Menken, Kleyn, and Chae 2012), the practice stands in sharp contrast to the general uniformity and centralized organization of the Norwegian school system.

Inasmuch as a sense of belonging is supported by interacting with the majority population and being included in a broad range of social institutions, sending children abroad may appear as counter-productive to such processes. Moreover, as social mobility is a goal for many immigrants from poorer countries to the affluent West, the practice of sending children "back" may appear somewhat puzzling. Therefore, a primary aim of this chapter is to contribute to a better understanding of this phenomenon.

In this chapter, we explore the motivations for and the outcomes of sending children abroad for schooling or socialization. Does this practice represent an obstacle to integration and can it result in oppositional identities? Within this general framework, we are particularly interested in the role of Islam, both as a motivating force for parents, and as a "product" of stays abroad from the young people's perspectives. Does staying abroad result in a stronger Muslim identity, as the parents may have intended, and if so, what are the implications in terms of integration? We will begin this chapter by situating the current study within the literature on transnational family practices, before going on to describe the Norwegian context. This is followed by a descriptive account of patterns of transnational movement of children of Pakistani and Somali backgrounds, based on Norwegian public registries. We then use interview data to address our research questions by analyzing the ways in which parents and young people talk about the role of Islam in their motivations for, and experiences with, stays abroad. We conclude the chapter with a discussion of our findings, focusing on the question of whether the stays abroad are contributing to or disrupting integration processes.

Transnational families and Islam in a Western context

Migration scholars have been grappling with the complex relationship between transnational practices and immigrant integration for some time (Levitt and Schiller 2004; Nadim 2014; Smith 2006). Levitt and Schiller (2004: 1003) emphasize immigrants' "simultaneity" of connections: living lives that incorporate daily activities, routines, and institutions located both in a destination country and transnationally. Children's experiences of migration and transnational living may include various forms of return mobilities, such as return visits, return migration and transnational circulation (King and Christou 2011: 459). The double engagements of migrant families in countries of origin and settlement often result in split families (Grillo and Mazzucato 2008), in which considerations about children, their upbringing and education as a whole become significant for decisions about mobility. Research on children's return migration includes studies of return with family members, split families, and children who stay by themselves with relatives (Erdal et al. 2015; Carling, Menjívar, and Schmalzbauer 2012; Zontini 2010; Aakesson, Carling, and Drotbohm 2012).

Experiences of otherness coupled with sharing a common ground with other immigrants constitute a central background for the identification and orientation of the descendants of migrants (Andersson 2010; Kasinitz et al. 2008). Global religious communities and transnational identifications form part of this orientation, offering a feeling of inclusion and connection that is sometimes difficult to achieve with native-origin peers. However, Amit (2012) points out that the turn within migration studies towards transnational connections has led to a strong emphasis on continuity. She calls for "a more measured appreciation of the balance and dialectic between continuity and rupture" (Amit 2012: 506). The ways transnational practices affect integration, and vice versa, depend on the specific context and practices in question. Thus, migration scholars such as Erdal and Oeppen (2013) have called for moving beyond merely describing the co-existence of integration and transnationalism and focus more on identifying the nature of that co-existence. We address this question in our analysis of changes and continuities in religious identities as products of temporary stays abroad.

Some international studies of children's experiences of return migration have focused on transitions between different school systems and cultural contexts (Wen 2010) or exploring narratives of childhood return (Ní Laoire 2011; Hatfield 2010). A few Norwegian studies have analyzed the movement in and out of Norway among school- aged children from different country backgrounds, including transnational practices among Norwegian-Pakistani youth (Dzamarija 2004; Erdal et al. 2015; Lidén et al. 2014; Ostberg 2006). However, little is known about what role religion plays for the motivation for and experiences of these children's stays abroad. In this chapter we are specifically interested in investigating religion as a site for negotiating continuity and rupture. Before moving on to our analyses, we will briefly sketch some central features of the Norwegian context.

The Norwegian context

Three aspects of the Norwegian national context are particularly relevant for the framing of the findings in this chapter: the central position of Muslim immigrants in the Norwegian integration discourse, the overall position of children of immigrants in the Norwegian education system, and the relatively strict central regulation of Norwegian schools.

When the so-called guest workers started arriving in Norway in the late 1960s, they came predominantly from countries with majority-Muslim populations. Migrant networks and emerging migration restrictions in other European countries such as Denmark and Germany created a migration flow dominated by Pakistani labor migrants to Norway, with smaller contingents of other nationals such as Turks and Moroccans. These migrants became the anchor point for a growing male chain migration to Norway, replaced by family reunification and family formation after the official immigration hiatus came into force in 1975. The bulk of refugees that have arrived in Norway since then have also come from Muslim countries, such as Somalia, Iraq, Afghanistan, and Bosnia, although non-Muslim countries such as Vietnam and Sri Lanka are also among the core sending countries.

This chapter is mainly based on interviews with parents and young adults with Somali and Pakistani backgrounds in Norway, who had current or previous experience with temporary stays abroad. There are two main reasons why we chose to focus on these two origin countries. First, they are currently the largest groups of children of immigrants from outside the European Economic Area (EEA) in Norway[1]. Second, the two groups represent (children of) very different waves of immigration to Norway.

Compared to the Pakistani immigrants who arrived as labor migrants in the 1960s and 1979s, the Somalis came to Norway much later, in the late 1990s and early 2000s, predominantly as refugees. A considerably larger proportion of their children that have reached school age today were born abroad. Somalis are currently the largest immigrant group from outside the EEA and the group with the largest number of children. The contrasting migration histories of these two predominantly Muslim groups make them particularly interesting for the study of transnational practices and the role played by religion.

Recent research shows that children of immigrants do relatively well with regard to indicators normally associated with structural integration, such as educational attainment and social mobility, particularly those who are born in Norway (Bratsberg, Raaum, and Røed 2012; Hermansen 2015). Children of non-European immigrants are overrepresented in Norwegian higher education, and even though they lag behind their native-origin peers with regard to labor market access, once they enter the labor market they do not seem to suffer any disadvantage with regard to occupational positions (Hermansen 2013). At the same time, some children of immigrants seem to be in more vulnerable positions, most often men who arrived in Norway as older school children (Støren 2005).

From a comparative perspective, the relatively small social differences and the uniform public school system in Norway seem to help mitigate some of the educational and socioeconomic disadvantages that many immigrant families arrive with. Research shows, for example, that attending a school with a high concentration of immigrants does not have a negative effect on student performance in Norway (Hermansen and Birkelund 2015). The flip side of the uniform public school system is that private religious day schools are relatively rare. Only 3.1 percent of students in Norwegian elementary and lower secondary schools attended private schools in the school year 2013–2014 (Utdanningsdirektoratet 2013).[2] Due to strict regulation of private schooling in Norway, there are currently a number of Christian schools of different denominations throughout the country, but no regular day schools based on Islam or other religions.

Patterns of transnational movement

To map the scale and scope of stays abroad among children of immigrants in Norway, we analyzed public register data from Statistics Norway with information about movement in and out of Norway, citizenship, country of origin, gender and age. The data available from Statistics Norway are not ideal for our purpose, since not all movement is officially registered, but they are the best data available nonetheless. Because they are based on public registries, they mainly capture those who have reported to the local authorities that they are leaving Norway, in which case the destination country is also registered. In our extracted data, we have information about everyone registered as having moved abroad or returned for every year between 2004 and 2012, as well as a cumulative count of people who have left Norway without returning by January 1, 2012. We also have information linking parents and children together.

Over time, the number of children that move either temporarily or permanently abroad from Norway has fluctuated. Among Norwegian-Pakistanis, absolute numbers have gone down, whereas for the Norwegian-Somalis the numbers have gone up quite drastically in recent years (Figures 8.1a and 8.1b). There are three main reasons for these diverging patterns. First, the Somali minority has been growing in numbers during the period, both because of continued immigration and family growth. Second, an increasing proportion of the Somali diaspora in Norway have reached the required minimum age of seven years that allow them to obtain a Norwegian citizenship. A stronger formal attachment to Norway seems to encourage some Somalis to leave the country, at least temporarily, without the fear of being unable to return. Third, the increased numbers may also reflect that parts of Somaliland and Puntland are safer travel destinations now than they were at the beginning of the period. By contrast, the Pakistani minority is not growing as rapidly, and if anything, the security situation in Pakistan has become worse over the period. Our in-depth interviews also suggest that the practice of sending children to Pakistan for schooling or "cultural rehabilitation" is in fact on retreat, so that the numbers we observe may reflect a realistic picture of the development of the practice over time.

Figure 8.1a Number of children registered as moved abroad: Somali background

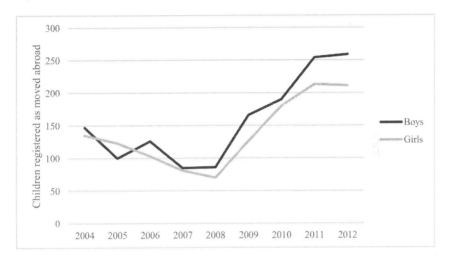

Source: Authors' own calculations based on register data from Statistics Norway

Figure 8.1b Number of children registered as moved abroad: Pakistani background

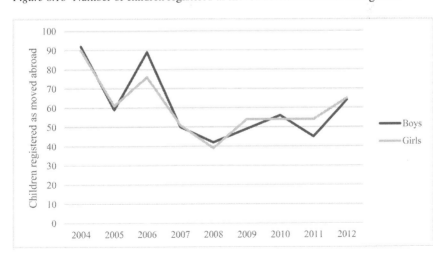

Source: Authors' own calculations based on register data from Statistics Norway

Our analyses of registry data show that destination countries vary considerably among children of immigrants from outside the EEA. We analyzed the extent to which children who leave Norway return to their parents' home countries, travel to other Western countries, to other non-Western countries, or are registered without a destination country. Figure 8.2 shows destinations for the children of immigrants of Somali and Pakistani origin in Norway, who left Norway in 2012. We find that it is much more common for those with Pakistani backgrounds to temporarily or permanently move to Pakistan, than it is for those of Somali background to move to Somalia (see Figure 8.2). Further inquiries show that while children of Pakistanis who move abroad from Norway primarily move to Pakistan, followed by Great Britain and Denmark, children of Somalis in Norway primarily move to Great Britain, followed by Kenya and Somalia (figures not shown).

Among those who leave Norway, far from all return. Still, a considerable proportion of these young people do come back to Norway, with implications for further schooling, integration into the labor market and society as a whole. Notably, however, the rates of return vary across the two groups. The following graph shows that among children of Somali background who left Norway in 2004, only about a quarter had returned eight years later (Figure 8.3). The return rates are similar six and four years after leaving. By contrast, about half of the Norwegian-Pakistani children had returned in the same period.

The low return rates and the mobility patterns with regard to destination countries indicate that some of the Somali migration from Norway may be more permanent and it likely includes secondary migration of whole families. Yet despite low return rates, the highest *number* of returning children in Norway are still of Pakistani and Somali background, since the number of Somali children leaving Norway is generally higher than that for other immigrant groups. With these patterns in mind, we now turn to the qualitative data and the narratives of Pakistani and Somali families engaging in these transnational practices.

Figure 8.2 Destination countries for children ages 0–17 who left Norway in 2012

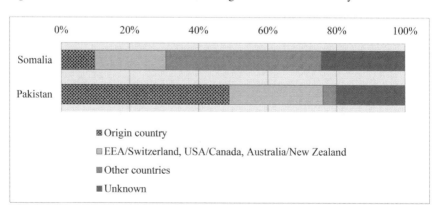

Source: Authors' own calculations based on register data from Statistics Norway

Figure 8.3 Share of children ages 0–17 returned by January 1, 2012

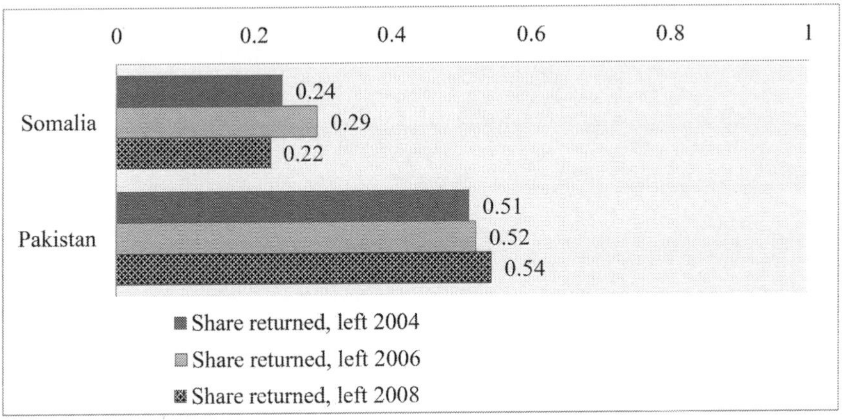

Source: Authors' own calculations based on register data from Statistics Norway

A note on the qualitative data

In all, we interviewed 24 children and young adults and 23 parents of Somali background. About half of the interviews were conducted in Kenya, Somaliland, and Puntland. The other half were conducted in Norway, with interviewees who had spent some time back in Norway after a stay abroad. Using snowball sampling methods, interviewees were recruited from organizations and social networks by two research assistants with Somali language skills. These assistants also conducted the interviews, except for the interviews in Kenya, which were conducted by one of the authors. Additionally, headmasters at schools with diaspora pupils in Kenya, Somaliland, and Puntland were interviewed, as were representatives of the Department of Education in Somaliland and Puntland. The Pakistani material includes interviews with 18 young adults and eight parents, most of them conducted in Norway by the researchers and an Urdu-speaking assistant. Thirteen additional interviews conducted in Pakistan included headmasters, teachers, and a few other individuals with more indirect experience with Norwegian Pakistani children in local schools. These were interviewed by a local research assistant. All interviews were carried out in 2013.

In both groups, our interviewees represent a broad social spectrum including both well integrated and more marginal families in the Norwegian context. The Pakistani material is likely skewed toward middle-class families, while the Somali interviewees are of more mixed social backgrounds. Some are seemingly well integrated, while other families are in more marginal positions, with mothers outside the labor market and children who are struggling in the school system.

Parents' motives and family practices

> Life here is better than in Norway. Here one experiences happiness, joy. It is less stressful and more motivating compared to Norway.
>
> (Mother, Norwegian-Somali)

The findings from our in-depth interviews with Pakistani and Somali families suggest that the parents' motivations can be sorted into three main categories: a) family issues, b) strengthening cultural or religious identity, and c) education. Motivations are often mixed, with cultural and religious learning being part of a cluster of several motivating factors. In both groups the father often stays behind in Norway, to provide the family with stable income, while the children stay abroad, sometimes alone but more often with their mother and other siblings.

Family issues

This set of motives typically refers to care needs of elderly and sick relatives in the country of origin, which in particular obliges women to move "home" for a period of time, bringing their children with them. For the men, going back may be prompted by family business enterprises, such as a joint venture with male relatives. These family-oriented moves are not always planned ahead. For instance, several interviewees talked about how they had come to stay on after what originally was planned as a holiday, or the opposite, how what was intended as a permanent return turned into a temporary stay. Such patterns of temporality were typical of the women living as stay-at-home mothers in Norway. As there was no job to hold them back, they would go on open-ended stays with relatives and stay on with their children as they found life "back there" more attractive. Family issues may act as both pull and push factors. Descriptions of the companionship and easy life of a familiar environment "at home" should be seen in contrast to their life on the margins of Norwegian society due to limited language skills and social network. Some also leave because they are afraid that the childcare authorities in Norway will disrupt their family life by removing one or more children from their households.

Success stories of other relatives inspired some of our interviewees to give schooling abroad a try for their own children. A mother who had lived in Kenya for three years explained:

> We came as tourists to my husband's family. Here we met the children in the family at similar ages and saw how well they were doing. That's why I decided to stay. We have lived here for almost three years, I live with the children, while my husband lives in Norway and provides for us. I live here with my mother and two ladies that take care of the house and live with me. We also have a tutor that comes to me and provides homework help. They particularly need help with math.

Some, mostly among the Pakistani interviewees, also emphasize the opportunity to live a more privileged life, with a big house and even servants, contrary to the limited possibilities they have for such luxury in Norway. For the Somali migrants a more privileged life abroad was mainly possible outside their home country, in Kenya or Egypt, which are typical countries for secondary migration among the Somali diaspora, and where our interviewees had often been reunited with other family and kin members.

Strengthening cultural or religious identity: to live in a community – with Islam

The desire to strengthen their children's cultural and religious identity was among the parents' main motives for sending them "back" or to a third country where the diaspora could stay together. These narratives tend to be about fostering a sense of belonging by living in a society where their own cultural and religious background is the norm. A father interviewed in Somaliland explains this as follows:

> One of the biggest benefits, even for me, has been; when Somali children return to Somalia or come to Somalia they get affirmation, or a very deep sense of belonging that they don't feel when they are in a country that they do not originate from, you are always a foreigner or a minority. When they come here it is different!

Parents express concerns that their daughters and sons do not get a proper religious education in Norway. They want them to acquire knowledge of Islam and to have a religious education that would shape them into people like themselves. Parents are concerned that in a busy Norwegian everyday life, they cannot manage to teach their children the proper religious codes and conducts, nor do the children learn the language of their parents adequately enough to communicate well. A young man of Somali background recounts his mother's motivation:

> The background for my stay abroad was mostly because of my mom. We often hear that Somali parents are not educated, that they do not have a good relationship with Norwegian schools and that they do not show up to the parent-teacher meetings. My situation was the opposite: my mother is religious and educated. My mother likes Norway because it is a civilized country, but she did not like the cold weather. She thought that we would benefit from being away for a while. In addition, she noticed that I had no Somali friends and networks, we didn't go to *dugsi* (Quran school), and we only spoke Norwegian. All of this was strange to her and she didn't like it. She wanted us to get to know the Somali culture, our relatives and our background.

Among the Norwegian-Pakistanis, the interviewees mostly referred to religion in general terms as one of several motivating factors, along with cultural values and the need to prevent children from becoming too Norwegianized or Westernized, as illustrated in this quote from a young woman:

> They wanted us to learn about the culture and religion of Pakistan. Those who live in Norway don't have that much respect for their parents. Those who have lived in Pakistan know more about the culture, respect and religion, the things that the parents want their children to have in them. That's on one side. On the other, it is about education.

Parents often want the child to gain a Muslim identity by living in a society where Islam permeates everyday life. However, for a young person who grew up in Norway, as a religious minority in a secular society where religious expressions in the public sphere may be controversial, the experience of living in a Muslim country can impose reflection. Our young interviewees said they were overwhelmed by how Islam was intertwined with general social life. They adjusted to the local practices as Muslims; however, when returning to Norway, rather than unreflectively continuing their religious practices, their experience became a frame of reference for how they related to Islam. Asad (2003) argues that the effort to define religion as different from cultural traditions, politics, and laws is part of the discursive practices within the history of the modern West and secularism (see Jacobsen 2006). In line with these developments, the young Muslims in our study tended to adopt a more discursive form of Islam, more compatible with the values of Western secular societies, and different from what the parents' generation may understand as the correct form of Islam.

Education

A common aim for parents from both Somalia and Pakistan was to improve their children's education. Among Norwegian-Pakistanis, private schools are seen as an instrument for social mobility, but also for display of social status and material wealth (see Erdal et al. 2015). As a father and grandfather of Pakistani background explained, his generation had grown up as village people in a highly stratified society. They were used to social status being reflected in a hierarchy of private schools. When he settled in Norway with his wife, they wanted the best for their family and it seemed natural to send the children to the kind of schools in Pakistan that his own family could only dream about.

Some children did not succeed in the Norwegian school system, and their parents wanted to give them a second chance to ensure that they would successfully attain higher education. This was the case particularly among the Norwegian-Somalis. They partly blamed the lack of success in school on negative social behaviors linked to their children's networks and friends. The parents prefer an educational system that they know, and as a diaspora family they may afford private schools with high prestige.

Both in Pakistan and in Kenya, there is an extensive private education market ranging from expensive international elite schools, to schools with moderate fees offering a choice between British GCE exams and national curricula, in English or the local language. These schools generally present themselves as highly academically oriented with modern teaching styles. At the other end of the continuum are cheaper schools with more traditional teaching and at the extreme end, Quran schools or *Madrassahs* with very low or no fees at all, typically catering to very poor families. Some of our interviewees were placed in these very strict Quran schools. However, most of our interviewees went to private schools or public schools with a good reputation. The parents also paid for additional private tutoring; thus, school activities made up a large part of the children's day.

Islam is a natural presence in all of the school curricula reported in our study. For instance, all Pakistani schools had Islam as an obligatory subject, so called *islāmiyat.* However, variation is great when it comes to the degree and form of teaching. In some schools, religious education is organized as a separate part of a mainly secular academic education. Other schools see Islam as a central framework for academic achievement, stressing the interconnections between the two. This includes offering courses leading to certification as *Hafiz-ul-Quran* (a person who is able to recite the entire Holy Quran).

One of the Pakistani principals presented his school as a modern pan-Islamic school in contrast to both old-fashioned *madrassahs* (Quran schools) on the one hand, and commercial profit-driven schools on the other. In the following quote he explains why parents choose his school:

> We do not adhere to any particular denomination (he uses the term *maslak*) or sect such as Sunni, Shia, or Wahhabi but emphasize being a good Muslim. Sectarian differences have led us to the problems we have today and spread hatred. We have a policy not to discuss sectarian differences and teachers do not give their interpretation. We also get them to learn the Quran, how to pray and basic Islamic manners. Our school combines modern education as in the Oxford syllabus and age-old Islamic manners – this is the basis for our creation.

In another school, the principal explains that today teachers and students are allowed to speak Urdu only in the Urdu classes. Previously, *islāmiyat* used to be in Urdu but they changed to English as this makes it easier to do O Level Islamic studies, which is part of the International Cambridge program. *Islāmiyat* content has also developed, he explains:

> We used to have a focus on Islamic education in a more traditional sense and all marks were for oral recitation, memorization that is. Now we have marks for translation and understanding of Quranic verses as well. It is important to get the concepts and know what it actually means.

However, we also heard of children attending schools where Islam was the main or sole focus of instruction. Such cases came from the Norwegian-Somalis, where some parents justified this choice with the fact that the children had not earlier received an adequate Islamic training. Some also mentioned their strict discipline as a reason for attending Quran schools. For others it was more about a lack of choice, as they could not afford good quality private schools.

Quran schools offer different types of education. Some teach several subjects, while others include only recitation of the Quran in Arabic. They tend to exercise strict discipline, including corporal punishment. Representatives of the Ministry of Education in Puntland emphasized that such schools apply traditional forms of teaching. While the students learn skills that are conducive to certain forms of learning, such methods are at odds with the type of cognitive skills necessary to succeed in higher education.

> You are teaching children very complex concepts in secondary school, intro-
> ducing highly technical subjects such as chemistry, biology and physics in
> a foreign language, so Puntland children, the only thing that they do is to
> memorize huge chunks of information, and they have the capacity to do so
> because of the strategies they have learned in *dugsi* (Quran school). But this
> type of strategy does not work in higher education. What I am trying to say
> is that necessary skills are not developed at all, the higher order skills are
> not developed at all; that is critical skills, research, analysis, assessment and
> application of the ideas that they have learned. . . . It is not difficult to memo-
> rize a formula when a child has learned such strategies; however, this creates
> another problem; that they get bored easily – since there is not a lot of inde-
> pendence in learning they get bored easily, if they get bored too much they
> drop-out of school, especially Somali boys.

Reflections on experience and outcomes

So far, we have looked predominantly at the parents' understandings and aspirations behind deciding to move their children or families "back" or to a third country. In the following section, we turn to the young people themselves and their views on the outcomes of their temporary stays.

Reintegration and schooling upon return

The consequences of being absent from Norwegian schooling tend to depend upon what kind of school the young men and women have attended, how motivated they are for schooling, and how long they have been away. A girl who was away for a year after lower secondary school said she adapted quickly to her Norwegian school after her stay abroad:

> I don't feel that I lost anything from being away. Learning has gone well after
> I returned. I adapted very quickly from being in Somalia to coming back to
> Norway. My Norwegian was just as good as it was before I left. What was dif-
> ferent was that I was more interested in school and motivated to learn. I had
> lost that when I was in my last year of middle school. It has made me more

determined and my goal is to continue studying after high school. I am more focused now and matured from the experience I had during my stay in Somalia. I really needed it. I thank Allah for having seen and experienced that.

Contrastingly, a young man who was sent to Somalia for two years when he was 15 because he had school problems, only attended *dugsi* (Quran school). He never managed to complete middle school after returning.

I never returned to school. I did not do well in school. I just wanted to find a job, but took it easy for a while. To find a job here in Norway is difficult. So I got some social benefits and got money here and there from friends. I also returned to Somaliland a couple of times and took it easy. I don't know what to say. I think that the lifestyle there affected me. I take life day by day and I don't need much, you know.

Other interviewees confirm that the transition back to the Norwegian school system can be challenging. Many report losing Norwegian language skills while they are abroad, with consequences for their schooling upon return to Norway. Some say that the skills they got from the school abroad were not recognized in the Norwegian context. On the other hand, the practice of younger children going "back" for longer stays is also frowned upon in some parts of the community. Particularly among the Pakistanis, it seems to have an old-fashioned, backward ring to it. Those who want to portray themselves as forward-looking, realistic, and socially mobile people stress the need to keep up with Norwegian and Western education and language. As one young man puts it:

That's something that was quite common in our parents' generation. But they came to realize that it was not such a good idea if you envisaged your future in Norway. And add to that the deterioration of the situation of Pakistan. Security, electricity, corruption, you name it. There is nothing there for us now, except a few weddings maybe. But weddings are also increasingly held in the West as most relatives live in the diaspora.

Several parents said that if they were given the choice, they would have preferred to send their children to private Islamic schools in Norway. That way, they would have the best of all worlds: retaining their Norwegian language skills, being subject to more discipline (which many parents believe is all but absent in Norwegian schools), and learning and practicing Islam as a natural part of their everyday life.

Culture, religion, and self-understanding

Among the more positive narratives are stories of adolescents who get a deeper understanding of their heritage as well as a better understanding of their parents. They find a clearer identity that helps them stay grounded and stay out of trouble when they return to Norway. Such positive narratives also include stories about learning discipline and appreciating the opportunities and standard of living in Norway.

Several of our interviewees emphasize the great contrasts between the conditions they met abroad and Norwegian everyday life. Their reflections upon these dissimilarities have given them an enhanced sense of self and a new direction in their lives after returning to Norway. They have realized how privileged they are and relate this to the Norwegian standard of living and the education system. They have been inspired to use these opportunities and to explore how to be a "good Muslim" in a Western context, in effect strengthening their identity as hyphenated Norwegian-Somali or Norwegian-Pakistani. To this end they emphasize the importance of developing a safe base from where to combine different cultural inputs and interests in their everyday life as a minority in Norway. One girl of Somali background says:

> Somalia made me. I became stronger and more independent. Since I got back, I have tried to do the best for me and my family.

Many say they obtained a different and more personal relationship to practicing their religion and to their parents' cultural background. In particular, the young Norwegian-Somalis and Norwegian-Pakistanis seem more conscious about separating between what they see as religion and what they see as cultural traditions. For instance, they would be opposed to certain discriminatory practices based on gender, as well as caste, clan, and class, on the grounds that these are cultural and un-Islamic concepts.

For some, practicing a more pious way of life made them more visible. However, their new frames of reference and a more independent relation to Islam helped strengthen their identity and religious self-confidence. One young woman expressed how she became more reflexive on these issues when attending a Quran school in Pakistan:

> I was a non-practicing Muslim when I left [Norway] and not that concerned about religion. During my stay I got a different impression of religion. I started to wear the *hijab*. Now that I am back I notice this very strongly. People look at me as a foreigner, as an asylum seeker. They look at me, I get negative stares. But never comments. Some of my friends reacted "And you with your pretty hair." I tell them I am not different.

However, stays abroad are not seen as the only or even the best way to achieve a confident Islamic identity. When asked about what advice she would give to parents today, a young woman of Pakistani descent made a pertinent distinction between effects on education and integration more generally, and the role of religion. She says she would have advised against sending children away, at the same time pointing to some unresolved issues pertaining to Islamic upbringing:

> I can understand that parents want their children to stay in touch with their religion and culture, but at the same time, it is not smart to send them

abroad. It splits up the education and their lives. The children may experience emotional defeats as they get back. It is a struggle. I remember the time in the reception class, I felt quite helpless, no one understood me and I was afraid of being bullied. And I don't want other children to experience the same. For me, I don't care about culture, but religion is important to me. But you can be just as religious in Norway. I think an Islamic school would solve the problem. I have seen it in Sweden and Denmark; they are ordinary schools except they have religion and Arabic as well. It would make the parents more secure and prevent many of them from sending their children abroad.

Structural and cultural implications of stays abroad

As indicated earlier in this chapter, there are significant differences between the two Muslim groups studied. We have particularly emphasized their migration timelines on the one hand, and their transnational movement patterns on the other. As Somalis are still a new immigrant group in Norway, their practice of sending children "back" in some ways resembles the practice described by Norwegian-Pakistanis, which now seems to be in decline. The parallel between Somalis now and Pakistanis at an earlier point in time is, however, not complete. While the Pakistani movement primarily was a bilateral one, going back to relatives and the old village in Pakistan, the Somalis show a more dispersed pattern of movement.[3] The Somali diaspora in Norway is still in a period of adjustment, characterized by the desire to maintain links with and support for their relatives in other countries. While the lure from Pakistan in terms of kinship bonds and commitments has waned over time, such factors are still very much in play for many Somalis.

Despite these differences, we find that the motivations for going abroad are very similar. Our data show a wide range of motives for sending children on temporary stays in other countries, of living and schooling arrangements while abroad, and of experiences and reflections upon return. Transnational lives are both commonplace and contested within the diaspora communities. While our research shows considerable convergence when it comes to parents' motives, the content and outcomes of such stays vary considerably. Furthermore, the children and young people themselves have their own perceptions of the outcomes and meanings of temporary stays abroad, which do not necessarily align with parental aspirations.

Our analyses indicate that outcomes differ depending on the quality of education the children have received, their ambitions and motivation for studying, the length of their stay, and at what age and school year(s) they were away. For some, it seems that the stay abroad represents a turning point or functions as a "vitamin injection" to their school performance. Some of our interviewees insist that their present school achievements in Norway are a consequence of their school years abroad. Similar patterns have been found in other research on children of Somali refugees from Europe returning to Somaliland to attend school there for a limited time, before moving back to Europe (Lindley 2008).

Yet, our findings also suggest that there are valid reasons for the concern that temporary stays abroad may hamper the structural integration of children of immigrants. A number of our interviewees had less optimistic narratives and some struggle to establish themselves as returnees in Norway, whether in coping with school or accessing the job market. In particular, in the case of longer stays abroad, it seems that language skills deteriorate significantly, with the risk of considerable academic set-backs upon return, as Norwegian schools teach in Norwegian. Shorter stays, however, do not seem to have the same adverse effects.

While our study gives some support for the concern about structural dimensions of integration, the picture seems more complex when it comes to cultural integration. In the following, our main focus will be on religious identity and implications for transnational children's identification with Norwegian society and their sense of belonging.

Our young interviewees are positioned at the intersection of different, ambivalent, and contrasting discourses and practices of Islam. In her research on young Muslims in Norway, Jacobsen (2006; 2011) explores the transformation of Islamic identity in the context of migration and social mobility in a secular Western society. In public discourse on immigrant youth, there has been a tendency to treat them as socially and culturally embedded in close-knit families and networks of co-ethnics. According to this view their religious identity is determined by such belongings, placing them within the same tradition of their parents, mixing religion and cultural traditions. In contrast, Jacobsen finds that Islam becomes a central means for reinterpreting certain forms of cultural traditions for the young generation, as part of their identity politics directed at both majority society and the parent generation. This seems to be the case also in our study.

What then are the results of these temporary visits and education abroad, in religious terms? Have the adolescents become *more* Muslim? Some speak of a stronger Muslim identity. They have improved their knowledge and skills to define the way they will live as a Muslim. The stay made them reflect more upon what it means to be a Muslim. Others emphasize that their identity both as a Muslim and Somali or Pakistani has become more integrated and less problematic. In that sense it may be seen as becoming both weaker, by being less of a constant focus of attention, and stronger, by being more secure and mature. They are not as vulnerable to other people's opinions and verbal attacks as before. They are more confident and self-assured about who they are, and not necessarily in a way that rules out a sense of belonging to Norway. On the contrary, several interviewees would claim that their stays abroad have made them appreciate Norwegian society and culture more, as they have been able to, or forced to, compare with the other country (see Waldinger 2015).

In fact, the Pakistani case is a good illustration of the multiplicity of meanings of transnational practices when it comes to religion. The fact that Norwegian-Pakistani parents no longer send their children to Pakistan to the same extent as before could suggest that Islamic education and values are less important to them. However, as one of the Norwegian-Pakistani interviewees pointed out, it has become easier to practice Islam in Norway now than it was in the 1980s and

1990s, with increasing number of mosques in most cities, Quran lessons, and even the alternative of online Islamic education (Aarset 2015). In other words, among some of our Norwegian-Pakistani interviewees, Islam no longer represents a pull factor toward Pakistan. This does not mean that religion has lost its importance. Rather, in this narrative Islam becomes part of the reason for staying in Norway.

It is often assumed that the more time a child or a young person spends in her country of origin, or any other country of similar cultural background, the more influenced they are by that culture and religion. Furthermore, this influence is often understood in terms of increased loyalty to and identification with that culture, with a corresponding decrease in identification with Norway. Our findings indicate a less unilineal identification development among children and young people who spend time abroad. In fact, exposure to conditions "there" may result in processes that bring children closer to Norway, while at the same time allowing them to establish new emotional links to their parents' homeland. The transnational identity work of the second generation is thus an ongoing reflexive process. The outcome of this process is likely to be influenced by the opportunity structures available upon return, and to what extent they support both emotional and practical reintegration.

Notes

1 https://www.imdi.no/om-integrering-i-norge/innvandrere-og-integrering/innvandrerbe folkningen-i-norge/
2 www.utdanningsforbundet.no/upload/Publikasjoner/Faktaark/Faktaark%202014/ Faktaark_2014.01.pdf
3 However, our data show a considerable proportion of Norwegian-Pakistani and Norwegian-Somali children moving to Great Britain and other Western countries. While this chapter focuses on the "old" pattern, the motives for and outcomes of movement across Western countries in terms of religious education and belonging should also be investigated.

References

Aakesson, Lisa, Jørgen Carling, and Heike Drotbohm. 2012. "Mobility, Moralities and Motherhood: Navigating the Contingencies of Cape Verdean Lives." *Journal of Ethnic and Migration Studies* 38(2): 237–260.

Aarset, Monica Five. 2015. "Transnational Practices and Local Lives. Quran Courses Via Skype in Norwegian-Pakistani Families." *Identities* 23(4): 1–16.

Amit, Vered. 2012. "The Raptures and Ruptures of Mobility." *Identities* 19(4): 501–509.

Andersson, Mette. 2010. "The Social Imaginary of First Generation Europeans." *Social Identities* 16(1): 3–21.

Asad, Talal. 2003. *Formations of the Secular: Christianity, Islam, Modernity*. Stanford, CA: Standford University Press.

Bratsberg, Bernt, Oddbjørn Raaum, and Knut Røed. 2012. "Educating Children of Immigrants: Closing the Gap in Norwegian Schools." *Nordic Economic Policy Review* 3(1): 211–253.

Carling, Jørgen, Cecilia Menjívar, and Leah Schmalzbauer. 2012. "Central Themes in the Study of Transnational Parenthood." *Journal of Ethnic and Migration Studies* 38(2): 191–217.

Dzamarija, Minja Thea. 2004. "Norske barn i utlandet – uvalgte land: Pakistan, Marokko, Tyrkia og Spania." Notat 04/71. Oslo: Statistics Norway.

Erdal, Marta Bivand, and Ceri Oeppen. 2013. "Migrant Balancing Acts: Understanding the Interactions between Integration and Transnationalism." *Journal of Ethnic and Migration Studies* 39(6): 867–884.

Erdal, Marta Bivand, Anum Amjad, Qamar Zaman Bodla, and Asma Rubab. 2015. "Going Back to Pakistan for Education? The Interplay of Return Mobilities, Education, and Transnational Living." *Population, Space and Place* 22(8): 836–848.

Grillo, Ralph, and Valentina Mazzucato. 2008. "Africa< >Europe: A Double Engagement." *Journal of Ethnic and Migration Studies* 34(2): 175–198.

Hamann, Edmund T., Víctor Zúñiga, and Juan Sánchez García. 2010. "Transnational Students' Perspectives on Schooling in the United States and Mexico: The Salience of School Experience and Country of Birth." In *Children and Migration: At the Crossroads of Resiliency and Vulnerability*, edited by M. O. Ensor and E. M. Goździak, pp. 230–252. New York: Palgrave Macmillan.

Hatfield, Madeleine E. 2010. "Children Moving 'Home'? Everyday Experiences of Return Migration in Highly Skilled Households." *Childhood – A Global Journal of Child Research* 17(2): 243–257.

Hermansen, Are Skeie. 2013. "Occupational Attainment among Children of Immigrants in Norway: Bottlenecks into Employment – Equal Access to Advantaged Positions?" *European Sociological Review* 29(3): 517–534.

Hermansen, Are Skeie. 2015. "Coming of Age, Getting Ahead? Assessing Socioeconomic Assimilation among Children of Immigrants in Norway." Unpublished Ph.D. Dissertation: Department of Sociology and Human Geography, University of Oslo.

Hermansen, Are Skeie, and Gunn Elisabeth Birkelund. 2015. "The Impact of Immigrant Classmates on Educational Outcomes." *Social Forces* 94(2): 615–646.

Jacobsen, Christine M. 2006. *Staying on the Straight Path. Religious Identities and Practices among Young Muslims in Norway.* Unpublished Ph.D. dissertation. Bergen: University of Bergen.

Jacobsen, Christine M. 2011. *Islamic Traditions and Muslim Youth in Norway.* Leiden: Brill.

Kasinitz, Philip, John H. Mollenkopf, Mary C. Waters, and Jennifer Holdaway. 2008. *Inheriting the City: The Children of Immigrants Coming of Age.* New York: Russell Sage Foundation.

King, Russell, and Anastasia Christou. 2011. "Of Counter-Diaspora and Reverse Transnationalism: Return Mobilities to and from the Ancestral Homeland." *Mobilities* 6(4): 451–466.

Levitt, Peggy, and Nina Glick Schiller. 2004. "Conceptualizing Simultaneity: A Transnational Social Field Perspective on Society." *International Migration Review* 38(3): 1002–1039.

Lidén, Hilde, Anja Bredal, and Liza Reisel. 2014. "Transnational oppvekst: Om lengre utenlandsopphold blant barn og unge med innvandrerbakgrunn." Report 2014: 05, Oslo: Institute for Social Research.

Lindley, A. 2008. "Transnational Connections and Education in the Somali Context." *Journal of Eastern African Studies* 2(3): 401–414.

Menken, Kate, Tatyana Kleyn, and Nabin Chae. 2012. "Spotlight on 'Long-Term English Language Learners': Characteristics and Prior Schooling Experiences of an Invisible Population." *International Multilingual Research Journal* 6(2): 121–142.

Nadim, Marjan. 2014. "Forerunners for Change: Work and Motherhood among Second-Generation Immigrants in Norway." Unpublished Ph.D. Dissertation, Department of Sociology and Human Geography, University of Oslo.

Ní Laoire, Caitríona. 2011. "Narratives of 'Innocent Irish Childhoods': Return Migration and Intergenerational Family Dynamics." *Journal of Ethnic and Migration Studies* 37(8): 1253–1271.

Ostberg, Sissel. 2006. "Skolegang i Pakistan – barn med innvandrebakgrunn som går på skole i foreldrenes opprinnelsesland." Oslo: Høgskolen i Oslo.

Smith, Robert Courtney. 2006. *Mexican New York: Transnational Lives of New Immigrants.* Berkeley, CA: University of California Press.

Støren, Liv Anne. 2005. "Ungdom med innvandrerbakgrunn i norsk utdanning–ser vi en fremtidig suksesshistorie?" In *Utdanning 2005 - deltakelse og kompetanse,* edited by M. Raabe, pp. 70–97. Oslo/Kongsvinger: Statistics Norway.

Waldinger, Roger. 2015. *The Cross-Border Connection: Immigrants, Emigrants, and Their Homelands.* Cambridge, MA: Harvard University Press.

Wen, Ma. 2010. "Bumpy Journeys: A Young Chinese Adolescent's Transitional Schooling across Two Sociocultural Contexts." *Journal of Language, Identity and Education* 9(2): 107–123.

Zontini, Elisabetta. 2010. *Transnational Families, Migration and Gender: Moroccan and Filipino Women in Bologna and Barcelona.* New York: Berghahn Books.

Part IV

Reconstructed and misconstrued identities

9 Second-generation Muslim American advocates and strategic racial identity

Erik Love

Advocacy organizations are the venues where Muslim American advocates most often craft strategies around racial politics and policy. Within these organizations, advocates from diverse backgrounds in ethnicity, nationality, and generation of immigration frequently discuss issues and objectives which involve racism toward Muslims. Over the past three decades, advocacy organizations with significant Muslim American constituencies have struggled to gain a foothold as racial politics have been transformed. In part, these transformations have come about because of the repeated electoral successes of far-right and center-right politicians who have used Islamophobia as a "wedge issue" to generate votes in their favor. These struggles have coincided with difficult conversations among advocates about how to engage in effective political advocacy. First- and second-generation immigrants often disagree on priorities and strategic approaches to bringing about reforms, and the strategic use of racial identity has been a crucial point of debate and disagreement among advocates. This chapter will describe some of the discussions around these issues that take place in these advocacy organizations. These conversations, often between first- and second-generation Muslim American civil rights advocates, represent critically important efforts by Muslim American communities to navigate the shifting terrain of race and racism in the United States.

To discuss these dynamics, I present results from a study based on interviews with twelve Arab, Muslim, Sikh, and South Asian American civil rights advocates. My conclusions are further supported by ethnographic observations of various discussions between advocates and community members over more than ten years. I argue that beginning around 2010 and continuing until at least 2016, some second-generation Muslim American advocates led renewed efforts to codify and co-opt a new racial identity category that would include Arab, Muslim, Sikh, and South Asian Americans. I argue that resistance to recognizing such a racial identity category, seen as insurmountable in the 1990s and in the first decade of the 2000s, is beginning to wane in the 2010s, in large part due to the work of second-generation Muslim American activists.

These efforts developed as Muslim American immigration has increased significantly in the past three decades. Almost half (45%) of all Muslim immigrants have arrived after 1990 (Pew Research Center 2011). A recent survey of

Muslim Americans found that first-generation immigrants comprise over 60% of the entire Muslim American population. Moreover, the vast majority of these immigrants (87%) arrived after 1980 (Pew Research Center 2011). They arrived during the rise of the New Right, led by President Ronald Reagan and other conservative leaders. Among the keys to the success of the New Right have been the steady erosion of civil rights protections and the re-articulation of racial and anti-immigrant stereotypes using political "dog whistles" (Perlstein 2014; Omi and Winant 2015). By speaking as though race has nothing to do with immigration and counter-terrorism policy proposals, American leaders have successfully painted civil rights advocates as "playing the race card," as vestiges of an obsolete race-conscious society. These dynamics present tremendous tensions for all civil rights advocates, and Muslim American advocates have occupied a particularly challenging position in this field.

Despite the New Right's success, the creation of advocacy organizations designed around identity categories enabled the development of recognized and legitimated strategies that seek to leverage racial identity in the construction of anti-racist political power. These strategies have proven effective for a number of communities in the United States, including Asian Americans, African Americans, Latinos and Native Americans. The use of racial identity to gain additional political leverage has taken many forms, and it is difficult to generalize about these efforts. Across several different historical moments, however, advocacy organizations have promoted the acceptance of an ascribed racial identity in order to expand the number of adherents and participants in reform efforts. For example, civil rights advocates in the 1970s and 1980s encouraged Chinese, Filipino, Japanese, Korean, and many other Asian ethnic communities to join together in unified political campaigns under an Asian American racial identity (Okamoto 2014). They successfully made the case that hate crimes, discrimination, and stereotypes affecting any of these ethnic groups actually impacted all of them, because of race. While never achieving anything close to perfect unity, these civil rights advocates nonetheless managed to propel the Asian American identity into the mainstream, and in part because of that, they won several major political reforms. In this way, race-based strategies for advocacy found some significant successes in the late-1900s.

In so-called identity politics campaigns like those by Asian American advocates, discussions between first- and second-generation advocates have been crucial. Even though race is central in American life, it remains a mysterious and even a taboo topic for many Americans. People who have lived in the United States for their entire lives struggle to understand and navigate the treacherous terrain of race as it affects daily life. Indeed, relatively few Americans ever fully appreciate how deeply structural racism affects them. For this and many other reasons, race presents a particular challenge for newcomers to the United States. First-generation immigrants frequently have difficulty picking up the social cues and idiosyncrasies associated with the production of race in the United States. Even gaining an understanding of the day-to-day realities of race and racism does not necessarily provide insights into how racism remains embedded in the foundations of American social institutions. Many advocates understandably have struggled to craft effective strategies given the realities of racial politics in the U.S.

In short, the difficulty in conceptualizing race, for all Americans, including first- and second-generation immigrants, presents a complex challenge for civil rights advocates representing Muslim American communities. Given that civil rights advocates frequently disagree or have contentious conversations around race and racism, in this chapter I focus on how such discussions inside Muslim-American advocacy organizations – including discussions frequently led by second-generation advocates – have shaped advocacy strategies for dealing with Islamophobia.

Islamophobia and racism

There can be no doubt that racism operates at the very core of Islamophobia in the United States. While other factors are always present – class, ethnicity, gender, geography, religion, sexuality, and more – this does not negate the central role that race plays in the reproduction of Islamophobia. Racial formation of a "Muslim" category, which in fact encompasses myriad ethnic, religious, national-origin, and cultural groups, has developed in parallel with Islamophobic discrimination over the past century in the United States (Rana 2011; Volpp 2002). Race is the only possible explanation for why Arabs, Sikhs, South Asians, and other communities frequently face Islamophobic discrimination and hate crimes in America. Because of race, the communities vulnerable to Islamophobia extends beyond those who have a Muslim-American identity. Of course, Muslim Americans have endured a seemingly endless string of injustices in recent decades, ranging from violent hate crimes to systematic discrimination, and political exclusion. Yet consider the many, all-too frequent attacks on Sikh Americans by perpetrators attempting to harm "Middle Easterners" or "Muslims," like Balbir Singh Sodhi, who was murdered in September 2001 by a White man who said he wanted to avenge the attacks of 9/11. It is likely that the White supremacist who opened fire at the Sikh Temple of Wisconsin in August 2012, killing six worshippers, had similar motivations. Islamophobia lay behind yet another attack in Illinois, when Inderjit Singh Mukker was brutally beaten in September 2015 by a man who shouted "Terrorist! Go back to your country!"

The motives behind any individual hate crime have as much to do with the structures of power as they do with whatever churns inside the mind of the perpetrators when they decide to strike. Moreover, the effect of hate crimes resonates beyond the slain, beyond those dealing with injuries (physical and mental), and beyond even the families who lose loved ones. Because they target entire communities, hate crimes threaten to create profound chilling effects that affect people locally and globally. After the attack in Wisconsin, Sikhs at *gurdwaras* across the nation and around the world immediately wondered whether they were safe, and many beefed up security in the wake of the massacre. Similarly, because of the racialized identity that links Arab, Muslim, Sikh, and South Asian Americans, many communities must confront the awful legacies of attacks like these. Hate crimes affect more than just the families who lost loved ones and more than just the Sikh community – they affect Muslim American communities as well, because of race. The climate in which racist hate crimes targeting "Muslims and those mistaken for Muslims" develops is a result of the ways that discriminatory policies and Islamophobic rhetoric reinforce one another. When Sikhs are shot for "looking Muslim" while political leaders decry the threat from "radical Islamic terrorists," these same leaders often propose that police "patrol and secure Muslim neighborhoods," showing that the racist environment for politics and policymaking is obvious and deeply troubling.

In determining how to navigate racial dynamics in this environment, civil rights advocates occupy a pivotal position. When advocacy organizations generate campaigns for social change, the national understanding around race can undergo profound reconfigurations. Therefore, the debates between advocates working with organizations such as the Muslim Public Affairs Council (MPAC) and the Council on American Islamic Relations (CAIR) have the potential to contribute in significant ways to the social construction of race for their constituents. Whether to talk about "Islamophobia" as a form of racism or not represents a key strategic consideration for advocacy organizations like these (Love 2017).

Given the recent large-scale immigration of Muslims to the United States, it is not surprising that most of the historically prominent Muslim American advocacy organizations have emerged only in the last three decades. Of course, many communities of Muslim Americans, especially African American Muslims (or so-called indigenous Muslims), have a long history of civil rights advocacy and activism. However, restricting the discussion to immigrant Muslim communities allows a focus on the first and second generations, and on two of the best-known organizations that came to prominence in the 1990s, i.e., CAIR and MPAC. Arab American advocacy organizations, like the American-Arab Anti-Discrimination Committee (ADC) and the Arab American Institute (AAI), and South Asian American advocacy organizations such as South Asian Americans Leading Together (SAALT) have also worked on Islamophobia extensively in recent years. These organizations have had their work cut out for them as hate crimes, exclusionary political rhetoric, media stereotypes, and new governmental policies and initiatives implemented in the 1990s and 2000s have had tremendous impacts across all of these communities. An apparent rise in Islamophobia has been noted in a wide range of recent research.

Indeed, there may be an emergent field of "Islamophobia studies," as Garner and Selod (2014: 2–3) describe the plethora of new publications on this topic. They argue that this research has established that "Muslims and those mistaken for Muslims" bear the brunt of the racialized stereotype of "the terrorist." Although the impact of race on "Islamophobia" seems somewhat obvious, in a survey of the scholarly discussion, Meer (2013: 386) found a "virtual absence of an established literature on race and racism in the discussion of Islamophobia." This perhaps results from the recent shift, during the period of significant immigration in the 1980s and 1990s, of the racial character of the term "Muslim." This term has been rearticulated to have a clear, unambiguous connection with Middle Eastern Americans, even though Muslim American communities, of course, include large numbers of Black, White, and Asian Americans.

The transfiguration of the Middle Eastern American racial category occurred amidst many well-publicized and spectacularly violent events, including the Black September organization's attacks in the 1970s, then the 1979–1981 Iran Hostage Crisis, the 1984 assassination of Indira Gandhi by two of her Sikh body-guards, and the 1993 bombing of the World Trade Center by al Qaeda. Even before these and similar events, and even more so afterward, American popular culture consistently reflected the images of Middle Eastern villains as seen in the news media. As portrayed in films and television programs, terrorists largely stuck to a stereotypical caricature of "Arab Muslims," almost always wearing a turban, *keffiyeh*, or *hijab* (Shaheen 2014; Alsultany 2012). The actors portraying these repetitive villains often had brown skin, or sometimes they wore makeup to darken their skin tone. With the end of the Cold War, the meteoric rise of the "clash of civilizations" paradigm (Huntington 1993), which posited Islam writ large as the new existential threat to so-called Western Civilization, built upon and served to reaffirm this stereotype. Unfortunately, some militants in the Middle East took their U.S.-supplied arms and military training and turned them against their former American mentors. They signaled their displeasure with changes in U.S. foreign policy by bombing New York in 1993, and then with simultaneous terrorist bombings in 1998 at the American Embassies in Nairobi and Dar es Salaam. Of course, these were hardly the only terrorist attacks happening in the 1990s – many similar attacks were carried out by dissidents in Spain, Colom-bia, Ireland, and Sri Lanka, to name only a few examples of non-Islamic terror-ist groups active in recent decades. The terrorism carried out by al Qaeda and other Middle Eastern militants, however, attracted the most attention of American policymakers and Hollywood filmmakers. To make a long story short, by the mid-1990s, the false stereotype that terrorists are almost always Arab or Muslim led not only political pundits but also professional investigators to presume that Middle Eastern terrorists were at fault in both the bombing of the federal build-ing in Oklahoma City, which was perpetrated by right-wing Christian Americans, and also in the explosion of TWA Flight 800 after takeoff from New York, which was a mechanical failure. Recent "Islamophobia studies" scholarship illuminates the pervasive, longstanding racialization that is at work in stereotypes that led to premature, damaging conclusions like these (Aidi 2014; Beydoun 2013; Bakalian and Bozorgmehr 2009; Meer 2013; Rana 2011; Volpp 2002; Werbner 2005).

In short, the racial formation process has ascribed an identity – variously rendered as "Arab," "Muslim," or "Middle Eastern," or a similarly crude amalgamation – that ignores and obscures tremendous ethnic, religious, and cultural diversity. The banal stereotypes about this racially-bound group are known to just about anyone who has been in the United States for even a short time: violent, lecherous, misog-ynistic, religiously devout, and so on. Like any racial grouping, this ascribed iden-tity uses visual, phenotypic indicators as a shortcut to indicate membership in the socially constructed category. And the racial identity "Muslim" becomes part and parcel of the dehumanization process in the various American wars in the Middle East region, and in so-called counterterrorism efforts as well.

Despite the powerful effects of the "Middle Eastern" racialization, it remains a nebulous and often unrecognized identity category in contemporary discussions about race. There is no universally accepted term for the collection of groups swept into the "Middle Eastern" category. Some insist that there is no racial category at all, and that religious persecution is the sole issue, with "those mistaken for Muslims" getting unintentionally exposed to Islamophobia. But racialization is the best way to explain how this "mistaken identity" happens – an ascribed racial identity is operative here.

The lack of a clearly recognized and easily discussed racial category is partly why Meer (2013) finds a surprising lack of discussion of race and racism in the existing literature on Islamophobia. Moreover, this is because Islamophobia is overdetermined. Religion, gender, class, nationality, and other factors happen simultaneously in the reproduction of Islamophobia. Therefore, it is both understandable and productive to look at any and all of these factors in studying it. However, it is important not to ignore the role of race when analyzing Islamophobia, particularly when considering how advocates in the United States confront it (Love 2017).

Another reason that race remains obscured in so many analyses of Islamophobia comes about because the mere presence of an ascribed identity (like "Middle Eastern American") is a necessary but not sufficient condition for the establishment of a well-recognized panethnic category in the mainstream. In other words, simply because many Americans associate those physical features – turban, brown skin, etc. – with the social category of "Middle Eastern," that is not by itself enough to codify a racial category. Recent research finds that unlike the 1960s, in recent years "potential contemporary panethnic groups" have to contend with a "hostile climate" that may discourage the creation of broader coalitions like "Middle Eastern Americans" (Bozorgmehr, Ong, and Tosh 2016). The "hostile climate" includes state actions – like discriminatory policies – that have "punitive" effects on some Middle Eastern American groups. In any climate, however, the mere ascription of an identity category (through discrimination, cultural representations, day-to-day interactions, and all other racial projects) is not sufficient to codify a racial category in the mainstream. Advocates must organize collective action in such a way as to intentionally "bridge" groups together under an umbrella panethnic grouping (Okamoto 2014; Espiritu 1992; Omi and Winant 2015). This brings us to the focus of this chapter – the discussions in advocacy organizations about how to navigate racial politics.

Racial contentions inside advocacy organizations

Comparing the work of Muslim American advocacy organizations in the 1990s with their more recent efforts can illuminate how much of a role race plays in determining strategies and tactics for civil rights advocates. In particular, the past thirty years have seen "colorblindness" ideology rise to dominance in the

United States (Bonilla-Silva 2006). According to "colorblindness," recognizing the mere existence of racial identity serves mainly to perpetuate racism, and therefore the best way to overcome discrimination is to act "blind" to race. Therefore, any explicit discussion of racism is a mistake from this point of view. The best approach is to find the "real" causes of discrimination (economic inequality, for example) rather than pointing to something supposedly ephemeral, like race. By the end of the 1900s, colorblindness was the dominant ideology in America, and almost any enunciation of racism was met with skepticism. As this ideology took hold in the center of American politics and culture, new and prominent Muslim American advocacy organizations began to emerge.

New Muslim American organizations specifically tailored to political advocacy began to emerge in the late 1980s. MPAC began as a political action committee at the Islamic Center of Southern California in 1986, before spinning off into an independent organization two years later. CAIR was founded in 1994 in Washington, DC. Both of these organizations aspired to represent the entire Muslim American community, but especially in the early years, their work clearly centered around issues affecting immigrant Muslims. They joined an advocacy scene that already had several Arab American organizations, including AAI and ADC. In the 1990s, all of these organizations dealt with a large number of issues, ranging from denouncing media stereotypes, to providing aid to people who faced discrimination at their workplaces, to lobbying the government for changes in foreign policy.

One longtime advocate described the model of advocacy developed during the 1990s as an "old model, based on ethnic stereotyping in the entertainment industry" (Interview September 2008a). He explained that "most of the negativity" in that era, the sort that today we would call Islamophobia, "was ethnicized – it was anti-Arab, really. And it was located, for the most part, the most blatant stuff, was in the entertainment industry." Indeed, Shaheen (2014) and others have described the repetitive use of demeaning "Arab" caricatures in American film and television. As a result, a large proportion of the early civil rights work of groups like MPAC and CAIR was dedicated to protesting Hollywood productions. Several advocates noted that the "old model" of advocacy resembled the work of Italian American organizations that protested stereotypical portrayals of organized crime figures and the like. This was seen as an effective approach in part because the advocates, like most in the communities they served, saw themselves as ethnically and religiously distinct from most native-born Whites, but not strictly speaking as racialized minority groups. This "old model" of approaching the issue of discrimination and stereotyping of Arab and Muslim Americans as "defamation" rather than racism, fit neatly into the colorblindness mold. It enabled these organizations to describe the problem without referring to race.

After the 1995 bombing of the federal building in Oklahoma City, while officials speculated that "Arabs" or "Mideasterners" were likely responsible for the attack, advocacy organizations were "at a weak stage," according to an ADC advocate active at the time (Interview February 2008). He felt that the crisis was an opportunity for the advocacy organizations, given the widespread, bigoted assumption of investigators and pundits, who were eventually proved wrong when two Christian, White, native-born Americans were found guilty of the massacre. "A crisis like [the Oklahoma City bombing] was a gold mine," he said, adding, "If [ADC] had responded affirmatively, it could have built itself eternally as part of the civil rights constituency in the country" (Interview February 2008). Instead, he lamented, the major organizations remained "weak" due to a variety of factors, including an inability to overcome ethnic and religious divisions.

These examples illustrate the trajectory away from unity among these advocacy organizations, despite a racialization process that collectivized their communities. This trend was firmly in place by the end of the 1990s, which partly explains why, in the months after 9/11, there was no immediate effort to build coalitions among Arab, Muslim, Sikh, and South Asian American organizations. Instead, these organizations, which were under tremendous strain in the aftermath of the terrorist attacks as reports of hate crimes and discrimination skyrocketed, relied mainly on the model they had developed over the previous few years. Moreover, there was no obvious reason, following the colorblindness view, to seek out a broad coalition, even with the racist nature of the post-9/11 "backlash" in hate crimes and discrimination.

Consider, for example, the lack of an effort toward such a broad coalition even after violent hate crimes targeting Sikhs, including the murder of Balbir Singh Sodhi. These attacks, which occurred with alarming frequency in 2001 and 2002, did not spur Arab and Muslim American organizations to build bridging organizations with Sikh and South Asian American organizations. Apart from some (important) joint efforts at condemning these attacks, and statements of support, the racist nature of even the most violent attacks like these did not result in any apparent support for bridging efforts. Compare this with the response to the murder in 1982 of Vincent Chin, a Chinese American man, in Michigan. An angry group murdered Mr. Chin because they believed he represented the "Japanese" destruction of the automotive industry in Detroit. The brutal murder led to renewed efforts by civil rights advocates from Chinese, Japanese, Filipino, Korean, and other Asian American organizations to forge panethnic ties (Espiritu and Omi 2000). This was a crucial moment in the recognition of the Asian American identity itself, along with the rise of Asian American political clout over the following decade. This kind of response was thought to be representative of the "post-Civil Rights era," but for Middle Eastern Americans after 9/11, this pattern did not hold.

Just as the immediate crisis over 9/11 began to fade, and civil rights advocacy organizations perhaps had a chance to gain some new traction in the struggle against Islamophobia, there was a concerted effort beginning around 2005 by New Right institutions to leverage the legacy of the 9/11 attacks to support neoconservative political goals like the Iraq War. One of the advocates I interviewed noted that the period immediately after 9/11 was relatively not as bad as what came years later:

The reputation of Islam right after 9/11 was on par with [the reputation of] Catholicism. . . . It wasn't 9/11 that caused a lot of Americans to be fearful and uneasy and have some intolerant views about Islam and Muslims. It's something else. It's a discourse, designed to do it.

(Interview September 2008a)

That discourse, explicitly Islamophobic, was apparent beginning in 2006. During that year, the neologism "Islamo-fascism" appeared all over mainstream American political rhetoric. That term was used in various efforts, like the desperate attempt to retroactively justify the 2003 invasion of Iraq as a stand for "freedom" and not a misguided mission to rid the Middle East of weapons of mass destruction. Islamophobic hysteria continued during the 2008 national election, as Senator Barack Obama faced widespread rumors that he was somehow a "secret Muslim" and part of a vast, nefarious conspiracy to infiltrate the American government. That such rumors spread so far and so wide is testament to the efficacy of the explicitly designed Islamophobic discourse described by this advocate. Because calling Obama "Muslim" was not, strictly speaking, racial, it still fit the pattern of colorblind New Right rhetoric perfectly. Then, in 2010, an unprecedented controversy about a proposed mosque building in lower Manhattan, then known as the Cordoba Center, portended yet more Islamophobic outbursts in the years to come. Concerns about "self-radicalized" Muslim Americans pervaded political discourse around counter-terrorism, even as the Obama Administration moved to drop the "War on Terror" terminology of its predecessor. Amidst all of these challenging developments, there were very few efforts at sustained coalition building among Arab, Muslim, Sikh, and South Asian American organizations.

Debates around racial identity became prominent in 2014, when talk of a racial awakening seemed premature at the ADC Annual Convention. A panel on "Arab American Identity in the 21st Century" featured several young Arab-American activists who gave contentious presentations about the need for "race-based activism" (American-Arab Anti-Discrimination Committee 2014; Interview November 2014). Scholars on the panel discussed the complexities of racial identity among Arab Americans. Many ADC members in attendance voiced opposition to accepting any singular racial identity, preferring various national, ethnic, and religious identity terms. One woman said she was "offended" at the idea that she was required to identify a certain way in order to participate in the political process, adding, "I'm not going to accept an identity just for the convenience of the political structure."

Meanwhile in 2014, AAI led the effort to place a Middle Eastern and North African (MENA) identity category on the 2020 Census, but specifically as an ethnic and not a racial category. After gathering more than two dozen Arab and Muslim American advocacy organizations into a coalition to press the Census Bureau for revisions to the ancestry question on the 2020 Census survey, the Census Bureau announced plans to conduct a National Content Test using the MENA category. Advocates promoting the MENA category told the Philadelphia Inquirer that the effort was specifically not about racial identity, but rather ethnic origin (Matza 2014). AAI Executive Director Maya Berry explained that Arab Americans are "a diverse constituency with a great deal of ethnic pride," adding that the "MENA category allows us to honor that and arrive at a better count" (quoted in Matza 2014). In an interview, a leading Arab American advocate told me that characterizing the MENA category as ethnic was intended in part to ensure participation of advocates who reject the very concept of racial classification (Interview December 2014). In addition, this non-racial tactic helps to circumvent regulations that make it difficult to change the racial categories listed on the Census questionnaire. Specifying MENA as an ethnic category on the Census would be possible without the approval of the Office of Management and Budget, which has oversight over the racial categories used on the Census form. The Census Bureau can independently make changes to ethnic categories, although final approval will require congressional support among other regulatory hurdles. Still, the Census Bureau can more easily make changes to ethnic – not racial – categories. The Arab American advocates leading this effort have attempted to use this situation to their advantage.

Elsewhere that same year, as #BlackLivesMatter protest events continued, a few prominent, young Muslim American leaders called for solidarity between Middle Eastern Americans and Black Americans as "people of color." For example, Linda Sarsour, then- Executive Director of the Arab American Association in New York City, traveled to Ferguson to participate in "Ferguson October" protests and to engage in workshops with Arab and South Asian American business owners. Sarsour spoke with *Colorlines* and expressed her opinion that Arab Americans must "build solidarity with people and communities who have been impacted for decades by police brutality, by racial profiling, by stop-and-frisk and by broken windows policing" (quoted in Hing 2014). She identified her goals as "integrating Arab-Americans and South Asian and Muslim communities within the larger work around combating racism in the US" (quoted in Hing 2014). Finally, she criticized the opinion that passing as White is effective, adding that when people say Muslim is not a racial identity, but a religious faith, she responds by arguing that:

> whether we like it or not, based on government policies, we've been racialized as a community. There are specific policies being implemented by the US government and some law-enforcement agencies on the federal and local level targeting people who are Muslim or perceived to be Muslim. So we have become a racialized community. Stop-and-frisk focuses on black and brown young people. Well, surveillance programs are focusing on Muslim communities in all of their diversity. And, I'd add that at least a quarter of our community is African-American Muslims. These people have to deal with issues that Black communities already have to deal with, plus the additional layer of anti-Muslim hate preventing them from doing things like going to mosque and dressing traditionally.
>
> (Quoted in Hing 2014)

Sarsour is a second-generation activist calling for racial solidarity. In this interview, she references a common counter-argument that she faces, that Muslim (like Arab) is not a racial identity, which therefore makes it impossible to join coalitions based on non-White, "people of color" status.

Broader impacts: the debate among Arab American advocates around race

The debates between activists who advocate for a strategy based on racial understanding and those who reject racial classification will in many ways determine the tactics of advocacy organizations seeking to confront Islamophobia in the decade ahead. On several occasions, younger, second-generation advocates working at organizations like CAIR expressed to me their desire to supplant their mainly first-generation Muslim American leaders. They felt that the "old guard" had too much trouble understanding the political and social concerns relevant to younger Americans. The debate over whether and how to use a broad racial identity in advocacy campaigns was one of the most contentious issues in these conversations. No consensus had emerged in the mid-2010s, despite the flurry of activity and discussion among advocates.

Given the dominance of the "colorblindness" paradigm in contemporary American racial politics, the stakes for this debate are even higher. Colorblindness presupposes that merely acknowledging race perpetuates racism. The solution to racism, in this view, is to ignore race entirely. Even keeping basic statistics on race, such as the number of people from different racial groups living in a particular city or attending a particular school, is considered a problematic application of race that serves only to perpetuate racism. The impact of colorblindness on civil rights advocacy represents a huge shift in American politics, and a significant rollback of the legal and political framework put into place by the 1950s- and 1960s-era Civil Rights Movement. The effects of this shift on civil rights advocacy are only now becoming apparent.

If Arab and Muslim American advocates effectively articulate a "colorblind" perspective, such that Arab American or even MENA identity is understood as ethnic and not racial, that might serve to extend the "colorblind" paradigm. John Tehranian (2008) notes that Arab, Iranian, Muslim, Sikh, and South Asian Americans have signed a "Faustian pact with Whiteness," wherein even a provisional White status is better than staking a claim as a member of a racialized minority group, because of rapidly weakening American legal protections for minority groups. Andrew Shryock (2008) agrees that the "status quo," with its ambiguous, officially White racial position, carries certain advantages for political clout, advantages that would be lost in a campaign using identity politics to make what he calls a "moral analogy."

The stakes of this debate, once again, are quite high. If Arab and Muslim American advocates effectively articulate a race-conscious perspective, such that a MENA identity is understood as racial, as part of a non-White, "people of color" status, then the dominance of the "colorblind" paradigm might be challenged significantly. Discrimination affecting Arab, Muslim, Sikh, and South Asian Americans remains among the most controversial and widespread in the United States in the 2010s. This is an era when war, torture and mass surveillance, racial profiling by police, and continued discrimination in workplaces have relied upon stereotypes of dangerous Arabs and an inherently violent Muslim culture. If this discrimination is seen specifically as racist – in addition to restricting religious freedom and suppressing ethnicity – then the idea of anti-racist civil rights advocacy might gain a new foothold in American politics and policy. Strategic decisions made by Arab American advocates and organizations like MPAC, CAIR, AAI, and ADC will have an important effect on these issues and on the social construction of race generally.

Advocacy coalitions and race

Anny Bakalian and Mehdi Bozorgmehr's extensive study of Middle Eastern and Muslim advocacy, *Backlash 9/11*, described a considerable amount of coalition work across ethnic and religious divides among Middle Eastern American advocates (2009: 199–211). They found that "the number of umbrella organizations among Middle Easterners has increased" in the years since 2001 (Bakalian and Bozorgmehr 2009: 202). They cite the creation of the National Network of Arab American Communities, its success in obtaining funding and support, and the expanded role of the Council of Arab American Organizations as evidence of the expanding role of coalitions across ethnic and religious dividing lines. Rights Working Group (RWG) was another of these formal coalitions that emerged in the years after 9/11. The "working group" contained more than 100 advocacy organizations, including ADC, AAI, MPAC, Muslim Advocates, Sikh Coalition, SAALT, and a number of local community organizations (RWG 2010). The campaigns initiated by RWG centered mostly on comprehensive immigration policy reform and against racial profiling, both areas of wide agreement for its member organizations.

RWG met with some success using a strategy that was straightforward and fit with a standard, mainstream Washington DC political advocacy model. RWG brought legitimacy by partnering with as many so-called grassroots advocacy organizations as it could sign up, but it asked for little in return other than the right to add the name of each organization to its growing list. In that way, RWG and similar "coalitions" were in fact independent organizations that imported a grassroots base through these weak "partnerships." The weak nature of the coalition did not contribute to the creation of panethnic ties like the strong bonds produced by bridging organizations among Asian Americans as described by Okamoto (2014). RWG's strategy did not meet with much success. Comprehensive immigration policy reform did not occur, and the organization lost most of its key staff by 2014. It dissolved altogether in 2016, less than ten years after it was founded (Rights Working Group Executive Committee 2016).

By contrast, a local advocacy coalition emerged in Chicago in 2008 which did appear to argue for inclusion of Middle Eastern Americans in "people of color" coalitions. The Illinois Coalition for Immigrant and Refugee Rights (ICIRR) undertook a remarkable electoral campaign, in an effort to increase voter turnout amongst immigrant communities in and around Chicago. Dubbed "New Americans Democracy Project," the effort reportedly registered more than 25,000 new immigrant voters, from "Latino, Asian, Middle Eastern" communities (Illinois Coalition for Immigrant and Refugee Rights 2008). In addition to get out the vote efforts, the New Americans Democracy Project also held training sessions for dozens of "immigrant electoral organizers" from around the country (ICIRR 2008).[1]

I spoke with organizers working with CAIR's Chicago branch and ICIRR, who told me that CAIR-Chicago decided to partner with ICIRR as part of what they called "Project Organize" (Interview June 2008a; Interview June 2008d). CAIR-Chicago initiated this program in 2006 to improve Muslim American voter turnout. The organizers noted that CAIR-Chicago immediately saw a need to connect with other immigrant communities in order to effectively coordinate any kind of political issue campaign. CAIR-Chicago partnered with ICIRR and had volunteers scrub through their lists of potential supporters looking for "Muslim names," and then they generated targets for door-knocking and phone banking (Interview June 2008d). This kind of targeted, grassroots outreach to Muslim Americans on the issue of immigration reform was the only one of its kind in the nation in 2008.

These two examples, the work of RWG and CAIR's partnership with ICIRR, illustrate the kind of coalition building that was characteristic in Muslim American advocacy between 2005 and 2015. Importantly, RWG and ICIRR both carefully maintain a non-racial rhetoric about their advocacy. Their mission statements, membership, and the documents produced in their work do not seek to leverage a common "people of color" or otherwise racialized identity in order to advance their cause. Instead, the only common identity connecting their supporters is immigrant status, which is often but not necessarily racialized. There is arguably no need to appeal to a "people of color" community for political work like this, especially when looking to broaden the base of supporters for immigration reform. But the reasons RWG and ICIRR choose not to use the rhetoric of the civil rights era is telling. Moreover, it seems that neither race nor religion (nor anything else) has been effectively utilized to form the basis of coalition building among Muslim American organizations.

While some advocates I spoke to indicated that there is some coordination amongst Muslim American advocacy organizations to create a pan-Muslim effort, the overwhelming evidence shows that there are serious and persistent divisions among Muslim American advocacy organizations. They are divided by ethnicity, by sect and theology, and by political priorities.

First, the largest ethnic split among Muslim Americans is undoubtedly the division between African American (or "indigenous") Muslims and Muslims in immigrant communities.[2] There are many reasons for this split, described most thoroughly by Sherman A. Jackson (2005: ch. 4). Stated simply, African American Muslims have a much different history than immigrant Muslims. The advocacy priorities of African American and immigrant Muslims do not always concur. CAIR and MPAC have relatively few staff or volunteers who are African-American

Muslims – they are perceived as organizations that serve the immigrant Muslim community first and foremost. One executive staffer at MPAC confirmed that outreach from MPAC to African American Muslim communities is not a priority: "A lot of our work is limited in terms of trying to keep up with everyone as much as we want" (Interview September 2008b). He expressed a desire to connect with African American Muslims but presented the lack of any effective outreach as a "capacity issue."

Second, there are at least two competing "umbrella" coalitions of Muslim Americans that are deeply divided by policy goals, advocacy strategy, and political philosophy. One such umbrella group is led by CAIR and another is led by MPAC. CAIR has, broadly speaking, conservative social priorities, and their advocacy strategy is typically centered on mosque-level grassroots organizing. MPAC, on the other hand, has a generally centrist political position that largely seeks to avoid controversy, and its advocacy strategy involves mostly direct lobbying with very little grassroots organizing capacity.

When I asked a prominent CAIR leader – a first-generation immigrant – how race affects the advocacy strategy of CAIR, I got a complex answer:

> The American Muslim community doesn't consider itself a unique racial group in America. For one reason. If you go to any mosque now, you'll see the diversity that America represents at that mosque. you'll see the Mexican Muslim, the Pakistani Muslim, the Anglo Muslim, the Latino Muslim, the African American Muslim, Chinese Muslim. You'll be sitting there and you'll see like what you see outside, but inside. Obviously, with a larger Arab and Pakistani ratio, but what I mean is: you don't see one race.
>
> (Interview December 2007)

I pointed out that Sikh Americans and Muslim Americans that look a particular way tend to face the most discrimination and hate crimes, and I suggested that this is because of racism. I then asked whether that fact influences CAIR's relationship with the Sikh American community. He replied: "I'm not sure I understand the question, to tell the truth" (Interview December 2007). The concept that Sikhs and Muslims could work together on civil rights advocacy had clearly not occurred to him before. This executive, and several others I spoke with at CAIR and MPAC, had no sense that joining with a racialized coalition for civil rights would make much sense for Muslim Americans.

Conclusion

In many ways, Muslim American advocates are encountering the same challenges that all advocates face when contending with the mysteries of race in America. There are contradictions, inconsistencies, and inadequacies generated by race and racism, and no advocacy strategy can effectively deal with all of these issues.

On the one hand, based on a very old pattern of racialization that began in premodern times and continues largely unbroken until the present, people from the "orient" – including but not limited to immigrant communities of Muslims, Arabs, Sikhs, and South Asians – have faced animosity and outright hostility in the West. On the other hand, for many reasons, it has thus far proved difficult effectively to aggregate this "group" in the United States along any axis where social scientists typically observe groups: class-based, cultural, religious, ethnic, racial, political ideology, or anything else.

Struggling against the American legacy of racism has led many Muslim American advocates, both as individuals and as collectivities, largely to eschew identifying themselves along racial lines. Instead, they insist both on their internal diversity and on their civil liberties. That this perfectly valid approach has no doubt contributed to the durability of Islamophobia is no small irony. American civil rights may require racialization, as is strongly indicated by the predicament facing all these communities. This situation has been only deepened by the national failure, thus far at least, to construct Middle Eastern Americans as a legally and socially protected group.

This process of decision-making, at the individual as well as collective level, where Muslim American advocates have chosen this path, was the subject of this research. The crucial conversations continue among advocates as they respond to racist and Islamophobic hate crimes. The strategic choices made by advocates, including many leading second-generation advocates seeking a more nuanced approach to the politics of racial identity, will continue to play a significant role in the formation of racial categories in the years ahead.

Acknowledgements

The author wishes to thank the National Science Foundation and the Richard Flacks Fund for the Study of Democratic Possibilities for supporting this research. The author accepts sole responsibility for the text, analysis, and discussion presented here, which do not reflect in any way upon these institutions.

Notes

1 In compliance with regulations, ICIRR did not coordinate its efforts with any particular candidate's campaign.
2 There are also ethnic splits within African American communities and within immigrant Muslim communities – too numerous to detail in this space.

References

Aidi, Hisham. 2014. *Rebel Music: Race, Empire, and the New Muslim Youth Culture*. New York: Pantheon.
Alsultany, Evelyn. 2012. *Arabs and Muslims in the Media: Race and Representation After 9/11*. New York: New York University Press.
American-Arab Anti-Discrimination Committee. 2014. "2014 ADC Convention Program." Available online at http://convention.adc.org/2014-adc-convention-program/ (accessed 31 March 2015).

Bakalian, Anny, and Mehdi Bozorgmehr. 2009. *Backlash 9/11: Middle Eastern and Muslim Americans Respond.* Berkeley, CA: University of California Press.

Beydoun, Khaled A. 2013. "Between Muslim and White: The Legal Construction of Arab-American Identity." *New York University Annual Survey of American Law* 69: 29–79.

Bonilla-Silva, Eduardo. 2006. *Racism without Racists: Color-Blind Racism and the Persistence of Racial Inequality in the United States.* Lanham, MD: Rowman & Littlefield.

Bozorgmehr, Mehdi, Paul Ong, and Sarah Tosh. 2016. "Panethnicity Revisited: Contested Group Boundaries in the Post-9/11 Era." *Ethnic and Racial Studies* 39(5): 727–745.

Espiritu, Yen Le. 1992. *Asian American Panethnicity.* Philadelphia, PA: Temple University Press.

Espiritu, Yen Le, and Michael Omi. 2000. "'Who Are You Calling Asian?': Shifting Identity Claims, Racial Classifications, and the Census." In *The State of Asian Pacific America: Transforming Race Relations,* edited by Paul M. Ong, pp. 43–101. Los Angeles: Leadership Education for Asian Pacifics, Asian Pacific American Public Policy Institute and University of California, Los Angeles Asian American Studies Center.

Gallup Center for Muslim Studies. 2009. *Muslim Americans: A National Portrait.* Washington, DC: Gallup.

Gallup Abu Dhabi Center. 2011. *Muslim Americans: Faith, Freedom, and the Future.* Washington, DC: Gallup.

Garner, Steve, and Saher Selod. 2014. "The Racialization of Muslims: Empirical Studies of Islamophobia." *Critical Sociology* 41(1): 9–19.

Hing, Julianne. 2014. "Facing Race Spotlight: Palestinian-American Activist Linda Sarsour." *Colorlines.* Available online at http://colorlines.com/archives/2014/10/facing_race_spotlight_linda_sarsour.html (accessed 31 March 2015).

Huntington, Samuel P. 1993. "The Clash of Civilizations?" *Foreign Affairs* 72(3): 22–49.

Illinois Coalition for Immigrant and Refugee Rights (ICIRR). 2008. "New Americans Vote: 2008 Results." Chicago: ICIRR. Available online at http://icirr.org/en/nadp (accessed 24 April 2010).

Illinois Coalition for Immigrant and Refugee Rights (ICIRR). 2010. "New Member Application." Chicago: ICIRR. Available online at http://icirr.org/sites/default/files/Revised New Member Application FY2011_NG.doc (accessed 24 April 2010).

Jackson, Sherman A. 2005. *Islam and the Blackamerican: Looking Toward the Third Resurrection.* New York: Oxford University Press.

Love, Erik. 2017. *Islamophobia and Racism in America.* New York: New York University Press.

Matza, Michael. 2014. "Report: More data would make 2020 Census more accurate." *Philadelphia Inquirer.* Available online at http://articles.philly.com/2014-12-16/news/57077009_1_census-officials-american-community-survey-origin (accessed 31 March 2015).

Meer, Nasar. 2013. "Racialization and Religion: Race, Culture and Difference in the Study of Antisemitism and Islamophobia." *Ethnic and Racial Studies* 36(3): 385–398.

Okamoto, Dina. 2014. *Redefining Race: Asian American Panethnicity and Shifting Ethnic Boundaries.* New York: Russell Sage Foundation.

Omi, Michael and Howard Winant. 2015. *Racial Formation in the United States.* 3rd ed. New York: Routledge.

Perlstein, Rick. 2014. *The Invisible Bridge: The Fall of Nixon and the Rise of Reagan.* New York: Simon & Schuster.

Pew Research Center. 2011. *Muslim Americans: No Signs of Growth in Alienation or Support for Extremism.* Washington, DC: Pew Research Center. Available online at www.people-press.org/2011/08/30/muslim-americans-no-signs-of-growth-in-alienation-or-support-for-extremism/ (accessed 31 March 2015).

Rana, Junaid. 2011. *Terrifying Muslims: Race and Labor in the South Asian Diaspora.* Durham, NC: Duke University Press.

Rights Working Group (RWG). 2010. "About RWG." Washington, DC: RWG. Available online at http://rightsworkinggroup.org/content/about-rwg (accessed 24 April 2010).

Rights Working Group Executive Committee. 2016. Email message to RWG Supporters mailing list. March 10.

Shaheen, Jack. 2014. *Reel Bad Arabs: How Hollywood Vilifies a People.* Revised and Updated Edition. Ithaca, NY: Olive Branch Press.

Shryock, Andrew. 2008. "The Moral Analogies of Race: Arab American identity, color politics, and the limits of racialized citizenship." In *Race and Arab Americans Before and After 9/11: From Invisible Citizens to Visible Subjects,* edited by Amaney Jamal and Nadine Naber, pp. 81–113. Syracuse, NY: Syracuse University Press.

Tehranian, John. 2008. *Whitewashed: America's Invisible Middle Eastern Minority.* New York: New York University Press.

Volpp, Leti. 2002. "The Citizen and the Terrorist." *University of California Los Angeles Law Review* 49: 1575–1599.

Werbner, Pnina. 2005. "Islamophobia: Incitement to Religious Hatred – Legislating for a New Fear?" *Anthropology Today* 21(1): 5–9.

Interviews

CAIR Staff Member. December 2007. In person. Audio recorded and transcribed.

ADC Staff Member. February 2008. In person. Audio recorded and transcribed.

CAIR Staff Member. June 2008a. By telephone. Audio recorded and transcribed.

RWG Staff Member. June 2008b. In person. Audio recorded and transcribed.

RWG Staff Member. June 2008c. In person. Audio recorded and transcribed.

ICIRR Staff Member. June 2008d. By telephone. Audio recorded and transcribed.

ADC Staff Member. September 2008a. In person. Audio recorded and transcribed.

MPAC Staff Member. September 2008b. By telephone. Audio recorded and transcribed.

MPAC Staff Member. January 2008. In person. Audio recorded and transcribed.

ADC Staff Member. June 2014. In person. Not audio recorded.

ADC Volunteer. November 2014. In person. Not audio recorded.

AAI Staff Member. December 2014. By telephone. Not audio recorded.

10 Second-generation Muslims and the making of British Shi'ism

Kathryn Spellman Poots

The central argument of this chapter is that belonging to a Twelver or *Ithna Asheri*[1] Shi'i Muslim community, in addition to the wider British Muslim minority and ethno-national diasporic groupings, has become a more salient identity for young Twelver Shi'is in recent years. The formation of Twelver Shi'i communal identity will be investigated in relation to identity politics of the wider British Muslim population, day-to-day life in Britain's secular society, and against the background of the gradual rise of sectarianism in the Middle East and South Asia. Simultaneously this chapter examines how Twelver Shi'i pan-religious identity is debated and informed by sources of religious authority (i.e., *marja*s) across a number of spatial and mediated transnational spaces. By focusing specifically on the transmission and transformation of quintessential Twelver Shi'i religious practice, the chapter aims to demonstrate how young British Twelver Shi'is are negotiating and reconfiguring local, national, and transnational authority structures, creatively forming a cross-ethnic Twelver Shi'i community, and striving to establish themselves as social/political actors in British society.

The results of the 2011 Census indicate that the general Muslim population in England and Wales has risen from 1.5 million to almost 3 million between 2001 and 2011.[2] This increases the proportion of Muslims from 2% of the total population to 5%, making Islam the most popular religion after Christianity. Furthermore, over half of the British Muslim population is under the age of 24. Based on the national-origin of the Muslim population, it is thought that 15% to 20% of the total Muslim population is from a Shi'i background, resulting in approximately 450,000 individuals in England and Wales. British Twelver Shi'i Muslims come from a wide range of backgrounds, including South Asian, East African, Iranian, Iraqi, Afghan, Lebanese, Indian, Bahraini, and Saudi Arabian as well as, among converts, Brritish. The majority of British Shi'i Muslims are Twelvers or *Ithna Asheri*s, the focus of this chapter.

The "British Muslim" category

While the majority of Shi'i Muslims are embedded in intra-ethnic relations, my research findings show that Twelvers, particularly the younger generations, are also building new institutional, performative, and mediated connections with

Twelver Shi'is from other ethno-national backgrounds. This is despite contestations and power struggles linked to regional differences, ethnicities, religious leadership, gender, and social class. Theoretically, in line with scholars such as Brubaker (2002), Hall (2003), Zubaida (2007) and Werbner (2002b), this chapter approaches the formation of a supranational collective identity, such as "British Shi'i" or the more general term "British Muslim Community," as fluid, and therefore not exclusive and unchangeable. As Brubaker (2002: 168) has argued, this "means taking as a basic analytical category not the 'group' as an entity, but groupness as a contextually fluctuating conceptual variable." The formation of "Shi'i Muslim" groupness, especially over generations, needs to be placed in the broader context of the wider British Muslim population and the development of the "British Muslim" category in post-WW II Britain. As with ethnic groups, social scientists have demonstrated analytical limitations in the conceptualization of pan-religious groupings. For example, the more generalized umbrella term "British Muslim community" has been criticized for masking other important social, cultural, economic, and political identifications (see Gilliat-Ray 2010; Zubaida 2007; Vertovec and Peach 1997). It glosses over the wide range of theological schools of thought, reformist movements, and religious practices within the British Muslim population, and conceals the many different ways people orient themselves to their faith or Muslim backgrounds. Whereas some British Muslims are conservatively pious, others have liberal orientations or feel indifferent to their religious background – and these outlooks might all be experienced during the course of one person's lifetime (Eade 1996; Gilliat-Ray 2010; Modood 2005; Spellman 2004). Furthermore, aggregating diverse Muslims into a "Muslim Community" overlooks the subsequent generations and how they might question or re-examine the religion they have inherited (Geaves 2007; Lewis 2007; Knott and Sadja 1993).

In addition to these factors, the social, economic, and political experiences of British Muslims are greatly influenced by a combination of overlapping factors in the migration and settlement process. To draw on the model developed by Alba and Waters (2011: 4), the character of the migration (ethnic proximity and cultural/religious familiarity with natives), the type of migration (labor, professional, entrepreneurial, or refugees/asylum seekers), the citizenship regime (i.e., citizenship rules and access to political and legal rights), the key institutions of the host society that immigrants and their children must pass through (i.e., the configuration of schools and labor market), and the varying experiences of growing up in local contexts within the receiving country are all important factors when considering incorporation across generations. The historic, often postcolonial, relations between the country of origin and Britain further continue to provide important conditions for navigating migration and settlement. Moreover, the transnational dimensions of the migration and diaspora experience must also be part of the analysis. For example, digital communication links and cheap travel enable immigrant groups and their progenies to maintain varying degrees of social, religious, economic, and political connections with homelands. Notwithstanding all of these diverse orientations, profiles, and experiences, there has been an increasing prioritization of "Muslim" self and group-identification among some immigrants and their children in the West (La Brooy 2008; Modood 2005; Saint-Blancat 2002). Studies have also shown increased antagonism toward Muslims in Britain, and reified and largely unfavorable stereotypes of "Islam" grafted on to immigrants and their children of Muslim extraction (Modood et al. 1997).

Asserting "Muslimness" and totalizing the "British Muslim community"

Prior to 9/11

The scholarly literature points to the following three shifts to explain the rising prominence of "Muslim" self- and group-identification in the post-Second World War UK. First, some immigrants from Muslim extractions joined together to make political demands for Islam and its exigencies (religious holidays, halal food, and so forth) to be officially acknowledged and recognized in British public life. This led to the emergence and mobilization of a "British Muslim community" – united as a single faith/cultural identity across Muslim sects – to counter racism and lobby for Muslim accommodation in a multicultural framework (see Modood 2005; Modood, Beishon, and Virdee 1994; Parekh 2004; Werbner 2002a).

The second shift, often referred to as a global "Muslim awakening," was understood to stem from different sources. These include: the 1978–1979 Iranian Revolution and its long-term ramifications; the effects of Saudi Arabian-backed international missions exporting *Salafi* teachings through mosques and schools; and relatedly, the rise of various other transnational Islamic social and political movements, such as the *Tablighi Jama'at*, *Hizb al-Tahrir*, or Muslim Brother-hood, responding mainly to failing nationalist and developmental projects in the Middle East and South Asia (see Eickelman and Piscatori 1996; Mandaville 2003; Zubaida 2011). These social and political trends, often conveyed with heightened religious practice and visibility of Islamic symbols, were and con-tinue to be expressed differently depending on varied interpretations of Islamic doctrine and practice. For instance, the increased public presence of religious dress, particularly the veil (*hijab*) for Muslim women, has become a paramount symbol of ideological difference and practice within and between Muslim and non-Muslim communities. The transnational concern about a number of "Mus-lim" issues, such as war and violence in Afghanistan, Palestine, and Bosnia, also became symbols of Muslim unity, and stimulated a shared perception that Muslims and Islam are under attack and have a need for defense (Eickelman and Piscatori 1996: 247).

The third shift was the reactionary "othering" and vilifying of Muslim prac-tices and principles, which started to surface in the 1980s primarily through some right-wing politicians, media channels, and popular discourses. The publication and reactions to Salman Rushdie's *Satanic Verses* in the late 1980s fuelled anti-Muslim sentiments and further objectified Muslims as outsiders, culturally different from "British culture." The Rushdie affair was additionally a turning point for many liberal and leftist intellectuals, historically anti-racist activists, who also began to question the compatibility of Western and Islamic principles. Perceptions that Muslims pose a threat to Western values – such as free speech, women's equality, and LGBT rights – continue to be at the heart of public debates and violent episodes.

Although not exhaustive, these three shifts provide a sense of the political and social environment that immigrants from all Muslim extractions have had to navigate and respond to in post-war Britain. The research that focused specifically on the second-generation immigrants found greater Muslim identity assertion as a response to families being dislocated from familiar cultural routines and institutions through the process of migration (Knott 1997; Jacobson 1998); a result of feeling marginalized and rejected by mainstream society (Ballard 1996; Berggren 2007); and a reaction to being "caught between" the customs of the first immigrant generation and the secular mores of mainstream British society. Instead of showing a linear pattern of "straight-line assimilation" for successive generations, these studies reveal how fluctuating local, national, and transnational conditions shaped and in turn are shaped by the migration and settlement experience. Indeed, in order to understand sub-religious formation, including internal differences within and between generations, we need to pay close attention to how people make sense of the changing world around them.

After 9/11 and the 7/7 bombings

The atrocities in the USA on 9/11 and the London 7/7 bombings greatly intensified the already complex social and political conditions for British Muslims. The dominant public discourses have reached new crisis levels in recent years with the threat of "homegrown" terrorists, the rise of the Islamic State in Iraq and Syria (ISIS), and deadly terrorist attacks on European soil in 2015 and 2016. The major political conflicts in the Middle East, the European refugee crisis, and the rise of anti-Western transnational jihadi networks have hardened positions on the "nature" of Islam and its compatibility with the West. What Islam is, and what being a Muslim implies, are at the very core of bitter academic and public debates on immigration and integration in Britain and Western Europe (Modood 2007; Zubaida 2007; Roy 2007; Kepel 2004). Concerns and hostilities about Muslims are so prominent in public discourse that it is no longer possible for Muslim immigrants and their offspring to escape the politics of Islam. Muslim "belonging," citizenship and identity have become "securitized" by policy makers and government initiatives such as the UK government's "anti-terrorism" strategies, known as PREVENT, CONTEST, and PET – Prevent Extremism Together. In turn, Muslim identity politics ensue in order to counter profiling, prejudice, and the rise of Islamophobia. As noted by Asma Mustafa (2015: 1):

> When people feel pressured, inspected, judged and targeted, it potentially breeds dissatisfaction, frustration, perceived inequality and double standards.

When it is asked why young second-, and third- and further-generation Muslims identify so strongly with their religion, it could be argued that their perceived alienation from being "British", "European" or "American" is pushing them further towards the only group identity they are familiar and comfortable with – their religious one.

It is for all of these reasons (pre- and post-9/11 and 7/7) that Muslim immigrants and their children have been compartmentalized into a politicized "category of analysis" (see Brubaker and Cooper 2000) and studied top–down, "from the perspective of the social engineers of integration and national security" (Sunier 2012: 193).

As a result, there is a research lacuna on the diversity of Muslim practices and outlooks *within* the British Muslim population and how they are intricately shaped by the historical, social, and political contexts in which they were/are formed. While scholarly studies have set out to "rebalance current discourse by focusing on issues that are perhaps much closer to the 'ordinary' daily lives of British Muslims" (Gilliat-Ray 2010), very little research has taken a bottom–up approach to the study of sub-religious community formation. As stated by Sunier (2012: 189):

The narrowing down of research foci in the field of Islam in Europe has caused a serious academic neglect particularly where it concerns the entanglement of Islamic practices with everyday life, the religious engagements, expressions and experiences among young people, and the transformation and reconfiguration of Islamic authority.

By focusing on ways that Islam is experienced by Shia youth in the UK, this chapter reveals the emergence of a new form of community, which is distinct from Sunnis and other Muslim groupings in the UK. But what are the social and political dynamics that have led to the formation of a Twelver British Shi'i communal identity? How have immigrants and their children from various Twelver Shi'i backgrounds responded to the shifting social and political conditions? What marks a British Twelver Shi'i communal identity? Who decides? By focusing on how Twelver Shi'i Muslims create their religious environment, we can gain a more precise understanding of practices and discourses within and between British Muslim communities. Moreover, this development demonstrates that "Islam" cannot be taken as a normative or fixed ideology that can be attached to a totalized "Muslim Community."

The making of British Twelver Shi'ism

The first sizable numbers of Twelver Shi'i immigrants in the UK were men from South Asia, eventually joined by their families, who came as guest laborers following World War II. During the 1970s and 1980s, revolution, sanctions, and wars in Iran, Afghanistan, and Iraq brought a substantial number of

Twelver Shi'is, followed by the *Khojas*,[3] who left East Africa due to the political turmoil in the newly independent countries. Other Twelver Shi'i Muslims include those from Lebanon, Bahrain, Saudi Arabia, and Kuwait as well as British converts.

As has become clear from similar research on Sunni British Muslims, religious life among the first-generation immigrants mainly took place privately in homes with devotees from similar regional, socioeconomic, and linguistic backgrounds. Informal gatherings in homes (particularly women-only ritual gatherings) have continued to be active among these networks and are often linked to social networks in their respective diaspora and country of descent. Important dates on the religious calendar (such as religious programs during the months of Moharram and Ramadan) are also commemorated by both men and women in mosques and community centers.

An increasing number of Twelver Shi'i centers – as opposed to centers that catered to both Sunni Muslims and Shi'i Muslims – started to develop in the late 1970s and 1980s. By the 1990s London was the primary destination for Shi'i religious leaders, institutions and communities in Europe and the West at large. It continues to be the international headquarter for the diverse and highly competitive global Shi'i networks. Some Shi'as, for example, follow Ayatollah Khamenei, the Iranian supreme leader and the doctrine of *Valayet-e faqih*.[4] They would be more inclined to attend gatherings and events at religious organizations such as the Islamic Centre of England (*Markaz-e Islmai-ye Englis*) and the Islamic Student Association (*Kanoon Towhid*) that are supported by the Iranian government. The Islamic Universal Association (*Majmah Eslami)*, supported by the Iranian-based Ayatollah Golpayegani, is financially independent from the Iranian government. It mainly attracts devout Iranian Shi'as who wish to stay clear of Iranian politics. Other British Shi'i, who do not endorse the doctrine of *Valayet-e faqih*, follow *marja*s such as the late Ayatollah Khoie (d. 1992), Ayatollah Sistani or (the late) Ayatollah Fadlallah (d. 2011), attend the religious programmes at the Shi'a centers such as the Khojas' World Federation of KSIMC (Khoja Shi Ithna-Asheri Muslim Communties), The Khoei Foundation, Dar al-Islam and the Imam Ali Foundation.

In addition to the building of mosques and community centres that catered to Twelver Shi'i theology and ritual practices, the strengthening of a Shi'i identity was also influenced by external forces such as the long-term effects of the Iranian revolution, the fall of Saddam Hussein in 2003, and the conflict between Hezbollah and Israel in 2006. Furthermore, the Wahhabi/Salafi anti-Shi'i campaigns in locations around the world, including the widespread diffusion of divisive Salafi teachings in British mosques, Islamic organizations and websites (Cesari 2013: 132–135), have provoked intra-community tensions and the sharpening of communal lines between Shi'i and Salafi-oriented Sunni groupings. The rise of sectarianism in the Middle East and South Asia, particularly in recent years with ISIS' anti-Shi'i propaganda and violence, has further pitted jihadi Salafis against "moderate" Shi'is. Indeed, the fear of home-grown terrorism and increasing securitization of Islam in Europe has prompted British

Shi'is to position themselves as the "good" Muslims and citizens who are also targeted by the "evil" de-territorialized terrorists.

Research methods

The British Twelver Shi'i population has been subject to very few studies in the UK.[5] My research has been based on a combination of structured interviews, focus groups, Internet-based analysis, and foremost ethnography. The ethnography has entailed spending time with networks of men and women, across generations that associate themselves with Twelver Shi'i communities in London, Manchester, Birmingham, Leicester, and Glasgow. I have spoken to over 200 men and women around the county who are mostly (but not entirely) middle class. I have spent the most time with 18–30-year-olds – both male and female – who are university students or employed in a range of occupations such as doctors, pharmacists, optometrists, computer engineers, accountants, academics, solicitors, and shopkeepers as well as in jobs in catering and retail. Some people described being employed in temporary jobs while actively looking for permanent positions.

My research, carried out largely between the years 2013 and 2016, included attending a number of religious rituals and events as well as spending time with people in their homes, cafés, student unions, and shopping malls. These individuals, who I met through chain-referral sampling, were from various diasporic groupings and different social networks within each diaspora. This wide sample allowed methodological insight as to how religious precepts and practice informs and is informed by other aspects of daily life. I conducted structured interviews with a number of Twelver Shi'i Muslim clerics and community leaders affiliated with the central Twelver Shi'i organizations. I also interviewed a number of controversial young orators and public figures who are hugely popular in these networks. It is important to stress that this research has focused on people who see their Twelver Shi'i Muslim communal identity as being important. Even though they might dip in and out of the various networks of activities – on or offline – they actively identify with Shi'ism.

To date, my research has found that the vast majority of the respondents are effectively holding multiple local, national, and transnational allegiances *and* feeling integrated into their local environments in Britain. There is, however, growing suspicion of the British government's policy shift from the "multicultural model," described as inclusive and accommodating of cultural and religious practice, to the doctrine of "community cohesion," deemed *de facto* as an assimilationist model. The doctrine, which stems from the government-commissioned Ritchie and Cantle Report, blamed the riots in the north of England in 2001 and other community tensions on the growth of isolated "self-segregated" communities around the country (Cantle 2008). My interlocutors are also critical of isolated Muslim or ethnic communities, particularly some Salafis, who maintain a separate stance to Western public institutions and lifestyles. They are also fearful of the influence of global jihadi networks and the threat of "homegrown" terrorists. But the majority of Muslims, they argue, are British (or Londoners, Mancunians,

Glaswegians, and so forth) and "Muslim" at the same time. I was repeatedly told that Britain has dealt with cultural diversity better than other European countries, most notably France. Mona, age 27, stated:

> I can be myself here. We have access to academic and political institutions and we've started to have more political representation. Like Mehdi Hassan and Hayder al-Khoie. Although I was the only *hejabi* in the office, I volunteered for both Tony Blair's and Ed Milliband's campaign. There's much greater communication between Muslim organizations and government institutions. But there needs to be more trust and interaction between people – and much better media coverage. Especially in today's hostile environment.

Although my respondents often report feeling misrepresented and negatively depicted by the British media and public discourses, they mostly feel at home in the UK and have no plans to emigrate or move permanently to their countries of origin. This research concurs with a BBC poll of 1,000 Muslims (presumably both Sunni and Shi'i) carried out in 2015 that found 95% of British Muslims feel loyalty to the country.[6] The same poll found that almost half (46%) feel that being a Muslim in Britain is difficult due to prejudice against Islam. In the wake of the rise of ISIS, the referendum in June 2016 to leave to European Union, and the latest terrorist attacks on Western soil, my respondents have reported feeling more conscious of negative public perceptions of Islam; they have noted an increase in prejudicial acts against Islam (particularly verbal abuse against women wearing *hijab*); and they have voiced serious concerns about increasing discrimination against Muslim populations at large. As such, there is added pressure to maintain a sense of coherency between their religious practices and national identities.

Transmission and transformation of Twelver Shi'i practices in Britain

Although there are different interpretations and performative ways to carry out Twelver Shi'i practices (depending on local customs, nation-state particularities, and *maraja*'s rulings), my research has shown increasing communication, coordination, and uniformity among the Twelver Shi'i centers and their respective leaders, especially with regard to marriage and funeral rituals, divorce proceedings, and honoring important days on the religious calendar (see Spellman-Poots and Zubaida 2013). Alliances between the Twelver Shi'i centers have also formed in response to British Muslim identity politics and leadership in the UK. Feeling dominated and marginalized by Sunni groupings, Twelver Shi'i religious and community leaders have made efforts to build a wider platform to represent their interests to the British government, the wider Muslim umbrella organizations, NGOs, and the media.

The younger generations regularly critique and challenge the religious/cultural centers and religious practices of the older generations. Similar to the second-generation Sunni Muslims, the religious life of the older generations is perceived by the second generation as antiquated, inauthentic, or imbued with language, customs, and politics from the home country. Unlike Sunni Muslims, however, Twelver Shi'is are expected to adhere to the transnational institution of the *marja'iyya*. All Twelver Shi'is are expected to select a top religious cleric or *marja al-taqulid* (source of emulation) to follow and emulate in daily life. The prominent *marja*s and their rulings are rigorously compared and contrasted. The most influential *marja*s in the UK and around the world are: Seyed Ali as-Sistani, Seyed Ali Khameneh'i, the late Seyed Abu al-Qasim al-Khu'i, the late Seyed Mohammed Husayn Fadlallah, Seyed Sadiq Al- Shirazi, Ayatollah Naser Makarim Shirazi, and Ayatollah Saafi Golpayegani. Many of these leaders have international headquarters in London and/or have representatives in the UK as well as interactive websites for adherents to query jurisprudential rulings on religious matters. In addition to the obligatory *zakat* (2.5% of assets) that all Muslims are expected to pay annually, Twelver Shi'is are expected to pay *khum*s (usually one-fifth of one's wealth) to their choice of *marja*. It is common practice for the *marja*s to give a portion of the money to the local representatives to spend on charitable and scholarly activities in the UK.

The intersection between the competing religious rulings and political ideologies of the *marja*s must also be examined in relation to other sources of power and influence from within and external to the Twelver Shi'i Muslim population. Internally, for example, they must navigate the politics of local Shi'i religious leaders and the different and at times conflicting ethnic/diasporic traditions and customs. Externally, as highlighted earlier, they must traverse the sectarian politics and violence in the Middle East and South Asia as well as anti-Shi'i sentiment stemming from Salafism and Islamist groupings, which spill over into heated debates in university common rooms, city streets, and online battles. Indeed, hate preachers – although shunned by the vast majority of British Muslims – have tried to nurture mistrust and further politicize communal boundaries between Sunnis and Shi'is in the UK and around the globe. Finally, an additional layer of navigation is the widespread and increasingly volatile public discourse about Islam and Muslims in the West.

The combination of these various forces is shaping and reshaping what it means to be a Twelver Shi'i in the UK, both socially and experientially. Let us now turn to some ethnographic material to see how young British Twelver Shi'is strive to make sense of and legitimize their religious subjectivities – in light of these forces and in relation to their day-to-day lives in British society.

Moharram ritual performances in the United Kingdom

The significance of Imam Hussain and the Battle of Karbala for Twelver Shi'is is well known.[7] Although Ashura commemorations vary among British Shi'is, the Karbala paradigm, particularly the martyrdom of Hussain, plays a key role in ritual performances, symbolism, and identity construction. Indeed, the legend of Imam Hussain enormously inspires and unifies the younger generations. While it is often associated with the ritualized self-flagellation of one's body in sorrow, bloodletting is greatly controversial among Twelver Shi'i leaders and the global Shi'i community at large. While several *marja*s like Sistani have discouraged the ritual performance, or barred it, like Fadlallah and Khamenei, others, like Shirazi, defend the ritual and locate it at the core of Shi'ism. Although self-flagellation is not practiced by the majority of British Twelver Shi'is, it is a topic of heated debate among its youth. This is partly due to the critical coverage that bloodletting rituals have received among segments of the Sunni population as well as in the British mainstream press.[8] Although the practice has been assessed by Twelver Shi'is and non-Shi'is – in relation to Sunni Muslim discourses, British law, and human rights discourses – it has been important for Shi'is of all ages to critically evaluate and debate the legitimacy of the ritual in relation to the precepts of Shi'i Muslim doctrine.

There has also been a long history of Shi'i Muslims using the Karbala paradigm as a metaphor for the present day and to rework the historical events to suit the personal, social, and political tasks at hand. A rich body of historical, anthropological, and sociological work has focused on the utilization of aesthetic devices and performative rituals to commemorate the tragic events at Karbala, which include not only self-flagellation but narrations and theatrical re-enactments of the Karbala story (*ta'ziyeh*), and women-only gatherings and ritual dinners (*sofrehs*).[9] Such work has demonstrated the various and changing forms and meanings of these religious performances across time and place, and in relation to gender, class, and religious sect.

Building on this scholarship, my research has located two central ways that young Shi'is are renewing or reworking Moharram rituals in the UK. First, by maintaining the form and aesthetics of the ritual, such as the ritualized street procession, but modifying the symbolic meaning to cohere to the present social and political conditions in the UK. Second, by challenging or rebuffing such customs as irrelevant and antiquated, and actively creating alternative ways to commemorate Imam Hussain. I will spend less time on the first point as I have published elsewhere about the transformation of the Ashura street procession in London's Hyde Park (Spellman-Poots 2012). There I argued that the Ashura procession executed by the older generations was an inward-looking communal religious experience that aimed to replicate the customary practices and aesthetics of "back home." The younger generation, while maintaining the ritualized form of the street procession, has made it more inclusive to Twelver Shi'i Muslims from all ethno-national backgrounds and more outward facing to reach wider British publics. In recent years, the Ashura procession in Hyde Park, for example, has brought together approximately 5,000 Shi'is of all ages from London and around the UK. In addition to Persian, Arabic, and Urdu, the banners and elegies to honor the Imam Hussain and his family have been written and spoken in the English language. Groups of youth have used the procession as a platform to promote a range of social, religious, or political messages. They have handed out English-language pamphlets with modern interpretations of Hussain's martyrdom to the press (both British mainstream and diasporic press) and to onlookers who happened to be in Hyde Park at the time of the procession.

Some student organizations, as often done in the past, have used the occasion as a metaphor for political injustices in the Middle East and South Asia. Since 2015, with the rise of ISIS and increased securitization of "Islam," many carried anti-*Daesh* (ISIS) banners in English while chanting damning slogans against ISIS in Syria and Iraq. Moreover, the procession was used as a space to position themselves as "good" Muslims and not the feared enemy, with participants holding banners that read "No to Terrorism," "No to Injustice, No to Racism," "Muslims United Against Terrorism," and women holding signs stating "We Are Equal to Men."

Others, however, argue that Ashura should not be politicized, but instead be a time for self-reflection, for personal purification, and to renew one's faith. They present Imam Hussain as a universal model for equality and peace and compare him to Jesus, Gandhi, and other iconic figures of peace. They complain that Ashura is notorious for self-harm and grief, portrayed by some Sunni groupings and the media as a violent and barbaric ritual. They talk enthusiastically about making the universal lessons of the Battle of Karbala known to the wider British public. Other groups, however, are critical of these approaches, and make the argument that the march has been hijacked by political and social-awareness agendas. They note that Ashura should be a day devoted to experiencing Hussain's suffering and not public relations. They defend bloodletting in private Muharram ceremonies as an integral part of the Shi'i faith.

The ethnographic vignettes reveal the internal conflicts and struggles about the meaning and enactment of Ashura commemorations. The organization, inclusivity, and openness of the event itself also demonstrate the efforts made to develop a wider sense of Shi'ism, not only to other Twelver Shi'i Muslims, but also more broadly to the British and other publics. There are parallels to Pnina Werbner's ethnographic research in early 2000 on how Sunni Muslims in Manchester negotiate the boundaries of minority citizenship by creatively using appropriate public spaces. She examines how this process, which has usually been peaceful, has been shaped and reshaped by events from the Rushdie affair to the Gulf War to the post-September 11th crisis (Werbner 2002b: 16).

Following Ashura, it is customary for devoted Twelver Shi'is to carry out street processions to mark the fortieth day after Imam Hussain's death. Since the fall of Saddam Hussain, and despite security issues, a reported 20 million Twelver Shi'is attend the Arbaeen procession in Iraq each year. This religious, social, and political event has become a new rite of passage for young Twelver Shi'is in the UK and around the world. As millions of pilgrims walk from Najaf to Karbala (70km), they are provided with food, tents, and even massages throughout the five days, in what many describe as a carnivalesque atmosphere. It has become a media event, with all the major Twelver Shi'i and other TV stations broadcasting the spectacle around the world. Pilgrimage tours are organized by the growing number of popular English-speaking religious leaders who are linked to Twelver Shi'i tour agencies around the UK. The Arbaeen pilgrimage is another example of a long-standing ritual that has been transformed and renewed under new social and political circumstances. It has become an important religious and social space for young British Twelver Shi'is, across ethnic and national lines, to also feel a part of a wider global Twelver Shi'i community.

New ways to commemorate Moharram

As noted earlier, young Twelver Shi'is have also been actively finding new or alternative ways of commemorating Ashura and other important dates on the Shi'i religious calendar. For example, due to the negative images of Ashura conveyed to wider publics, the Islamic Unity Society pioneered a program called the Imam Hussain Blood Donation Campaign.[10] The organizers, "as a method of giving for the sake of all humanity," set out to encourage British Muslims to donate blood to benefit others *and* honor the memory of Imam Hussain. Every Ashura the Society, in collaboration with the British National Blood Service, sets up blood-donation centers in Glasgow, Bradford, Leeds, Liverpool, Manchester, Birmingham, and several locations in London. According to Fatima, a University student in Manchester and an Islamic Unity member, "Giving blood on Ashura has provided a positive and active way, equally for men and women, to commemorate Hussein and the battle of Karbala." While some young Twelver Shi'is think donating blood is a "bourgeois" practice, and not a replacement for bloodletting, it shows how Ashura continues to adapt and evolve in British society.

Another important campaign, "Who is Hussain?", was first launched by Twelver Shi'i youth in London in November 2012. Inspired by the Arab uprisings, this grassroots initiative was spearheaded by a group of young British Twelver Shi'is aiming to promote social justice and the rights of others, using the example of the martyrdom of Imam Hussain and his heroism during the Battle of Karbala. Determined to remain anonymous and independent from any one Muslim organization, they raised enough seed money from private donors, and eventually a number of Twelver Shi'i centers, to launch the campaign. It quickly spread around the UK and to locations around the world. They designed a number of aesthetically pleasing posters, with questions such as "Have you got what it takes?", to provoke people to carry out good deeds or actions. They also referred to wider social movements, human rights discourses, and notable leaders such as Martin Luther King Jr., Mahatma Ghandi, and Mohammed Bouazizi (the Tunisian street vendor whose self-immolation inspired the Tunisian Revolution and the Arab Spring uprisings). The messages were disseminated through press releases, campaign posters in dozens of London's tube stations and bus routes, and well-designed social networking sites. The publicity prompted Twelver Shi'is around the UK, North and South America, East Africa, and the Far East to animate their locales with the posters and distribute water bottles with "Who is Hussain?" labels in public spaces. Although its impact is hard to measure, the "Who is Hussain?" campaign demonstrates novel ways in which young British Twelver Shi'is are striving to be recognized as social actors in British society.

There is a long list of other examples of Moharram events that have gained currency among young Twelver Shi'i Muslims across ethnic divides. These occasions – which are English speaking, cross ethnic lines, and mix genders – include lecture series, black-tie dinners in five-star hotel banquet rooms, knowledge-raising and fundraising events in student unions and other public spaces, and simultaneous "academic" conferences such as the Imam Hussain conference in London and Dearborn, Michigan. Concurrently, there has been an emergence of a British and transnational Twelver Shi'i industry, which encompasses Twelver Shi'i TV stations and press; NGOs and charitable organizations; Twelver Shi'i poets, artists, and filmmakers; and entrepreneurs who sell Twelver cultural products to the Twelver Shi'i market.

This industry is fuelled by the hugely popular young thought leaders and speakers, such as Sayed Ammar Nakshawani, Sayed Ali Abbas Razawi, Sayed Mohammed Al-Hilli, and Sayed Mahdi Modaressi. Although the legitimacy and credibility of these community leaders are questioned by traditional clerics, they are in great demand at Twelver Shi'i programs in the UK and around the world. Unlike the older generations, they engage with pressing social, religious, and political contemporary issues. For example, they discuss the tensions surrounding Sunni–Shi'i relations, highlight the dangers of online hate preachers, and engage with questions surrounding citizenship, secularization, and integration in British society. Their lectures, which are uploaded on YouTube and circulated widely, include: "The characteristics of the model Muslim citizen;" "Does Ashura have any bearing to the lives of youth today?"; "Hijab as taught by Muhammad (*pbuh*) reflected in Karbala and role today;" and "Can a seventh century man be a role model in the twenty-first century?"

All of these draw from Islamic sources and lessons from Karbala in order to support and encourage the fashioning of a moral, ethical self in the West. Significantly, it is at these events that Twelver Shi'is from across ethnic divides discuss, compare, and debate these points and many others, such as being Muslim in a Western secular society, Islamophobia, sectarian and ideological tensions, dress and *hijab*, dietary prohibitions and ritual differences, family life, and so forth. These discussions are used to evaluate different *marja*s' rulings, their parents' religious traditions and practices, and normative British and Western values. They can also be used as bargaining chips or negotiation tools for navigating micropolitics at home. Examples include: arranged vs. love marriages; the style of one's wedding – with or without music; funeral and burial customs – whether women can attend a burial; how Twelver Shi'i rituals such as Ashura and temporary marriage are carried out. These are but a few examples of practices that vary among Twelver Shi'is.

Conclusion

Many second-generation UK Shi'i Muslims, including those who are doing well at university or are employed in good jobs, are struggling to find a sense of coherency between their religious subjectivities, family and intradiasporic tensions, rising Shi'i–Sunni (mainly Salafi) tensions, and increasing anti-Muslim sentiment in the West. In distancing themselves from Salafi-styled separatism, young Shi'i leaders promote social and political participation in the UK and search out appropriate platforms from which to speak out against social ills in the UK and beyond. As second- and even third-generation immigrants, many with strong links to their country of descent – and increasingly to Shi'i sacred sites in the Middle East – they also acknowledge the challenges of these networks that stretch across nation-state borders. By looking at the experiential and discursive dimensions of Shi'i religious performances, I have tried to capture the creative ways in which the younger generations are articulating a new sense of belonging, both in the UK and to a wider global Shi'i community. Instead of being relegated to the social margins, they have been finding ways to be politically and socially active and relevant. Rather than evaluating such practices simply as integration issues, they should be viewed as important insights into the building of local and transnational community among Twelver Shi'i Muslims, who simultaneously have a multiplicity of other attachments and identities.

The ethnography of manifestations of Moharram rituals, which included renewal of past practices or legitimization of new ones, has enabled us to see how young British Shi'is are engaging with and critiquing the overlapping and shifting conditions they have to navigate in British society. Among these conditions are the wider identity politics of the "British Muslim community," as well as family and religious relations, and intra-diasporic relations with non-Shi'i Iraqis, Iranians, Pakistanis, and so forth – all of which are actively tied to social and political dynamics back in their countries of origin. By questioning and negotiating their parents' religious traditions and practices, young Shi'is are gaining the confidence to question ethno-national characteristics and expectations of the older generations while in turn building a Twelver Shi'i communal identification and platform across ethnic divides. So, while mindful of the volatile political and social environment over the past three decades and the trend to totalize a British Muslim Community, this chapter has shed light on complex religious and social transformations among the Twelver Shi'i British Muslim population and the varying ways in which they have responded to the politics that surrounds them.

Notes

1 The term *Ithna Asheri*, or Twelvers, refers to the belief in twelve divine leaders or Imams. The twelfth Imam, *Mahdi*, is believed to be in occultation but will one day return to establish a just society.
2 The Census information cited in this section is taken from Office for National Statistics, 2011 Census: aggregate data (England and Wales) [computer file], and National Records of Scotland, 2011 Census: aggregate data (Scotland) [computer file]. Available online at www.nationalarchives.gov.uk/doc/open-government-licence/version/2
3 Deriving from the Persian word *Kh'aja* meaning lord and master, the term *Khoja* is used to describe Shi'i Muslims who originate from Gujarat in India. Within Twelver Shi'i communities, *Khoja* is a term used more specifically to describe people who dissented from Aga Khan and the Shi'i Imami Ismaili community in a dispute in the 1860s in India. In turn, they declared themselves as Twelver Shi'i Muslims in line with the Shi'i religious establishment in Iran and Iraq.

4 The Guardianship of the jurist, or *Valayat-e Faqih*, is a concept that empowers religious scholars with the exclusive right to interpret Islamic law. It was first applied as a form of government when Ayatollah Khomeini came to power in 1979.

5 As pointed out by Gilliat-Ray, "Shias in Britain are under-researched, and as yet there has been no systematic study of this diverse community" (2010: 61).

6 See www.comres.co.uk/polls/bbc-radio-4-today-muslim-poll/ (retrieved March 29, 2015).

7 Shi'i Muslims place great significance on the historical Battle of Karbala in 680, where Imam Hussain (the grandson of the Prophet Muhammad), along with seventy-two of his family members and supporters, was killed by the troops of the second Umayyad caliph, Yezid.

8 Reports and images of the bloody activity have made their way to the British mainstream press, especially during the high-profile child cruelty case that took place in the Manchester Crown Court in 2008. A man, aged 44, was convicted of child cruelty for encouraging his two sons, aged 13 and 15, to self-flagellate until their backs bled during an Ashura ceremony at an Islamic center in Manchester.

9 See Abrahamian (1993); Mottahedeh (1986); Keddie (1983).

10 Note that donating blood during the month of Moharram is widely practiced in Twelver Shi'i communities around the world.

References

Abrahamian, Ervand. 1993. *Khomeinism – Essays on the Islamic Republic*. London and New York: I. B. Tauris.

Abu Lughod, Lila. 1991. "Writing Against Culture." In *Recapturing Anthropology: Working in the Present*, edited by Richard G. Fox, pp. 137–162. Santa Fe, NM: School of American Research Press.

Alba, Richard, and Mary Waters (eds.). 2011. *The Next Generation: Immigrant Youth in a Comparative Perspective*. New York: New York University Press.

Ballard, Roger. 1996. "Islam and the Construction of Europe." In *Muslims in the Margin: Politcal Responses to the Presence of Islam in Western Europe,* edited by Wasif Shadid and Pieter Sjoerd Van Koningsveld, pp. 15–51. Kampen: Kok Pharos Publishers.

Berggren, Jason. 2007. "More than the Ummah: Religious and National Identity in the Muslim World." *The American Journal of Islamic Social Sciences* 24(2): 71–93.

Brubaker, Rogers. 2002. "Ethnicity without Groups." *Archives Européennes de Sociologie* 43(2): 163–189.

Brubaker, Rogers. 2005. "The 'diaspora' diaspora." *Ethnic and Racial Studies* 28(1): 1–19.

Brubaker, Rogers, and Frederick Cooper. 2000. "Beyond Identity." *Theory and Society* 29(1): 1–47.

Cantle, Ted. 2008. *Community Cohesion: A New Framework for Race and Diversity*. Basingstoke, UK: Palgrave Macmillan.

Cesari, Jocelyne. 2013. *Why the West Fears Islam: An Exploration of Muslims in Liberal Democracies*. Basingstoke, UK: Palgrave Macmillan.

Eade, John. 1996. "Nationalism, Community, and the Islamization of Space in London." In *Making Muslim Space in North America and Europe*, edited by Barbara Metcalf, pp. 217–233. Berkeley, CA: University of California Press.

Eickelman, Dale, and James Piscatori. 1996. *Muslim Politics*. Princeton, NJ: Princeton University Press.

Geaves, Robert. 2007. "A Reassessment of Identity Strategies amongst South Asian British Muslims." In *Religious Reconstruction in the South Asian Diasporas: From*

One Generation to Another, edited by John R. Hinnells, pp. 13–28. Basingstoke, UK: Palgrave Macmillan.

Gilliat-Ray, Sophie. 2010. *Muslims in Britain*. Cambridge: Cambridge University Press.

Hall, Stuart. 2003. "Cultural Identity and Diaspora." In *Theorising Diaspora: A Reader*, edited by Jana Evans Braziel and Anita Mannur, pp. 233–246. Oxford: Blackwell.

Jacobson, Jessica. 1998. *Islam in Transition: Religion and Identity among British Pakistani Youth*. London and New York: Routledge.

Keddie, Nikkie (ed.). 1983. *Religion and Politics in Iran: Shi'ism from Quietism to Revolution*. New Haven, CT: Yale University Press.

Kepel, Gilles. 2004. *The War for Muslim Minds: Islam and the West*. Cambridge, MA, and London: Harvard University Press, Belknap Press.

Knott, Kim. 1997. "The Religion of South Asian Communities in Britain." In *A New Handbook of Living Religions*, edited by John Hinnells, pp. 756–774. Oxford: Blackwell.

Knott, Kim, and Khokher Sadja. 1993. "Religious and Ethnic Identity among Young Muslim Women in Bradford." *New Community* 19: 593–610.

La Brooy, Camille. 2008. "To Essentialise or De-essentialise: That is the Question." University of Melbourne. Available online at www.tasa.org.au/wp.../uploads/2008/12/La-Brooy-Camille.pdf (accessed September 30, 2016).

Lewis, Philip. 2007. *Young, British and Muslim*. London: Continuum.

Mandaville, Peter. 2003. *Transnational Muslim Politics: Reimagining the Umma*. London: Routledge.

Modood, Tariq. 2005. *Multicultural Politics: Racism, Ethnicity and Muslims in Britain*. Edinburgh: Edinburgh University Press.

Modood, Tariq. 2007. *Multiculturalism: A Civic Idea*. Cambridge: Polity Press.

Modood, Tariq. 2011. "Capitals, Ethnic Identity and Educational Qualifications." In *The Next Generation: Immigrant Youth in a Comparative Perspective*, edited by Richard Alba and Mary Waters, pp. 185–206. New York: New York University Press.

Modood, Tariq, Sarah Beishon, and Satnam Virdee. 1994. *Changing Ethnic Identities*. PSI Research Report 794. London: London Policy Studies Institute.

Modood, Tariq, Richard Berthoud, J. Lakey, James Nazroo, and Philip Smith. 1997. *Ethnic Minorities in Britain: Diversity and Disadvantage – Fourth National Survey of Ethnic Minorities*. London: London Policy Studies Institute.

Mottahedeh, Roy. 1986. *The Mantle of the Prophet*. New York: Chatto and Windus.

Mustafa, Asma. 2015. *Identity and Public Participation among Young British Muslims*. London: Palgrave Macmillan.

Parekh, Bhikhu. 2004. *The Report of the Commission on the Future of Multi-Ethnic Britain (2000) revisited in 2004*. Runnymede Trust Briefing Paper April 2004. London: The Runnymede Trust.

Roy, Olivier. 2007. *Secularism Confronts Islam* (trans. George Holoch). New York: Columbia University Press.

Saint-Blancat, Chantal. 2002. "Islam in Diaspora: Between Reterritorialization and Extra-territorialization." *International Journal of Urban and Regional Research* 26(1): 138–151.

Spellman, Kathryn. 2004. *Religion and Nation: Iranian Local and Transnational Networks in London*. Oxford and New York: Berghahn Books.

Spellman-Poots, Kathryn. 2012. "Manifestations of Ashura among Young British Shi'is." In *Ethnographies of Islam*, edited by Baudoin Dupret, Thomas Pierret, Paulo G. Pinto, and Kathryn Spellman-Poots, pp. 40–49. Edinburgh: Edinburgh University Press.

Spellman-Poots, Kathryn, and Sami Zubaida, eds. 2013. *Middle Eastern Religious Minorities*, special issue of *The Middle East in London Magazine* 9(3). London: School of Oriental and African Studies.

Sunier, Thijl. 2012. "Beyond the Domestification of Islam in Europe: A Reflection on Past and Future Research on Islam in European Societies." *Journal of Muslims in Europe* 1: 189–208.

Torab, Azam. 1996. "Piety as Gendered Agency: A Study of Jaleseh Ritual Discourse in an Urban Neighbourhood in Iran." *The Journal of the Royal Anthropological Society* 2(2): 235–252.

Vertovec, Steven, and Ceri Peach (eds.). 1997. *Islam in Europe: The Politics of Religion and Community*. New York: St. Martin's Press.

Werbner, Pnina. 2002a. "The Place which is Diaspora: Citizenship, Religion and Gender in the Making of Chaordic Transnationalism." *Journal of Ethnic and Migration Studies* 28(1): 119–133.

Werbner, Pnina. 2002b. *Imagines Diasporas among Manchester Muslims: The Public Performance of Pakistani Transnational Identity Politics*. Woodbridge, UK: James Currey Press.

Zubaida, Sami. 2007. "The Many Faces of Multiculturalism." *Open Democracy* 6(5). Available online at www.opendemocracy.net/faith-europe_islam/many_faces_4677.jsp (accessed March 24, 2016).

Zubaida, Sami. 2011. *Beyond Islam: A New Understanding of the Middle East*. London: I. B. Tauris.

11   Imagining the "Muslim terrorist"

Media narratives of the Boston Marathon bombers

*Nazli Kibria, Saher Selod and
Tobias Henry Watson*

On April 15, 2013, at the annual Boston Marathon, one of Boston's most iconic and beloved public events, tragedy struck, resulting in what has been widely described as one of the most significant acts of "homegrown" terrorism on U.S. soil since 9/11. As runners began entering the finish line, two pressure cooker bombs exploded, killing two persons and injuring an estimated 264 others. By the late evening hours of April 18 the suspects had been identified. They were the brothers Tamerlan and Dzhokhar Tsarnaev, residents of Cambridge, Massachusetts and members of a family of refugees from Chechnya who had resettled in the U.S. in the early 2000s. A dramatic series of events unfurled; Tamerlan was killed in a shootout with police and Dzhokhar, the younger brother, was arrested following an extensive manhunt. In 2015, Dzhokhar was found guilty and sentenced to death in a Massachusetts federal court.

The Boston Marathon bombings are widely seen and remembered as an act of Islamic terrorism against Americans that was "homegrown," committed by young Muslims living and settled in the U.S. Public narratives of the Tsarnaev brothers – about the course of their lives and especially their motivations for violence – form part of a wider discourse about Muslims that has important consequences for the experiences of young Muslims growing up in the U.S. With the goal of exploring this discursive terrain, this chapter examines media discussions of the marathon bombers as revealed in news reports and accompanying readers' comments in the days that followed their identification.

We find the popular narrative of the Boston Marathon bombers to be embedded in a conception of deep-seated, indeed primordial, tendencies towards extremism and violence within Muslims, especially young male Muslims. Muslims growing up in the U.S. are seen as persons who have these inclinations, which may become activated or lie submerged, depending on life conditions, including those of social and cultural assimilation into America. In this narrative, the failed assimilation of young Muslim Americans is signaled by their engagement and involvement with Islam and Muslim institutions – they turn towards Islam rather than away from it. Anchored in the framework of a "clash of civilizations" between Islam and the West, the story of the Tsarnaev brothers emerges as a cautionary folk tale, of young Muslims who fall into a spiraling cycle of radicalization and extremism as they embrace their Muslim identities and reject American values and loyalties.

The "Muslim terrorist" folk devil and media frames of Islam

Rooted in long-standing historical antipathies and contemporary global conflicts, the early Twenty-First century is a time of sharply visible anti-Muslim sentiments. Drawing on long-standing Orientalist narratives, Islam and Muslims are seen as antithetical to Western civilization and indeed at militant odds with it – the essential enemy of the West (Meer 2013; Rana 2011). Undergirding these hostilities is the War on Terror, launched by the U.S. and its allies following the September 11, 2001 attacks on New York and Washington D.C. by the Islamic terrorist group al-Qaeda. Subsequent Western military interventions in Afghanistan and Iraq, along with programs of surveillance and policing directed towards Muslim communities, have strengthened an understanding of division and conflict between the West and Islam.

Writing of the emotionally charged moral panic that surrounds Islam and Muslims in North America and Europe, Pnina Werbner (2013: 451) describes a social imaginary that is "formed out of the fantasies, fears, symbols, caricatures, stereotypes, jokes, myths and nightmares of a threatening Other, as they are encapsulated in images of inhuman violence and a capacity for cruelty and violation." At the heart of this social imaginary is the figure of the "Muslim Terrorist" – the central antagonist in the War on Terror. The "Muslim Terrorist," as it emerges in the public imagination is a mythical figure, a "folk devil" (Cohen 2002). Typically understood as male, he captures the inhuman savagery and evil that is consonant with terrorism and fuses these qualities with Islam and its followers (Devji 2008; Rana 2011). Stampnitsky (2014: 4) has described the development, since the 1970s, of a terrorism discourse that describes the perpetrators of illegitimate political violence in a language of irrational evil: "[r]ather than simply judge terrorists' reasons as unworthy, the terrorism discourse places such actions outside the realm of moral consideration entirely." Thus the "Muslim Terrorist" is devoid of humanity and his monstrous actions require no further explanation beyond that of the identity itself. In short, the "Muslim Terrorist" commits savage violence simply because he is a Muslim Terrorist.

Scholars have noted how both cultural and physical characteristics are implicated in the social imaginaries of Muslim difference (Rana 2011; Selod and Embrick 2013). Thus the Muslim Terrorist is defined not only by cultural dispositions towards savagery and violence, but also by an "enemy body." Indeed, the Muslim Terrorist is a somatic imaginary, embedded in visual images of bodies that are mediated by local histories. In the contemporary U.S., Muslims are widely understood to "look Middle Eastern or Arab" with brown skin color and other physical features such as beards that are associated with these origins. These perceived body features fuse with visible expressions of Muslim culture and identity, such as the *hijab* and the *keffiyeh* (Middle Eastern head-dress for men) to create an image of "looking Muslim." Along with other signs such as an "Arabic-sounding" name, these cues are used to identify and target Muslims, whether it is in the course of anti-Muslim hate-crimes or security screening practices at airports (Selod 2015).

Like other social imaginaries, the Muslim Terrorist is a potent and contested set of ideas and images (Cohen 2002; Werbner 2013). Its hegemonic place in the Western imagination is challenged by a variety of conditions, including the growing prominence of the radicalization paradigm. As Kundani (2012) describes, since the mid-2000s, policy analysts are increasingly inclined to reject the "terrorist as irrational evil" framework in favor of that of "radicalization." The latter draws attention to individual life journeys of pathology, in which psychological factors and exposure to relevant social networks coalesce and push individual Muslims towards an extremist interpretation of Islam, from which terrorist engagements emerge. A notable omission is political context, or the greater political conditions within which these individual life journeys take shape. But, appealing to liberal sensibilities, "radicalization" is responsive to the need to address "homegrown terrorism," in which it is not foreign nationals but rather U.S. citizens, born and raised in the U.S., who are the perpetrators of terrorism. In essence, the radicalization framework challenges the social imaginary of the Muslim Terrorist not by denying his evil but rather by seeing it as an outcome of a pathway rather than a given matter. The Muslim Terrorist develops a human past and becomes the Radicalized Muslim.

Through its framing of events and occurrences, the news media play a critical role in the production of social imaginaries such as the Muslim Terrorist. The emerging literature on Western media depictions of Muslims affirms the presence of negative, threatening images as well as the shifting and uneven character of these depictions. Studies show the prominence, in news content, of a "clash of civilizations" narrative in which Islam and Muslims are associated with terrorism and violence (Abrahamian 2003; Powell 2011; El-Aswad 2013; Saeed 2007). Morey and Yaqin (2011: 1) write of how media portrayals paint Muslims as "unenlightened outsiders" and as "a homogeneous zombie-like body . . . liable to be whipped into a frenzy at the least disturbance to their unchanging backward worldview." The work of Bail (2012) further highlights the prominence in news content since 9/11 of an emotionally charged "Muslim as Enemies" frame that is actively promoted by anti-Muslim organizations.

Media analyses also show these negative portrayals of Islam and Muslims to be evolving and uneven rather than constant and unidirectional in their course of development (Trevino, Kanso, and Nelson 2010). In their study of *New York Times* headlines about Islam or Muslims from 2005 to 2013, Bleich, Nishar and Abdelhamib (2016) find a general trend of improvement over time, with a noticeable jump in positive tone in the four weeks following terrorist attacks. Similarly, in their research on depictions of American Muslims and Arabs before and after 9/11 in four daily newspapers (the *New York Times*, the *New York Daily News*, the *New York Post*, and *USA Today*), Nacos and Torres-Reyna (2007) find an increase in positive stories after 9/11. However, they also find a subsequent movement back to negative coverage by the time of the one-year anniversary of 9/11.

The strong yet evolving presence of stigmatizing images of Islam and Muslims in the media points to the need for a closer understanding of the content of these depictions and the contests and shifts that surround them. In this chapter, we suggest that media narratives of the Boston Marathon bombers and the causes of their violence offer a window into the ongoing construction of Muslim difference and stigma in the popular U.S. imagination.

The Boston Marathon bombers in the news

Our study of Boston Marathon bomber narratives draws on news reports and reader comments. The latter, part of the new world of participatory journalism, offers an extended lens into media frames, one that goes beyond the authoritative voices of established news sources (Maratea 2008). However, while we examine reader comments for insight into emergent discursive themes, we refrain from treating them as opinion data or measures of the public scope and strength of these themes. Among the many challenges and limitations of reader comments as a data source is the absence of social and demographic information about those who are behind them. In addition, news sources are increasingly likely to monitor and block comments that are offensive or inappropriate, thus offering only partial access to the range of comments that are actually submitted.

We focus on materials that appeared from April 18 (the day that photographs of the suspects were released) to April 22, 2013. This five-day period, a time of dramatic unfolding events, was one of intensive media coverage and high levels of public interest in the bombings. Our data are drawn from the *Boston Globe*, the *New York Times* and the online news site *CBS.Boston*. As a leading local paper, the *Boston Globe* was especially important during this event, often serving as a primary source for other news outlets. The *New York Times* is a major national and international news source that is frequently cited and plays an agenda-setting role; it ranks second in digital traffic among U.S. papers (Markens 2011; McCoombs 2006; Pew Research Center 2015). We note that both of these papers are viewed as politically liberal and in the case of *The New York Times* especially, geared towards an elite readership; paid subscriptions are required in order to gain full access to content and only registered paid readers can post comments. In order to diversify our news sources, we also looked at *CBS Boston*, a digital national online news site affiliated with the local WBZ TV and radio stations, which has an open comments section.

We examined a combined total of 247 news reports from the April 18 to 22 time period. Of the 12,239 reader comments that accompanied these reports and were available to us, we eventually narrowed our analysis to those that commented directly on the Tsarnaev brothers in some manner, whether it was to condemn them or to provide information and views about their identity, character and motives (n=499). The comments that we did not analyze touched on a range of topics, from the architecture of Watertown to gun control; some mentioned Islam and Muslims, but without reference to the Tsarnaev brothers or their actions.

We coded all of the news reports and the direct comments in an iterative process that involved multiple coding episodes across different segments of the data (Charmaz 2014). We searched for organizing narratives and explanatory frames or ways of understanding the Tsarnaev brothers in relation to their violent actions (Riessman 2008). When looking at the comments, we coded the presence of multiple themes within a comment rather than classifying comments according to one theme, when applicable. We took note of dialogue about explanatory frames as reflected in reader comments directed towards the news article under which they were published or those directed to the comments made by other readers. While we did find instances of such dialogue, we also found a large proportion of the reader comments to not be specifically directed towards anyone in particular; in some cases, these were geared towards imagined friends or more often towards foes on the political left or right. Similar findings are reported by Szpunar (2013) in a study of reader comments in response to news coverage of the 2009 Fort Hood shooting in which Nidal Hasan, a U.S. Army major, fatally shot 13 people and injured more than 30 others. He offers a conceptualization of reader comments as "dissemination" or "communication as imparting, as 'speaking into the air', as broadcasting to an imagined or invisible audience over which the sender has no control and receives no guarantee of recognition or response" (Szpunar 2013: 187). He argues that the undirected character of these communications can shroud their significant role in the development of national myths and narratives.

Public sleuths, vigilantes and "Middle Eastern looking" suspects

In the hours following the blasts at 2: 49 pm on April 15, video clips of the horrific bombing scene went viral; Boston's famed Boylston Street had become "a place of blood and horror and chaos" (Powers 2013). Heartbreaking accounts of injuries and deaths were accompanied by inspirational stories of the heroic acts of runners and onlookers who had struggled to bring the wounded to safety. "Boston Strong," a slogan of Boston's unity and resilience in the face of adversity, was evident everywhere, proudly displayed on t-shirts and banners across the city.

In the intervening hours between the bombing on April 15 and the identification of the Tsarnaev brothers as the culprits on April 18, there was intense public speculation about the perpetrators of the bombing. In both implicit and explicit ways, suspicions of Islamic terrorism were a core theme of these discussions. News reports noted broad similarities, such as the type of casualties inflicted and the weapons (i.e., pressure cooker bombs) used, between the marathon bombing and attacks on allied forces in Iraq and Afghanistan. Comparisons were also drawn between the marathon bombing and the 9/11 attacks (*Boston Globe* 2013a; *Boston Globe* 2013b). Furthermore, the campaign of "technologically enabled vigilantism" (Volpp 2014: 2211) that developed at this time was guided by established visual cues of the Muslim Terrorist. On social media outlets such as Reddit. com and 4chan, photos of suspects were submitted along with circled notations of why they were suspicious, which included references to them as "brown."

Indeed, the racialized character of the April 15 to 18 manhunt was also evident in the string of false accusations that it generated. Those erroneously accused included a Saudi Arabian student who had come to Boston to study English and an Indian American student who had been missing from his campus. On April 18, the *New York Post* ran a front page cover ("Bag Men: Feds seek these two pictured at Boston Marathon") with a photograph of two unsuspecting Moroccan-American high-school track athletes from a running club who later brought a defamation suit against the paper.

The public search for "Muslim looking" suspects was vigorously defended at this time by conservative commentators such as Glenn Beck, who argued that the attackers had to be "Middle Eastern" terrorists (Wilstein 2013). On April 16, liberal commentator David Sirota (2013) published an online Salon.com article titled "Let's Hope the Boston marathon bomber is a white American" in which he voiced fears about the growth of retaliatory measures targeting Muslims if in fact the bomber turned out to be Muslim, as many suspected. What followed was a firestorm of responses from conservative and right-wing media in which Sirota was accused of "anti-white racism" and "political correctness" as evident in his refusal to acknowledge the inherently dangerous nature of Islamic doctrine and practice. Among other things, these commentary battles strengthened the role played by sharply drawn liberal-versus-conservative political rhetoric in framing the discussions of the Tsarnaev brothers that were to follow. That is, as we will see, in comments about the brothers, readers often self-consciously situated their opinions within broader discursive streams of liberal-versus-conservative politics. The comments that did not deal with the attackers tended to voice opinions, often with politically polarizing undertones, on such issues as gun control, the Tea Party, the role of the FBI, and U.S. foreign policy.

Not your average Muslim terrorist? Making sense of the Tsarnaev brothers

In the afternoon of April 18, a dramatic sequence of events began to unfold. The FBI released photographs and surveillance video of two suspects who had been at the Marathon finish line prior to the bombing. Flashing constantly on news screens, the images of men wearing baseball hats and carrying backpacks were the subject of intense public scrutiny, registering more than 2.5 million web hits by the late afternoon (Volpp 2011: 2210). Observers such as CNN anchor Erin Burnett expressed surprise about the identity clues offered by the photographs: "These two kids look like they're very, very stereotypically from here." Defying the "enemy body" of the Muslim Terrorist, the two men in the pictures wore baseball caps and jeans and they did not dress in Arab garb, sport beards or look "brown." Rather, they appeared to be quite "white" as observed by a *CBS Boston* reader:

> Ruby Ridge, Waco, Oklahoma City-white as they come. . . . My point is I see college kids straight up. Not what I expected.
>
> (comment, *CBS Boston* 2013a)

By the late evening the two men were identified as Dzhokhar and Tamerlan Tsarnaev. Besides their seemingly "white" appearance, the information that they were from Chechnya seemed to only compound the uncertainty about their identity. As highlighted by the confusion between the Czech Republic and Chechnya in the social media at the time, this is a region that is unfamiliar to many Americans. The Chechen origins of the Tsarnaev brothers both affirmed and complicated their perceived "whiteness." The idea that they were "Caucasian" was suggested by the location of Chechnya in the North Caucasus, next to Russia in the southernmost part of Eastern Europe. The word "Caucasian" is widely understood in the U.S. to mean "white," despite the fact that the two terms have not always been viewed as synonymous by legal courts in their decisions about access to U.S. citizenship (Kibria 1988). There is also the fact of Chechnya's location in Eastern Europe and proximity to Russia. In the U.S. today, persons of Eastern European and Russian origin are racially categorized as "white," notwithstanding the deeply contested history behind these understandings.

In the late hours of April 18, the brothers shot a police officer and carjacked a black Mercedes. In the shootout that followed Tamerlan died and Dzhokar escaped. During the massive manhunt for Dzhokhar that ensued, Governor Deval Patrick ordered a "shelter-in-place" request that residents of Boston and surrounding cities stay in their homes while law enforcement searched for the suspect. On the evening of April 19, Dzhokhar was captured. He was found in a residential area, hiding in a dry-docked boat. On the walls of the boat he had scrawled in pencil a message that the bombings were committed in retaliation for U.S. militarism and the killing of fellow Muslims: "we Muslims are one body, you hurt one you hurt us all."

With the identification of the Tsarnaevs and the capture of Dzhokar, the focus of public discussions about the bombings shifted, from the question of "who had done it" to "why they had done it." Confirming widespread expectations, the attackers, as it turned out, were in fact, Muslims who appeared to be motivated by anger towards the U.S. for its policies towards Muslims. But as reported in the media, they did not have any formal ties to Islamic terrorist groups, despite public speculation to the contrary. They were also Muslims who did not "look Muslim" and in fact looked white in appearance. As we will see, these intersecting conditions were fertile ground for vigorous public debates about what had led the young men to commit these horrific acts.

Reader comments: the Muslim terrorist as explanatory frame

Noting the visible presence of violent racist rhetoric on online commentary forums, Hughey (2012) argues that these forums have become a place for expressions of taboo racist talk that is disallowed in the mainstream public sphere. Affirming these insights, the reader comments we studied were prominently marked by a theme of sharp and overt hostility towards Islam and Muslims. Grounded in the Muslim Terrorist trope, these remarks suggest that the Tsarnaev brothers had bombed the marathon because they were Muslim. Islam is defined here by hatred of and conflict with the West, coupled with primordial inclinations among followers towards violence as promoted by its theological teachings:

> It's about Islam. We might be not at war with Islam, but Muslims are at war with us, non-Muslims.
>
> > (Comment, Seelye, Rashbaum, and Cooper 2013)
>
> Religion of peace . . . religion of peace . . . religion of peace. . . . Yeah, right.
> > (Comment, *CBS Boston* 2013d)
>
> All these new bomb-proof mosques being built in America need to be demolished and Islam should not be considered a religion. If this is allowed to spread in America we will be Third World in no time. . . . Get rid of all of them.
> > (Comment, *CBS Boston* 2013d)

As suggested by contemptuous references to "liberals" and "political correctness," comments such as the above are often self-consciously located within a wider politics of conservatives versus liberals. The often virulent hostility of many of these comments was at times greeted with protests from other readers who take them to task for their blanket condemnations of Islam and Muslims. A frequent theme in these protesting counter-remarks is that it is "extremism" that was to blame, and that the dangers of extremism are not specific to Islam but present everywhere. In the following exchange between *Boston Globe* readers, the first commenter angrily affirms the primary role of Islam in the bombing. He is then rebuked by the second commenter who reminds him of the potential for "nutty extremists" in any religion:

> [W]e have the Globe's Lisa Wangness's column "Islam might have had a secondary role in Boston bombings." MIGHT HAVE? MIGHT HAVE?? Even though most Muslim religious scholars interpret the Quran as a document of War? . . . How about a PRIMARY ROLE?? People like her and the whole Boston Globe are ready and willing to blame Whites and Christians and Conservatives for everything. But Muslims? The Quran? No, no, no.
> > (Comment, Arsenault, Murphey and Daley 2013)
>
> Oh, hey, equating Islam with this guy is like equating the Westboro Baptist Church with Baptists. He was a nutty extremist, and those can be found in any religion.
> > (Comment, Arsenault, Murphey and Daley 2013)

The explanatory frame of Muslims/Islam is thus both prominent and contested in the reader comment forums. The picture is further complicated when we turn to news reports of the Tsarnaev brothers – a forum in which frames rooted in the radicalization paradigm are prominent. In what follows we turn to an exploration of the explanatory frames offered by news reports and accompanying reader comments.

A tale of two brothers and angry young men

In the days following the death and capture of the Tsarnaev brothers, the news media drew on a variety of sources, from the Twitter postings of Dzhokhar to the press remarks of family members, to offer biographical sketches. Rooted in notions of radicalization, several intersecting themes emerge from these sketches. One is a tale of two brothers that hinges on their difference, a difference that also signals the oppositional dualism of America and Islam. Tamerlan, the older brother, is depicted here as angry, frustrated and socially isolated, an immigrant who never assimilates and remains a foreigner. He is quoted as saying: "I don't have a single American friend. I don't understand them" (Russell et al. 2013). In contrast to his older brother, Dzhokhar (or "Jahar" in his simplified American name), who came to the U.S. at the age of eight, is a typical American teen who is "laid-back" and fond of parties and smoking marijuana; his friends describe him as "sweet" and popular and find it difficult to believe that he would commit these terrible atrocities. Dzhokar is both American and likeable in nature, in contrast to Tamerlan who is foreign and unpleasant. The *Boston Globe* reports that Tamerlan is even disliked by his relatives:

> The question that remains is why the siblings would attack their adoptive nation. But a picture began to emerge Friday of Tamerlan Tsarnaev as an aggressive, possibly radicalized immigrant who may have ensnared his younger brother – described almost universally as smart and sweet – into an act of terror. "I used to warn Dzhokhar that Tamerlan was up to no good," Zaur Tsarnaev, who identified himself as a 26-year-old cousin, said in a phone interview from Makhachkala, Russia, where the brothers briefly lived. "[Tamerlan] was always getting in trouble. He was never happy, never cheering, never smiling. He used to strike his girlfriend. . . . He was not a nice man."
>
> (Arsenault 2013)

As Volpp (2014) observes, there was "a striking amount of public sympathy" (2217) towards the younger brother Dzhokhar (often described as "good-looking") in the immediate aftermath of the bombing. Expressing a sense of bewilderment with respect to the terrible violence that the attractive young man had committed, readers turn to Tamerlan and his negative influence as an older brother, over Dzhokhar, as a plausible explanation for Dzhokhar's actions:

> In no way shape or form do I condone any of the actions taken by the younger brother, and think he should be prosecuted to the fullest extent, but I almost feel sorry for him. When you read all the accounts from his acquaintances and family, it sounds like he was a good kid led astray by his older brother.
>
> (Comment, Seelye, Rashbaum and Cooper 2013)

The notion of "older brother's bad influence over younger brother" points towards youth, gullibility, and brotherly relations rather than Islam or Muslim identity as explanations. The humanizing implications of these alternative frames were not lost on dissenting readers who offer angry rebuttals to the idea that Dzhokhar could possibly be a "normal American kid." There is, they claim, a fundamental incompatibility between Muslim and American identities:

> A Muslim is NOT a normal American and never will be. Muslims are terrorists as they are directed to be if they follow the Koran, period.
>
> (Comment, *CBS Boston* 2013b)

> Just a normal American kid - EXCEPT HE IS A MUSLIM, WHICH MEANS HE IS PREDISPOSED TO BE A TERRORIST.
>
> (Comment, *CBS Boston* 2013b)

Drawing on the biographical sketches provided by news reports, readers also offer a frame in which the Tsarnaev brothers are compared to the perpetrators of other well-known incidents of rampage school shootings, such as those at Columbine High School in 1999 and the Sandy Hook Elementary School in 2012. The "school shooter" frame challenges that of the Muslim Terrorist by positioning Muslim identity as a secondary explanation for the violence and at times a symptomatic one, driven by other underlying conditions. Rather than an emphasis on their affiliation with Islam, the Tsarnaev brothers are depicted as alienated young men.

The school shooter frame is anchored in popular notions of youth as a problem population and male youth especially as threatening and dangerous. Fears of male youth are deeply racialized, as reflected in the pervasive criminalization of Black and Latino boys in the contemporary U.S. (Rios 2011). But the school shooter frame is one that is notable for its attention to young white men, often in rural or suburban and middle-class settings, who are depicted as being pushed into inexplicable violence by their alienation (Frymer 2009; Roque 2012). The association of the Tsarnaev brothers with this frame is suggestive, once more, of the putative, albeit contested, whiteness that was assigned to them in the aftermath of the bombings.

The school shooter frame is at times accompanied by references to the difficult life conditions of the Tsarnaev brothers, especially their fractured family life and separation from their father. These circumstances, it is suggested, led to frustration and to an anger violently taken out on others; the phrase "angry young men" laces through the reader comments. Along with these individual-centered explanations, readers refer to an underlying set of biological and social factors. Biologic understandings of youth and masculinity are evident in references to brain immaturity and a natural impulse towards explosive anger within young men. The difficulties embodied by young men are seen to further aggravate the larger problem of youth alienation in the contemporary modern world. The following set of comments highlights the wide scope of issues encompassed by the youth alienation critique, from the dangerous effects of video games and rap music to a lack of inner beliefs and goals:

> These kids are no different than the Sandy Hook kid. They are learning warfare and killing from their video games, these desensitize them to death and killing! In their minds they think they are playing a game until they wake up and realize what they have done is real. They are normal kids that are taking in evil games that are brain washing them.
>
> (Comment, *New York Times* 2013a)

> More fallen young men . . . at what point should we, as a society, take responsibility for making errors in raising boys and figure out how to help them? I say, it starts when they are very young, when the brain is developing and the ability to feel empathy must be taught.
>
> (Comment, *New York Times* 2013a)

> So, it's looking like another Columbine, another Newtown, another Aurora. There is plenty of inspiration for potential mass murderers out there. Video games, racist rants, al Qaeda blogs. Perhaps we need to take a deeper look at our society to see why some young people find carnage inspirational.
>
> (Comment, Schmitt and Schmidt 2013)

The school shooter frame is not an especially frequent one in the reader comments we analyzed. But its presence is notable, not the least because of the vigorous backlash to comments espousing it. Reflecting what Szpunar (2013) has described as the "disseminating" quality of reader comments, whereby they are often directed towards a general or invisible audience, we find opposition to the school shooter frame voiced even when the frame is actually not part of the accompanying news piece or the other surrounding comments. In these backlash comments, those who use the school shooter frame are rebuked, at times with great anger, for unnecessarily complicating what is simple and obvious. Recalling the imaginary of the Muslim Terrorist, "radical Islam" is offered as a total explanation, one so complete that there are no other legitimate questions to be asked about the lives and motivations of the Tsarnaev brothers:

> There seems to be an almost desperate effort on the part of many commentators to demonstrate that this mass murder is not anchored in Islamic terrorist jihad but rather is simply another sensational example of American domestic sociopathic violence in which downtrodden unhappy victims of the economic crisis are propelled into acts of quasi - understandable violence. Let's not try to spin this tragedy into meaninglessness. It's really quite simple. A couple of radicalized Muslims decided to kill a bunch of men, women, and children infidels.
>
> (Comment, Schmitt, Schmidt, and Barry 2013)

Such backlash comments as the one above are often situated within a broader political stance, typically of identification with a conservative political agenda and opposition to a liberal one. As in the comment below, proponents of the "school shooter" frame are chided for their "political correctness" as well as their presumed support of gun control measures:

> To suggest these [Tsarnaev brothers] are "homegrown" terrorists akin to Loughner, McVeigh and Lanza (all Americans by birth, btw) is ridiculous. They were radicalized Chechen Muslims who were born in Dagestan and in fact returned there, apparently, for training. That is an undeniable fact, as much as people would like to spin it otherwise. Radical Islam is and continues to be a threat to Americans. Why people want to engage in a rank suspension of disbelief just because they're been spoon fed a diet of political correctness doesn't make the problem go away. And yes, we need better gun control, but gun control would have done nothing in this case. The Tsarnaevs did their most murderous damage with two pressure cookers. Unless, of course, we should be banning pressure cookers.
>
> (Comment, Schmitt and Schmidt 2013)

Failed assimilation and the turn to Islam

The biographical sketches of the Tsarnaevs that appeared in news reports were also accompanied by a narrative of failed assimilation resulting in a turn to Islam. Broadly anchored in the radicalization paradigm and focused on the experiences of Tamerlan, the account is of a life gone awry, of an individual's spiraling experiences of failure and frustration culminating in horrific choices and outcomes. If in the tale of two brothers the "clash of civilizations" is expressed in the dichotomy of Tamerlan versus Dzhokhar, in the tale of failed assimilation the contradictions of American and Muslim identities play out in the twists and turns of Tamerlan's life.

Tamerlan arrived in the U.S. in his late teens with dreams of a professional career in boxing. Encouraged by his parents, he worked hard to cultivate his boxing skills and in 2009 he won the New England Golden Gloves championship. But a major disappointment followed when Tamerlan found himself disqualified from moving forward to the national Tournament of Champions because he was not a U.S. citizen. Media accounts emphasize the devastating impact of this disqualification, as the start of a downward spiral (Russell et al. 2013). Following the disqualification, Tamerlan dropped out of competitive boxing, withdrew from community college and distanced himself from friends. He also began to cultivate a visibly Islamic way of life. He stopped going to parties, cut off ties with friends, and took up studying the Koran and praying five times a day. Neighbors report that he had grown a beard and started wearing long white Arab clothing in the year prior to the bombings. In essence, he moves from aspiring American to committed Muslim. Anchored in the vision of a "clash of civilizations," the movement is so complete as to disallow hybridity or any middle ground. This is further highlighted by the story of Tamerlan's wife, Katherine Russell, and her conversion. After marrying Tamerlan in 2010, Katherine, a white woman from an upper-middle class family in suburban Rhode Island, converts to Islam and dons a long black robe and head covering. With her conversion to Islam she undergoes a dramatic transformation.

Among the notable features of this narrative of failed assimilation is the simultaneity of Tamerlan's subsequent turn to Islam and his radicalization. At no point is his involvement with Islam viewed to have been a potential route for him to actually cope with his frustrations in a healthy manner and to effectively integrate into American life. Instead, the turn to Islam is portrayed as the critical turning point in the story of his descent into violence. To be sure, news accounts and reader comments from a liberal stance are careful to describe Tamerlan's motivations for the attack to be rooted in "radical Islam" rather than in "Islam" more generally, reflecting an understanding of the importance of not condemning an entire religion. However, these distinctions undergo a process of blurring as they are situated within the story of failed assimilation and turn to Islam in which the latter is associated if not equated with a turn to violence. We see this in the following reader comment, in which the turn to Islam is understood as the key hinge that moves Tamerlan's towards sociopathy:

> His brother was a failed boxer, failed student, unable to make friends. He was in a foreign country that did not "accept" him. What does he do? He turns to Islam and turns into a sociopath. He acts revenge on the people that "shunned" him.
>
> (Comment, 2013c)

In contrast to the Muslim Terrorist, the tale of failed assimilation is one that lends a measure of humanity to the perpetrator, giving him a past in which he had not been angry and violent. Furthermore, by drawing attention to the formative life conditions and events of the attacker, the narrative seems to challenge the notion of intrinsic savagery that is a defining feature of the Muslim Terrorist. But of note is the notion of dormant violence and savagery that is woven into the story of failed assimilation. Even as readers acknowledge the frustrations and disappointments that had scarred Tamerlan's life, they also note the deep roots of violence among Muslims. That is, Muslim savagery might lie submerged and inactive under certain conditions, but it is always there beneath the surface, ready to rise up at the slightest provocation. The author of the comment below notes the futility of welcoming "Islamists" into the U.S., given their "sensibilities" which almost inevitably lead to anger and violence:

> Like the FT Hood shooter, no matter how much we try to appease Islamists and welcome them into our society, their easily offended sensibilities cause them to sympathize with extremism. And disgruntled Islamists will take up the bomb or the gun to get vengeance on their offended sensibilities.
>
> (Comment, *CBS Boston* 2013b)

The idea of a deeply rooted, inherent violence within the Tsarnaev brothers is further strengthened through reference to their Chechen origins. Despite the absence of evidence at this time of the brothers' ties to extremist groups in Chechnya or elsewhere, news reports offered extensive information on Chechnya as background to the Boston Marathon bombers (Filipov 2013). With such descriptions of Chechnya as "the most dangerous heart of darkness in the world" (Russell et al. 2013), they place a spotlight on its long history of war and conflict with Russia and the powerful rise of Islamic militancy and terrorism in the region. Chechnya is described by a *New York Times* article as:

> [O]ne of the darkest corners of nationalist and Islamic militancy [with] a campaign for separatism and vengeance responsible for some of the most unsparing terrorist acts of recent decades. Fired by a potent mix of blood codes, separatist yearnings and Islamic militancy, Chechen groups have staged a string of intermittent but spectacular attacks in Moscow and elsewhere in Russia since the 1990s.
>
> (Baker and Chivers 2013)

Depictions of a deep-seated, indeed primordially rooted Chechen history of violence, terrorism and Islamist militancy are a potent backdrop against which to infuse the story of the Tsarnaev brothers with the trope of the Muslim Terrorist. As in the following comment, the Chechen and Muslim Terrorist identities of the brothers are often invoked in simultaneous and interchangeable terms:

> I hope you are ready for an extended wave of these kinds of attack by this kid's father and his associates. Chechen militants are some of the most violent Islamic terrorists on the planet.
>
> (Comment, *CBS Boston* 2013d)

Conclusions

Fears of "homegrown" Islamic terrorism permeate the social and political landscape in which young Muslims in the contemporary U.S. negotiate their identities. Media narratives of the Boston Marathon bombers offer a lens on these fears and the fluid and multi-stranded discourse that organizes them. In the reader comment forums we studied, a racializing discourse of Islam and Muslims as inherently violent and savage is prominent, while newspaper articles take a different, seemingly neutral tone by emphasizing the precipitating factors in the Tsarnaev brothers' lives that led them down the path of violence. Ultimately however, we find these narratives of the Muslim Terrorist and the Radicalized Muslim mesh together through a discourse of violent potential in which Muslims are easily provoked to brutality because these inclinations are deeply rooted within them. Young male Muslims embody this potential for violence in particularly powerful ways, given that they are not only Muslim but also young and male – characteristics that are associated with impulsivity and aggression in popular American culture.

This discourse of violent potential legitimates young male Muslim as subjects of state surveillance and suspicion (Selod 2015).

The focus on radicalization as an explanatory frame is one that not only draws on the idea of the violent potential of Muslims but also on a classic assimilationist understanding of the immigrant experience in which Muslims growing up in the U.S. can either assimilate into mainstream America *or* embrace Islam. This is a framing that is silent on the possibilities of pluralistic integration for Muslim Americans. Instead, anchored in the idea of a core oppositional difference of values, sensibilities, and loyalties between Islam and the West, the young Muslim American is envisioned to be caught in an internal "clash of civilizations" struggle. Those who respond to this struggle by turning towards Islam signal their rejection of the path of assimilation.

References

Abrahamian, Ervand. 2003. "The US Media, Huntington and September 11." *Third World Quarterly* 24(3): 529–544.

Adams, Josh, and Vincent J. Roscigno. 2005. "White Supremacists, Oppositional Culture and the World Wide Web." *Social Forces* 84(2): 759–778.

Alsultany, Evelyn. 2012. *Arabs and Muslims in the Media: Race and Representation after 9/11*. New York: New York University Press.

Arsenault, Mark. 2013. "Second Marathon Suspect Captured, Manhunt Ends." *Boston Globe*, April 22. Available online at www.bostonglobe.com/metro/2013/04/20/second-marathon-suspect-captured-manhunt-ends/4ICVhfRArrGjgsiJnzJ2mM/story.html (accessed August 4, 2015).

Aresnault, Mark, Sean P. Murphey and Beth Daley. 2013. "Evidence mounts of radical turn for suspected bomber." *Boston Globe*, April 22. Available online at www.bostonglobe.com/news/nation/2013/04/21/dead-suspect-disrupted-speakers-mosque/zInGybr3sxsoAX6wkXbjLM/story.html (accessed August 4, 2015).

Bail, Christopher. 2012. "The Fringe Effect: Civil Society Organizations and the Evolution of Media Discourse about Islam since the September 11th Attacks." *American Sociological Review* 77(6): 855–879.

Baker, Peter, and C.J. Chivers. 2013. "Boston Attacks Turn Spotlight on Troubled Region of Chechnya." *New York Times*, April 20. Available online at www.nytimes.com/2013/04/21/world/europe/boston-attacks-turn-spotlight-on-troubled-chechen-region.ht (accessed August 4, 2015).

Barker, Kristen, and Tasha R. Galard. 2015. "Diagnostic Domain Defense: Autism Spectrum Disorder and the DSM-5." *Social Problems* 62(1): 120–140.

Bleich, Erik, Nisar, Hasher, and Rana Abdelhamid. 2016. "The Effect of Terrorist Events on Media Portrayals of Islam and Muslims: Evidence from *New York Times* Headlines, 1985–2013." *Ethnic and Racial Studies* 39(7): 1109–1127.

Boston Globe. 2013a. "A Grim Hunt for Answers in Wake of Marathon Attack." Available online at www.bostonglobe.com/metro/2013/04/16/investigation-mourning-continues-wake-attacks/irXykvV0YjDYfcaczbYN2H/story.html (accessed August 4, 2015).

Boston Globe. 2013b. "Investigators Scour the Area for any Clues." April 16. Available online at www.bostonglobe.com/metro/2013/04/16/boylston-street-now-one-boston-toughest-crime-scenes/UumF7TYgu098oBc2Jb065O/story.html (accessed August 4, 2015).

CBS Boston. 2013a. "FBI Releases Images of Boston Marathon Bombing Suspects." April 18. Available online at http://boston.cbslocal.com/2013/04/18/authorities-release-images-of-boston-marathon-bombing-suspects/ (accessed April 22, 2015).

CBS Boston. 2013b. "Bombing Suspect's Friend: 'Just a Normal American Kid.'" April 19. Available online at http://boston.cbslocal.com/2013/04/19/bombing-suspects-friend-just-a-normal-american-kid/ (accessed April 22, 2015).

CBS Boston. 2013c. "Dzhokhar Tsarnaev Under Heavy Guard, Unable to Speak Yet." April 20. Available online at http://boston.cbslocal.com/2013/04/20/dzhokhar-tsarnaev-under-heavy-guard-unable-to-speak-yet/ (accessed August 4, 2015).

CBS Boston. 2013d. "CAPTURED – Boston Marathon Bombing Suspect Caught in Watertown." April 19. Available online at http://boston.cbslocal.com/2013/04/19/gunfire-in-watertown-minutes-after-police-scale-back-search/ (accessed August 4, 2015).

Charmaz, Kathy. 2014. *Constructing Grounded Theory*. Los Angeles: Sage Publications.

Cohen, Stanley. 2002. *Folk Devils and Moral Panics: the Creation of the Mods and the Rockers*. New York and London: Routledge.

CNN. 2013. "Transcripts-Erin Burnett Outfront." Aired April 18. Available online at. http://transcripts.cnn.com/TRANSCRIPTS/1304/18/ebo.01.html (accessed July 1, 2016).

Devji, Faisal. 2014. *The Terrorist in Search of Humanity: Militant Islam and Global Politics*. London: Hurst Publishers.

El-Aswad, el-Sayed. 2013. "Images of Muslims in Western Scholarship and Media after 9/11." *Digest of Middle East Studies* 22(1): 39–56.

Filipov, David. 2013. "Tsarnaev Brothers' Background Runs Deep into History." *Boston Globe*. Available online at www.bostonglobe.com/metro/2013/04/19/chechen-bomb-suspects-link-conflict-chechnya-unclear/QoOy1stjYDOkjTpDrPkLjP/story.html (accessed April 5, 2015).

Franks, Myfanwy. 2000. "Crossing the Borders of Whiteness? White Muslim Women Who Wear the Hijab in Britain Today." *Ethnic and Racial Studies* 23(5): 917–929.

Frymer, Benjamin. 2009. "The Media Spectacle of Columbine: Alienated Youth as an Object of Fear." *American Behavioral Scientist* 53(10): 1387–1404.

Hughey, Matthew. 2012. "Show Me Your Papers! Obama's Birth and the Whiteness of Belonging." *Qualitative Sociology* 35(2): 163–181.

Kibria, Nazli. 1988. "The Racial Gap: South Asian American Racial Identity and the Asian American Movement." In *A Part, Yet Apart: South Asians in Asian America*, edited by Lavina Dhringa Shankar and Rajini Srikanth, pp. 69–78. Philadelphia: Temple University Press.

Kundani, Arun. 2012. "Radicalisation – The Journey of a Concept." *Race and Class* 54(2): 3–25.

Maratea, Ray. 2008. "The E-rise and Fall of Social Problems: The Blogosphere as a Public Arena." *Social Problems* 55(1): 139–160.

Markens, Susan. 2011. "The Global Reproductive Health Market." *Social Science and Medicine* 74(11): 1745–1753.

McCombs, Maxwell. 2006. "The Agenda Setting Function of the Press." In *The Institutions of American Democracy: The Press*, edited by Geneva Overhosler and Kathleen Hall Jamieson, pp. 156–168. Oxford and New York: Oxford University Press.

Meer, Nasar. 2013. "Racialization and Religion: Race, Culture and Difference in the Study of Antisemitism and Islamophobia." *Ethnic and Racial Studies* 36(3): 385–398.

Morey, Peter, and Amina Yaqin. 2011. *Framing Muslims: Stereotyping and Representation after 9/11*. Cambridge, MA: Harvard University Press.

Nacos, Brigitte, and Oscar Torres-Reyna. 2007. *Fueling Our Fears: Stereotyping, Media Coverage, and Public Opinion of Muslim Americans*. Lanham, MD: Rowman & Littlefield.

New York Times. 2013a – Live Update (April 19) "April 19th Updates on Aftermath of Boston Marathon Explosions." Available online at http: /thelede.blogs.nytimes.com/ 2013/04/19/updates-on-aftermath-of-boston-marathon-explosions-2/?_r=0 (accessed July 1, 2016).

Peters, John D. 2001. *Speaking into the Air: A History of the Idea of Communication*. Chicago: University of Chicago Press.

Pew Research Center. 2015. "State of the News Media 2015." Available online at www. journalism.org/files/2015/04/FINAL-STATE-OF-THE-NEWS-MEDIA1.pdf (accessed July 1, 2016).

Poole, Elizabeth. 2002. *Reporting Islam: Media Representations of British Muslims*. London: I.B.Tauris.

Powell, Kimberly A. 2011. "Framing Islam: An Analysis of U.S. Media Coverage of Terrorism since 9/11." *Communication Studies* 62(1): 90–112.

Powers, John. 2013. "Joyous Event Turns Shocking as Tragedy Halts Marathon." *Boston Globe*, April 16. Available online at www.bostonglobe.com/sports/2013/04/15/finish-boston-marathon-place-triumph-becomes-place-horror/aPXaZ1RlVvu13VVaE37lgL/ story.html (accessed July 1, 2016).

Rana, Junaid. 2011. *Terrifying Muslims: Race and Labor in the South Asian Diaspora*. Durham, NC: Duke University Press.

Riessman, Catherine. 2007. *Narrative Methods for the Human Sciences*. Los Angeles: Sage Publications.

Rios, Victor. 2011. *Punished: Policing the Lives of Black and Latino Boys*. New York: New York University Press.

Roque, Michael. 2012. "Exploring School Rampage Shootings: Research, Theory and Policy." *The Social Science Journal* 49(3): 304–313.

Russell, Jenna, Jenn Abelson, Patricia Wen, Michael Rezendes and David Filipov. 2013. "Brothers Veered Violently Off Track." *Boston Globe*, April 19. Available online at www.bostonglobe.com/metro/2013/04/19/relatives-marathon-bombing-suspects-wor ried-that-older-brother-was-corrupting-sweet-younger-sibling/UCYHkiP9nfsjAtMjJP WJJL/story.html (accessed July 1, 2016).

Saeed, Amir. 2007. "Media, Racism and Islamophobia: The Representation of Islam and Muslims in the Media." *Sociology Compass* 1(2): 443–462.

Santana, Arthur. 2011. "Online Reader Comments Represent New Opinion Pipeline." *Newspaper Research Journal* 32(3): 66–81.

Schmitt, Eric, and Michael S. Schmidt. 2013. "Investigators Dig for Roots of Bomb Suspects Radicalization." *New York Times*, April 22. Available online at www.nytimes. com/2013/04/22/us/boston-marathon-bombing-suspects-hoped-to-attack-again. html?pagewanted=all (accessed July 1, 2016).

Schmitt, Eric, Michael S. Schmidt, and Ellen Barry. 2013. "Boston Inquiry Turns to Motive and Russian Trip." *New York Times*, April 21. Available online at www.nytimes. com/2013/04/21/us/boston-marathon-bombings.html?pagewanted=all (accessed July 1, 2016).

Seelye, Katherine, Q., William K. Rashbaum and Michael Cooper. 2013. "F.B.I Post Images of Pair Suspected in Boston Attack." *New York Times*, April 18. Available online at www.nytimes.com/2013/04/19/us/fbi-releases-video-of-boston-bombing-suspects.html? pagewanted=all&_r=0 (accessed July 1, 2016).

Selod, Saher. 2015. "Citizenship Denied: Racialization of Muslim American Men and Women Post 9/11." *Critical Sociology* 41(1): 77–95.

Selod, Saher, and David Embrick. 2013. "Racialization and Muslims: Situating the Muslim Experience in Race Scholarship." *Sociology Compass* 7(8): 644–655.

Sirota, David. 2016. "Let's Hope the Boston Bomber is a White American." *Salon.* April 16. Available online at www.salon.com/2013/04/16/lets_hope_the_boston_marathon_ bomber_is_a_white_american/ (accessed July 1, 2016).

Stampnitsky, Lisa. 2014. *Disciplining Terror: How Experts Invented Terrorism.* Cambridge: Cambridge University Press.

Szpunar, Piotr. 2013. "The Horror at Fort Hood: Disseminating American Exceptionalism." *Media, Culture & Society* 35(2): 182–198.

Taras, Raymond. 2013. "'Islamophobia Never Stands Still': Race, Religion, and Culture." *Ethnic and Racial Studies* 36(3): 417–433.

Trevino, Melina, Ali M. Kanso, and Richard Alan Nelson. 2010. "Islam through Editorial Lenses: How American Elite Newspapers Portrayed Muslims Before and After September 11, 2001." *Journal of Arab & Muslim Media Research* 3(1–2): 3–17.

Volpp, Leti. 2014. "The Boston Bombers." *Fordham Law Review* 82(5): 2209–2220. Available online at http://ir.lawnet.fordham.edu/flr/vol82/iss5/10

Werbner, Pnina. 2013. "Folk Devils and Racist Imaginaries in a Global Prism: Islamophobia and Anti-Semitism in the Twenty-First Century." *Ethnic and Racial Studies* 36(3): 450–467.

Wilstein, Matt. 2013. "Beck Knows 'Middle Eastern' Terrorists Bombed Boston Because When Our Crazies Go Off, They Target The Govt." *Media-ite.* April Available online at www.mediaite.com/online/beck-knows-middle-eastern-terrorists-bombed-boston-because-when-our-crazies-go-off-they-target-the-govt/ (accessed July 1, 2016).

List of contributors

Richard Alba is Distinguished Professor of Sociology at the Graduate Center of the City University of New York. Among his many books are *Blurring the Color Line: The New Chance for a More Integrated America* (Harvard University Press, 2009), *Remaking the American Mainstream: Assimilation and Contemporary Immigration* (Harvard University Press, 2003, co-authored with Victor Nee), and *The Next Generation: Immigrant Youth in a Comparative Perspective* (NYU Press, 2011, co-edited with Mary Waters). Most recently, he co-authored with Nancy Foner *Strangers No More: Immigration and the Challenges of Integration in North America and Western Europe* (Princeton University Press, 2015).

Mehdi Bozorgmehr is Professor of Sociology at the Graduate Center and City College, City University of New York. He was the founding Co-Director of the Middle East and Middle Eastern American Center (MEMEAC) at the Graduate Center from 2001 to 2013. He is the co-author of *Backlash 9/11: Middle Eastern and Muslim Americans Respond* (University of California Press, 2009), which received an honorable mention (runner up) for the best book award from the International Migration section of the American Sociological Association (ASA). He is also the co-editor of *Ethnic Los Angeles* (Russell Sage Foundation, 1996), which won the best book award of the International Migration section of the ASA.

Anja Bredal is Senior Researcher at Norwegian Social Research at OsloMet, Oslo Metropolitan University, Norway. Her research interests are migration and integration, with a focus on family; gender and generation; public policy and service provision. Recent publications include *Fra særtiltak til ordinær innsats* (2017), a process evaluation of Norwegian policies on forced marriages and female genital cutting, and "Ordinary v. Other Violence? Conceptualising Honour-Based Violence in Scandinavian Public Policies" (2014) in *'Honour' Killing and Violence: Theory, Policy and Practice*.

Jan Willem Duyvendak is Distinguished Research Professor of Sociology at the University of Amsterdam. His latest books (co-edited) include *European States and their Muslim Citizens: The Impact of Institutions on Perceptions* *and Boundaries* (Cambridge University Press, 2014), *The Culturalization of Citizenship. Belonging and Polarization in a Globalizing World* (Macmillan, 2016). In 2013–2014, he was a Distinguished Fellow at the Advanced Research Collaborative (ARC) at the Graduate Center, City University of New York.

Fenella Fleischmann is Associate Professor at the Faculty of Social and Behavioral Sciences, the European Research Center on Migration and Ethnic Relations, Utrecht University, the Netherlands. She has published extensively on immigrant integration and political participation and on ethnic and gender inequalities in European societies.

Nancy Foner is Distinguished Professor of Sociology at Hunter College and the Graduate Center, City University of New York. She is the author or editor of eighteen books, including, most recently, *Strangers No More: Immigration and the Challenges of Integration in North America and Western Europe*, co-authored with Richard Alba (Princeton University Press, 2015); and *Fear, Anxiety, and National Identity: Immigration and Belonging in North America and Western Europe*, co-edited with Patrick Simon (Russell Sage Foundation, 2015).

Yvonne Yazbeck Haddad is Professor of the History of Islam and Christian-Muslim Relations at the Center for Muslim-Christian Understanding at Georgetown University. Widely regarded as a pioneer in the field of Islam in America and the West, she has published over a dozen books on the topic.

Serena Hussain is a sociologist and human geographer. She is Associate Professor at the Centre for Trust, Peace and Social Relations, Coventry University, where she is the course director for the Master in Global Diversity Governance. Her previous roles include Principal Scientist on Multiculturalism and International Migration at Charles Darwin University (Australia) and Postdoctoral Research Fellow at the School of Geography, University of Oxford. Her main areas of expertise are the social and spatial trends of Muslims in Britain. She is the author of *Muslims on the Map: A National Survey of Social Trends in Britain* (IB Tauris, 2008).

Philip Kasinitz is Presidential Professor of Sociology at the Graduate Center, City University of New York. He is the author of *Caribbean New York: Black Immigrants and the Politics of Race* (Cornell University Press, 1992), co-author of *Inheriting the City: The Children of Immigrants Come of Age* (Harvard University Press and Russell Sage Foundation, 2008), and co-editor of several books including *Handbook on International Migration* (Russell Sage Foundation, 1999), *Becoming New Yorkers: Ethnographies of the New Second Generation* (Russell Sage Foundation, 2004), and Global Cities, Local Streets (Routledge: 2015). He is a three-time winner of the Thomas and Znaniecki best book award from the International Migration section of the American Sociological Association.

Eric Ketcham is a doctoral candidate in Sociology at the Graduate Center, City University of New York, and a Demography Fellow at its Institute for Demographic Research.

Nazli Kibria is Professor of Sociology at Boston University. She is a scholar of global migration, families, and identity formations. Her recent books include *Muslims in Motion: Islam and National Identity in the Bangladeshi Diaspora* (Rutgers University Press, 2011) and, with Cara Bowman and Megan O'Leary, *Race and Immigration* (Polity, 2013).

Hilde Lidén is Research Professor at the Institute for Social Research in Oslo. Her research interests are transnational migration, childhood and family research, gender, migrants and national minorities, immigration policy, family policy. Recent publications include the chapter "Return to well-being? Irregular migrants and assisted return in Norway," published in the edited volume *Return Migration and Psychosocial Wellbeing* (Routledge, 2017). She is currently working on a monograph on children and migration.

Erik Love is Assistant Professor of Sociology and former Chair of Middle East Studies at Dickinson College in Pennsylvania. He is the author of *Islamophobia and Racism in America* (NYU Press, 2017). His research on civil rights advocacy has received the support of the National Science Foundation and the James Weldon Johnson Institute for the Study of Race and Difference.

Karen Phalet is Professor of Social and Cultural Psychology at the University of Leuven, Belgium. She has published extensively on the integration of the second generation, religious diversity, and educational inequality in European cities. In 2014–2015, Phalet was a Distinguished Fellow at the Advanced Research Collaborative (ARC) at the Graduate Center, City University of New York.

Jen'nan Ghazal Read is Professor of Sociology and Global Health at Duke University. Her primary areas of research focus on gender and health inequality and Arab and Muslim integration. A Carnegie Scholar, she has published widely on these topics, including a book and numerous book chapters and peer-reviewed journal articles.

Liza Reisel is Research Professor and Research Director at the Institute for Social Research in Oslo, Norway. Her research interests include comparative studies of inequality in education, multidimensional equality and social stratification, and gender and ethnic segregation in education and the labor market. Reisel recently edited a volume of *Comparative Social Research* on Gender *Segregation in Vocational Education* (2015). Other recent publications have appeared in *Journal of Adolescence* and *Nordic Journal of Migration Research*.

Saher Selod is Associate Professor of Sociology at Simmons College. Her research interests are in race, ethnicity, and religion. Her book, *Forever Suspect: Racialized Surveillance of Muslim Americans in the War on Terror*, was published by Rutgers University Press (2018).

Marieke Slootman is a researcher in Sociology at the Vrije Universiteit (VU) Amsterdam. Her University of Amsterdam dissertation, *Soulmates: Reinvention of ethnic identification among higher educated second generation Moroccan and Turkish Dutch* (2014), was awarded the national prize for the best dissertation in Sociology. She has published articles in journals such as *Identities* and *New Diversities*, and book chapters in the edited volumes *Fear, Anxiety, and National Identity* (Russell Sage Foundation, 2015) and *Citizenship, Belonging and Nation-States* (Palgrave Macmillan, 2016).

Kathryn Spellman Poots is a Visiting Associate Professor at Columbia University and Associate Professor at the Aga Khan University's Institute for the Study of Muslim Civilisations. Her research interests include Muslims in Europe and North America, the Iranian diaspora, transnational migration networks and gender and religion in the Middle East and North Africa, Her publications include the monograph *Religion and Nation: Iranian Local and Transnational Networks in Britain* (Berghahn, 2005) and the edited volumes *The Political Aesthetics of Global Protest: The Arab Spring and Beyond* (Edinburgh University Press, 2016) and *Ethnographies of Islam: Ritual Performances and Everyday Practices* (Edinburgh University Press, 2014).

Paul Statham is Professor of Migration and Director of the Sussex Centre for Migration Research at the University of Sussex, UK. He is Editor-in-Chief of the *Journal of Ethnic and Migration Studies* (JEMS). He has written several collaborative books, including *Contested Citizenship* (University of Minnesota Press, 2005), *The Making of a European Public Sphere* (Cambridge University Press, 2010), and *The Politicization of Europe* Routledge, (2013), as well as numerous journal articles and book chapters. His most recent book, co-edited with Jean Tillie, is *Muslims in Europe: Comparative Perspectives on Sociocultural Integration* (Routledge, 2018). In 2017, Statham was a Distinguished Fellow at the Advanced Research Collaborative (ARC) at the Graduate Center, City University of New York.

Marc Swyngedouw is Professor of Political Sociology and Methodology at the University of Leuven, Belgium. His diverse research and publications cover social science methodology, ethnic minorities, voting behavior, the extreme right, urban sociology, and public opinion. In 2015, he was a Visiting Fellow in Sociology at the Graduate Center, City University of New York.

Tobias Henry Watson is a doctoral candidate in Sociology at Boston University. He received his B.A. in Sociology from the University of Warwick, and an M.A. in Migration Studies from the University of Sussex. His dissertation research examines policies, practices, and discourses surrounding refugee resettlement.

Index

Page numbers in *italic* refer to tables.

Printed in Great Britain
by Amazon